ON THE WING

Wilson
ON THE WING
The *Davie Wilson* Story

DAVIE WILSON
AND ALISTAIR AIRD

First published by Pitch Publishing, 2020

Pitch Publishing
A2 Yeoman Gate
Yeoman Way
Worthing
Sussex
BN13 3QZ
www.pitchpublishing.co.uk
info@pitchpublishing.co.uk

A CIP catalogue record is available for this book
from the British Library.

ISBN 978 1 78531 633 3

Typesetting and origination by Pitch Publishing

Printed and bound by TJ International, UK.

CONTENTS

For my wife, Avril, my
children, Sheena and David,
and my grandchildren,
Carly, Harry, Anna
and David

ACKNOWLEDGEMENTS

SOMETIMES ACTING on an impulse can lead to great things. Back in March 2019 I had just finished the manuscript for *Rangers FC in the 1980s – The Players' Stories* and I wanted to get my teeth into another project. Although not old enough to see them play, the Rangers team of the early 1960s had always grabbed my attention when reading about the history of the club I love. And one of the key players in that team was a wee outside-left who had an incredible knack of scoring goals.

As an avid reader of all books about Rangers, it struck me as rather odd that Davie Wilson had never put pen to paper to chronicle his incredible career. So I took a flyer and messaged his Facebook page and asked him if he would be interested in working with me on his autobiography. The buzz I got when I got an almost instant 'yes' as a reply was incredible.

It has been an honour and a privilege to work with the great man on this book. The stories and anecdotes have been brilliant and brought his career to life. I only hope what we've pulled together does it justice and I can't thank Davie and his family enough for allowing me to work on this project.

I must also extend a vote of thanks to all those who generously gave their time to share their memories of Davie. For an ordinary punter like me to be afforded the opportunity to speak to the likes of Sir Alex Ferguson, Denis Law and Willie Johnston was very humbling. Lads like Sammy McGivern, Alistair Brown, Graeme Sharp and Murdo MacLeod were fantastic too.

Thanks also go to Jane Camillin at Pitch Publishing and Duncan Olner from Olner Design for yet another exceptional jacket design.

And finally, to my fiancée and soulmate Leona and our fantastic family, this is all for you. Better, stronger, ALWAYS together.

Alistair Aird
February 2020

FOREWORD
WALTER SMITH OBE

WHEN I first started to go to games at Ibrox with my grandfather in the late 1950s, Davie Wilson was starting to make the breakthrough into the Rangers first team. I have to confess that, as a boy at that time, I didn't really relate to the players. You knew who they were but I only really started relating to the Rangers players when the iconic team of the early 1960s started to evolve. That was, of course, Ritchie, Shearer, Caldow, Greig, McKinnon, Baxter, Henderson, McMillan, Millar, Brand and Wilson.

Jim Baxter was the main man but my favourite player was Jimmy Millar as I liked the way he played. He was a really good player and had such a competitive attitude. And although he maybe wasn't the most talented centre-forward, he was combative and I liked that. He would take the ball in with his back to goal and had a good touch and control. Most folk back then probably preferred Baxter, Willie Henderson or Davie Wilson, but Jimmy was the man for me.

Davie supplied a lot of the ammunition for Jimmy and, along with Ralph Brand, that talented trio made a huge contribution to that celebrated side. Davie and I knew of each other as he had worked with my dad at Redpath Brown's when he was younger. But when I first met him when he arrived at Tannadice to sign for Dundee United in August 1967, I was only a young lad playing in the reserve team.

I was working as an apprentice electrician so used to travel through on the train from Glasgow to Dundee. Davie stayed in and around Glasgow too and Jerry Kerr had sorted it out for him to train with Partick Thistle during the week. It was a wee bit surreal for me to have this guy travelling through alongside me. With Jimmy Millar also coming to United at that time, it was hard to fathom that I was now part of the same team as two guys who had been part of such a famous side I had idolised when I was watching them from the sloping terraces at Ibrox.

The chat on the train was all about football. There were a group of us who would travel through on a Saturday – all the kick-offs were 3pm back then – and some would get off the train at Stirling, others at Perth, while the likes of Davie and I would get off at Dundee. It was great for me just to be involved with guys like Davie who had had that level of success. What also came across was that, although these guys were maybe getting towards the end of their careers, their love of playing football and love of the game never diminished.

The first thing that struck me about Davie when he signed for Dundee United was his enthusiasm to play football. He was still a true professional and just wanted to play. As I said, he didn't attend training on a daily basis as he trained with Thistle, but any time he did come to train with us you could see that love of football and that passion come out of him. He had a terrific attitude towards each and every game that he played and his dedication to the sport was second to none.

To get the chance to train and play with guys like Davie and Jimmy Millar was a big thing for me, but they were really down to earth and there were no airs or graces. They still had a will to win, and even though it was perhaps regarded that the move from Rangers to United was a step down it didn't affect them. It didn't matter to them either that they were playing in front of smaller crowds and Davie, in particular, still wanted to work hard, get on the ball, take full-backs on, get crosses in and score goals.

I was actually his boot boy when he was at United. The young guys had lots of different jobs to do and, although he wasn't there all the time, Davie would leave his boots to be polished and I was quite happy to do that for him. In fact, it was a pleasure for me just to be involved with a player who had done so much in the game but was still prepared to give something to people like myself and others. He always offered encouragement and made sure we went about our game in the right way.

Davie was still able to influence games back then. When you get older, playing on the wing becomes more difficult as you still need to do a lot of running and take people on. It's a position that demands a great deal of fitness, and Davie had that. And while his natural enthusiasm shone through, we can't forget that he had a terrific level of ability.

When I came in to the United team I played mainly on the right-hand side of midfield. We had an experienced team with the likes of Davie, Doug Smith, Dennis Gillespie, Jimmy Briggs and Jimmy Millar so, as a youngster, I was in and out the team. I didn't have anywhere near the ability these guys did, but it didn't stop me looking at them and appreciating just how good they were.

Davie left United in 1972, not long after Jim McLean took over from Jerry Kerr as manager. Jim was a more modern type of coach and he decided to change the team and blood more youngsters. At that time players of the same vintage as Davie were deemed to be older players. I think Jim also wanted the players to live in and around Dundee. He wanted them to be at training all the time, so for guys like Davie that was always going to be a difficult move to make.

When Davie left United, he went to Dumbarton and had a spell playing there before he became assistant manager to Alex Wright. I actually played in opposition to Davie in his last match in senior football and he was instrumental in getting me to sign for Dumbarton in October 1975.

I had now moved up to live in Dundee, but although I was playing more often at United than I had been when Davie played there, I was still in and out of the team. As a youngster I could accept that, but once I reached my mid-20s, I realised that I wasn't going to be a player of any note. I was a good professional and I think Davie probably remembered that as much as anything else.

They were obviously looking for players and Jim McLean came to me one day and told me Dumbarton were interested in signing me. He was prepared to let me go so I went down there. Now it was my turn to do something similar to Davie, only in reverse. As Dumbarton were part-time, I would train at Tannadice then travel down and train with Dumbarton one night a week, either a Monday or a Thursday.

I got to know Davie a bit better in the year or so I played for Dumbarton. All the traits he had as a player he carried with him into his managerial career. You couldn't fail to be impressed by him. I can't emphasise enough how much his overall enthusiasm filtered through to everybody. He simply wanted us all to do well and enjoy playing football.

Davie was still keeping himself fit too and was still keen to take part in the games during training. You could tell, however, there was a frustration there that he had now stopped playing and had to sit and watch the game from the dugout.

Dumbarton did well in my time there and we had some good young players like Graeme Sinclair, who went on to play for Celtic, the McAdam brothers, Colin and Tom, and Ian Wallace. We managed to reach the last four of the Scottish Cup in 1976, where we lost to Hearts. We should actually have won the first game at Hampden when we missed a great opportunity in the latter stages of the game. But the replay is remembered for my spectacular own goal – the first goal of the evening, Hearts eventually winning 3-0 – and Davie still reminds me about it to this day!

Similarly to when Davie left United, the fact I was living in Dundee meant that when I got the chance to move back to United in February 1977 I was happy to accept. United had a bit of an injury crisis at the time, so I was back and played against Rangers at Ibrox a few days later, a match we won 3-2. But I was still in and out of the team and, as I was interested in going in to coaching, when I was 27 Jim McLean asked me to become player-coach.

After I left Dumbarton, it was a wee while before I bumped into Davie again, something like eight or ten years later. And when we did meet he still looked exactly the same as he had the last time we'd seen each other! In fact, even now he's still looking great and it's remarkable how he's managed to keep himself so fit. He's always kept that youthful look and although most folk know roughly what age he is, you wouldn't know that by looking at him. That's probably been helped by his outlook. He's always lively when you meet him and had that sparkle about him. Having seen him play and having met him then, you simply can't help but be influenced by his attitude.

CHAPTER 1

THE EARLY DAYS

PLEASE ALLOW me to introduce myself. My name is David Wilson and I am 83 years young. I was a professional footballer and I played predominantly as an outside-left for Rangers for 11 seasons. I made over 300 appearances for the club and scored 162 goals, which puts me in the top-ten goalscorers for Rangers since hostilities ended at the conclusion of World War Two. I also played for Dundee United and Dumbarton and represented Scotland on 22 occasions. After I finished playing, I had two spells as manager of Dumbarton – I became the first manager in their history to lead the club in to the Premier Division during my second spell – and also a couple of seasons as manager of Queen of the South.

But I'm getting ahead of myself, let's go back to the beginning and Sunday, 10 January 1937. That's the day my mother and father, Margaret – or Meg as she was better known – and Thomas, welcomed me into the world when I was born at the family home, 20 Clyde Street, in Newton. I was their second child, my big sister Nan being born just over three years earlier in July 1933.

I was a miner's boy and the house we lived in was one of the miners' houses. My father was more commonly referred to as Tommy or Big 'T' and he worked for A. G. Moore & Co at their Blantyre Ferme colliery on the Blantyre Farm Road. He was one of around 400 miners who worked there and he was the principal provider for the family. My mother stayed at home to look after me and Nan and then my two younger sisters, Grace and Linda. Grace was born on 21 January 1941, with Linda a late arrival on 10 November 1954.

Our house had a kitchen, living room, back room and an outside toilet. My siblings and I bathed in the scullery in a bath that was heated using a coal fire. We would use the coal my father got to heat the cold water in the big tin bath, so by the time I was the last one in the water was roasting!

We kept the coal in a coal house and one evening my mother was adamant the neighbours were stealing our coal. To confirm her suspicions, she drew a line in white chalk to mark where the coal was and put two padlocks on the door. Those measures did not deter the coal thieves, though, as the next day more coal had been taken, which left my mother perplexed as to how they were managing to gain entry. But my mother didn't take them to task as she knew those who were taking the coal didn't have much, and that summed up how generous she was.

My father worked for A. G. Moore & Co until 1953. He then moved on to work in the steelworks in Glasgow. As he spent most of his day waist-deep in water when down the pit, he ended up with sciatica. He stayed at the steelworks until it closed down, by which time he was in his late 50s. At that time it was difficult to get employment at that age, and my father tried countless places, even walking from Newton to East Kilbride to meet with one potential employer. Eventually someone he had worked with down the pit recommended the Gray, Dunn & Co. biscuit factory in Kinning Park and he remained there until he retired.

Like every boy, my father was my hero and it hit me hard when, in February 1977, he passed away. He used to walk for miles with his greyhounds before he went to work in the morning and would walk to the pit in Blantyre too. He took a stroke, though, and eventually his heart gave up. All the family were at his bedside when he passed.

My mother was a popular figure in the village but was very quiet. She didn't have a bad word to say about anybody and even after I made the grade with Rangers, she stayed humble and was never boastful about the burgeoning talents of her boy. Such was her popularity, the Hallside & Newton church the family attended was packed to the rafters for her funeral service when she died in 1989 at the age of 81.

My early days were good, but I hadn't yet turned three when a chap called Adolf Hitler started throwing his weight around, resulting in the declaration of war on 1 September 1939. But my dad wasn't called to the frontline as he was in what was considered to be a reserved occupation. A list of reserved occupations was published in April 1939 and included dock workers, miners, farmers, scientists, merchant seamen and railway workers. As these occupations were deemed essential to the war effort, my dad was therefore exempt from conscription.

As I was just a wee laddie at the time, I don't remember much about the war, but I do recall the occasions when the Luftwaffe were screaming overhead on a mission to bomb the Glasgow shipyards. Sometimes when it wasn't so bad the warden would come to the door and tell my mother just to stay in the house rather than go to the air raid shelters as Grace was just a baby at the time. But one night the guns were blazing with the Clyde Valley under attack and we were told to make for the shelters. We made our dash down the street huddled under a board that my big sister, Nan, did her tap dancing on. I remember rationing too but, although we didn't get as much as what we maybe usually got, my mum made sure we were still well fed and I don't recall going hungry at any stage.

When hostilities ended on 2 September 1945 I was at school, having started at Newton Primary School a couple of years earlier. I later moved on to Gateside Secondary and I loved my schooldays.

But I had developed a wee bit of an obsession with football and I was soon shooting to prominence. I always had a ball when I was out and about and me and my pals would play numerous games. My favourite was the one where we tried to keep the ball up for as long as possible, but I have to confess I was a wee bit accident prone, with one incident in particular almost ending my football career before it had even started. That was the day I dropped a drain cover – or stank as we called it – on my toe. I was always skinning my knees and picking up cuts and bruises, but this injury was so bad that my mum thought I would lose my toe. But in the end I got lucky, I only lost the nail, although that wouldn't be the last time my toe would be bandaged up as I was forever losing the nail due to kicking my football around as much as I did.

Our football matches used to take place in the field near our home. It could be challenging at times, though, as it was a pasture for cows. And the deposits left by our bovine friends made me extremely ill one day. The kickabout would invariably leave me with a thirst and to quench it in the winter I used to suck on the ice that formed on the puddles in the field. However, on this occasion one of the cows had evidently left a cowpat in the location of the puddle prior to it freezing. I was so thirsty that I didn't notice the ice had been contaminated and for a couple of days afterwards I was fine. But I then started to feel unwell and it got so bad an ambulance had to be called. I had contracted diphtheria and had to spend a few days in hospital as a result.

But even being in hospital couldn't contain my youthful exuberance. In those days family weren't allowed into the ward, they had to stand outside and look in through the window. And on one such visit I left my mother mortified. She looked in through the window and couldn't see me so asked one of the nurses where I was. The nurse pointed to the window ledge and there I was standing and getting myself ready to leap from the ledge on to my bed for what must have been the umpteenth time.

That wasn't the only time in my childhood the Wilson family had a need to call on the emergency services. My sisters and I were always getting up to something and one day Grace, who was only about five years of age at the time, decided to climb up towards the scullery roof. My pals and I had trapped some pigeons in a box, and as Grace climbed up to see I thought I would give her a fright. But when I did she let go of the poles she was using to climb and her head thudded against the concrete path. The impact was such that she was knocked unconscious. Fearing the wrath of my mother, I fled the scene and I was so scared that it must have been about 10pm that night before I returned home. Fortunately by then Grace had recovered but I thought twice the next time the notion came to give my wee sister a fright.

Those were great days. We were a really tight-knit community and I had lots of pals. We would be out playing morning, noon and night and it wouldn't just be football we'd play either. We had one game which we called 'the street versus the buildings' and the name of the game was to avoid the ash that the other participants threw at you. In a coal mining community where all the houses had coal fires, ash wasn't exactly scarce, and we would gleefully scoop up handfuls of the stuff from the dustbins and launch it at each other. Needleless to say, we traipsed home afterwards filthy, but we weren't scolded by our parents, it was all good fun.

Another popular pastime was something we called 'doing the dokies'. This involved following a leader down the street and you had to copy what he or she did. That could be a range of things, including jumping over walls and fences. Grace and I were really close and she was always wanting to run around with my pals and I. But there was a condition; she had to do 'the dokies' before we would let her play with us.

But, close as we were, there were times when my obsession for football took over. One day my mum agreed that I could take Grace to the cinema in Rutherglen. We caught the bus from Newton and Grace was really excited that her big brother was taking her to the movies. But when we arrived I heard my pals were playing football. I was desperate to join them so, noticing a girl in the queue that I knew from Newton, I paid her to take Grace to watch the film and then take her home!

As you can imagine, once again my mother wasn't best pleased, but the lure of football was just irresistible.

In addition to playing with my pals I was also turning out for the school team on a Saturday morning. We didn't have a school team at Newton Primary so I had to wait until secondary school to get a game. Mr Finlayson was the man in charge of the team, but although we had some good players, I was the only one who made it in the senior game. A lad called John Stark played in the juniors and I thought Jackie Tait, who was a left-back, had a chance of making it too. Jackie was over a year younger than me and he stayed in Dunlop Street, and while I went to Newton Primary he attended Hallside Primary. After he left school he became a steelman with Redpath Brown & Co. Ltd and played football for Burnbank Swifts, with whom he won the Scottish Juvenile Cup in 1958/59.

I have to confess, though, that my appearances for the school team used to drive my mother daft. On numerous occasions I would return home after a game minus the towel my mum had given me, and one time I came back without my navy blue overcoat. Clothes were hard to come by then, so you can imagine my mother's consternation when I returned not just without my own coat but with someone else's, which was much older than the one I had!

I was developing a reputation as a promising player and that led to an impromptu appearance for another school, the local Catholic school, St Charles. They were a player short for one game and they asked my head teacher if I could replace the absent player. He granted permission but that appearance earned my mum an apology from the whole school. She was walking back home one day when she was verbally abused by some boys from the school. My mum was quite upset by some of the names she was called and told my Aunt Agnes all about it. The children of the family who stayed next door to my aunt went to that school and when their mother heard what had happened she reported it to the headmaster. He had remembered me helping the school out by filling in when they were a player short and he was so angry about what had happened that he ordered the whole school to go down to our house and apologise to my mother.

At the age of 14, I started training at Ibrox two nights a week, Tuesdays and Thursdays, from 6pm to 8pm. The Rangers scout stayed near us in Newton and he had been watching me for a number of weeks in games at Halfway in Cambuslang. I was playing centre-forward and scoring goals, and after scoring ten in one match for the school team at Rutherglen, the deal was sealed. As a Rangers supporter I was delighted, and I hoped one day I could emulate my favourite player, Torry Gillick, and play for the first team.

My headmaster used to let me away from school early so I could get the bus in to Glasgow. I would get off at Carlton Place then walk to the subway, and from there it was out to Ibrox for training. I would train across the road from Ibrox at The Albion, alongside the first-team players that weren't full time, like the late Bobby Brown, who was a PE teacher.

I got the chance to meet the iconic Rangers manager Bill Struth too, although by then he was in failing health and consigned to a wheelchair after he had to have his legs amputated due to gangrene. He stayed in a flat at the stadium and still had a presence at the ground even after he was replaced by Scot Symon as manager in 1954.

I left school aged 16 – I stayed on so I could get picked for the Lanarkshire schools, but I wasn't too bad academically and I managed to pick up the school dux award before I left – and I ended up working with Redpath Brown. Founded in 1802, they made steel structures and had outlets in Glasgow, London, Edinburgh and Manchester. I started at the works, which were based on Canal Bank Street in Port Dundas, as a template maker. The gaffer there was a Rangers supporter so, just like my headmaster, he would also let me away early for training and games. I stayed with Redpath Brown for six years, leaving when I was 21 and conscripted for National Service.

I was paid the princely sum of £3 per week – which went straight to my mother – but it soon became clear that my career would be starting at Ibrox. There were no youth academies back then, so rather than go in to the reserves or third team, in common with other aspiring footballers of that era in Scotland, I was farmed out to a junior team. Rangers initially called Cambuslang Rangers when I was 14, but their hierarchy turned me down as it was felt I was too young and too small. I was also told that someone thought I wasn't good enough to be a footballer.

The rejection was just a minor bump in the road, though, and I was eventually signed by Baillieston Juniors. And by the end of August 1954, I was in the team, a team that were flying high at the top of the Central League, a 3-1 away win over Kilsyth Rangers, champions the previous season, putting us on 13 points after eight games.

I used to travel through to Baillieston on my push bike. It was roughly five miles from the house in Clyde Street, and I'd do this every matchday as I was still training two nights a week at Ibrox. I didn't believe in hanging around either. I was pacey on the park and it was the same on the bike. Initially I used my own bike, but eventually I borrowed my cousin Davie Cunningham's bike as it was faster than mine. Once in the saddle I was off like a rocket and it took me a mere 20 minutes to travel through to Baillieston.

My dad, who would work every Saturday morning down the pit, would go to all the games just as he had done when I was playing for the school team. Indeed, when I made the first team at Ibrox and got my six complimentary stand tickets for each game, I would go out and give them to my dad and he would distribute them to friends and family.

I alternated between centre-forward, where I had played for my school team, and outside-right and it was a tough baptism for me in a junior game that doesn't welcome any shrinking violets. But I wasn't overawed and pretty soon I was among the goals, scoring twice in a 3-0 win over Lanark United in the first round of the Lanarkshire Cup on 17 September.

A week later I scored again as we defeated Pollok, my strike after 22 minutes the second of our three goals in a 3-2 win. And at the end of September it was reported in the *Evening Times* that I was Baillieston's 'star forward' and that my 'clever play ought to have brought better results' as we lost 2-0 to Thorniewood in the first round of the West of Scotland Cup.

I was starting to make a name for myself and I had a really good game against Clydebank in the opening round of the Central League Cup on 16 October. Baillieston won 4-1 and I was fouled to win us a penalty for our second goal. And I followed that by bamboozling two defenders before rifling the ball in to the net to make it 3-0 before half-time.

The big prize in Scottish junior football was the Scottish Junior Cup and I made my debut in the competition playing at outside-right as Baillieston comfortably saw off St Anthony's by five goals to one at Station Park in the opening round. I played on the right wing again when we beat Lanark United 4-0 at home in round two, and in November I was selected when Baillieston hosted Wishaw in the third round. I was at outside-left for this one but we trailed 3-1 at half-time. It was soon 4-1 when, shortly after the restart, a chap called Maxwell scored his second goal for Wishaw. But we almost completed a stirring fightback, goals from myself and our left-back, Ross, making the final score 4-3 for our visitors.

I wasn't playing every week but I relished the chance when I was given the opportunity. And towards the end of 1954 I was part of the side that racked up convincing wins over St Anthony's (6-2) and Blantyre Celtic (5-0). A touch of flu kept me out of action over the festive period but I was back in the number-seven shirt for the league clash with Blantyre Victoria at Station Park on 8 January. In his match report for that match, George Manson of the *Evening Times* referred to me as a 'box o' tricks outside-right' and I played my part in our 4-0 win.

The junior game at that time was a rich breeding ground for talent and most of the games up and down the country would attract scouts, not just from Scotland but also from top senior sides in England. As I had already provisionally signed for Rangers, the presence of the scouts had no real impact on me. I was already being talked about as having all the necessary attributes to make a career in senior football, but I was conscious that I had to be playing well when selected as a report card on my progress was most likely being fed back to Ibrox on a regular basis.

The win over Blantyre kept Baillieston in touch with leaders Duntocher Hibs at the top of Division A. We were three points behind the team from West Dunbarton with a game in hand. But we missed a golden opportunity to apply pressure at the start of February. With our rivals on Scottish Cup fifth-round duty, we faced Renfrew away from home in the league but contrived to lose 4-2. We were pretty inconsistent after that and never really looked like winning the league. We won just three of our last ten league games and a 4-2 defeat away at Kirkintilloch Rob Roy on 7 May all but ended our title tilt. Baillieston eventually finished fifth, nine points behind Central League champions Ashfield.

We didn't end the season empty-handed, though. Junior football has numerous cup competitions and during the season I played in a total of six tournaments. I've already spoken about our early exits in the top two tournaments, the Scottish Junior Cup and the West of Scotland Cup, and Baillieston were eliminated early in the Central League Cup too, going out in the second round to Bridgeton Waverley. After a 4-4 draw at home, we contrived to throw away a 3-0 lead in the replay to draw 3-3. The tie was eventually concluded some five months after it started when Bridgeton won 3-1 at the neutral venue of Greenfield Park.

There was more joy in the other competitions, with Baillieston winning both the Eastern Charity Cup and the Pompey Cup. After receiving a first-round 'bye', we exacted revenge on Bridgeton Waverley in the Charity Cup with a 5-1 win. And we went goal crazy in the semi-final, my two first-half goals against Rutherglen Glencairn contributing to a stunning 10-3 win. I scored in the final as well. We trailed 2-0 against

Strathclyde before I got myself on the end of a Jim Tennant free kick to score. Three further goals from Baillieston after the interval secured the trophy.

The Pompey Cup also returned to Station Park. The trophy had been presented to the Central League by Portsmouth back in 1948 to mark the English club's golden jubilee and to recognise the close connection Pompey had with Scottish football. Baillieston had claimed the cup in each of the previous two seasons and we started our defence with a 2-0 win over Kilsyth Rangers in February. A tight 2-1 win over Renfrew followed before we comprehensively beat Shawfield 6-1 in the third round. St Roch's were next on our hit list in the semi-final before we lifted the cup with a 2-1 win over Petershill at Shawfield. The crowd was listed as 4,000 and I was, in the opinion of George Manson in the *Evening Times*, the 'big star' for Baillieston. George reckoned my opening goal in our 2-1 win was 'a real beauty' and it was nice to get such positive press at this early stage of my career.

It was, therefore, a pretty good first season in the junior ranks. I had established myself in the Baillieston team, predominantly at outside-right, although I had moved to centre-forward on the occasions that our regular number nine, Danny Park, had been absent through injury.

After our annual family holiday on the east coast of Scotland I was back at Station Park again for season 1955/56 and was joined in the Baillieston ranks by Jim Tennant, who had also signed provisionally with Rangers. Eventually, I was at outside-right and Jim was deployed on the opposite wing, but we both had to sit out the early matches of the season through injury. I had trouble with my ankle and was unavailable for selection as

Baillieston started off the campaign really poorly, losing heavily to Renfrew (2-5) and Petershill (1-6) in the Central League.

The start to the season was hectic to say the least. The Central League match against Petershill on 3 September was our tenth league match of the season, with the nine played in August taking place inside just 26 days. I was back on the pitch and free from my ankle issue for the match at Petershill Park, but I was unable to arrest our dreadful start to the Central League season, Baillieston winning just three of their opening ten league games. However, when the cup action kicked off we comfortably beat Thorniewood United in the opening round of the Lanarkshire Cup. We won 3-0 and I created our first goal, and Jim won the penalty that put us 2-0 in front.

Another Rangers connection at Station Park was the famous Jock 'Tiger' Shaw. Jock had played 527 games for Rangers, 289 of which were during the Second World War. He had picked up 23 honours and captained the club to the domestic treble in season 1948/49. He also won 24 caps for Scotland. A league championship and Scottish Cup winner at 38, he was still playing in his early 40s and was the oldest player to play for the club until Davie Weir surpassed his record in 2011.

Jock was part of the coaching team at Baillieston and, for a young lad like me, working with someone like him was fantastic. And Jock can take the credit for turning me into a winger. At school I always played as a centre-forward but, as he had been a full-back in his playing days so therefore knew a bit about wingers, Jock told me I had all the attributes to play in that position. He suggested watching the full-back I was up against and looking out for what foot they favoured. He advised that I should then take them on on the opposite side and I beat many a full-back in my time as a result of that guidance.

A couple of weeks after our win over Thorniewood, I was among the goals when Baillieston beat Vale of Clyde 4-1 in the Central League. I opened the scoring with a close-range finish after 20 minutes to set us on the way to our first league win since mid-August. And I was in the thick of the action again in the opening round of the Central League Cup in mid-November. We faced Vale of Leven at Millburn Park and it was from my cross that our inside-left, a chap called McEwan, opened the scoring. I added a second to give Baillieston a comfortable half-time lead and, although our hosts mounted a comeback in the second half, we progressed to the next round with a 3-2 win.

I was developing a bit of a goalscoring habit and I notched another goal before the end of the month when I opened the scoring in a league match against Shawfield. Although I was playing on the wing, I still had the instinct to get in to goalscoring positions and, on this occasion, I was able to capitalise on some defensive slackness to find the net.

There was a satisfying result for me too the week before Christmas when we hammered Cambuslang Rangers 7-0 in the second round of the Central League Cup. After being rejected by Cambuslang, I always wanted to do well against them and show they had made a mistake by not signing me. And I proved that point emphatically in one match I played against them when I scored the winning goal for Baillieston with, you've guessed it, a header!

That set us up nicely for our Scottish Junior Cup tie at home to Lochee Harp and we continued our scoring streak, with Danny Park notching up a hat-trick in our 5-2 win. In truth, the cups were really Baillieston's best hope of securing silverware as we just couldn't seem to find a consistent run of form in the Central League. We lost ten of our opening 19 matches to trail the leaders by a mammoth 15 points. We found form after that, winning nine of our last 11 Central League fixtures, but it was too late by then. For the second successive season, Baillieston finished fifth but this time we trailed champions Petershill by 13 points.

For me at this stage it was all about getting experience playing football, and I was certainly getting that as I was in the team virtually every week. And my performances were of such a standard that I earned an outing for Rangers Reserves against St Mirren Reserves on 16 April. The match was played under the floodlights at Ibrox and I was joined in the line-up by another provisional signing, John Bell, who was with Dalkeith Thistle. As you can imagine it was a real thrill to play under the lights at Ibrox, and I played very well in Rangers' 1-0 win, the goal coming courtesy of a Jimmy Walker penalty kick.

Back at Baillieston there was a memorable encounter with St Rochs and I was having a tough time against their red-haired left-back. My Uncle Jim, my mum's brother, was at that game and after one particularly robust challenge that sent me spinning off the park, he decided to take matters into his own hands. He jumped over the wall and landed a punch on the St Rochs player, knocking him clean out. When the referee came over to ask what had happened, my uncle told him that the lad had struck his chin against the railing and that was why he had been knocked out.

Baillieston found themselves knocked out as well when we faced Whitletts Victoria in the fifth round of the Scottish

Junior Cup. We trailed 1-0 at half-time in the first game at Voluntary Park but I equalised a minute after the restart. We fell behind again when the home side scored a second goal just shy of the hour mark. But we forced a replay when we levelled things up at 2-2. Alas, any aspirations of winning the trophy were ended when Whitletts came to Station Park for the replay seven days later. They won comfortably, 3-0, and the silverware coveted by Baillieston was gone for another year.

Our Scottish Junior Cup quest may have been ended but we were going well in the other cup competitions. March saw us progress to the fourth round of the Lanarkshire Challenge Cup at the expense of Douglas Water Thistle – yours truly opening the scoring in that one – and we also edged out high-flying Petershill in the third round of the Central League Cup, winning by the odd goal in nine at Station Park.

Although Baillieston relinquished the Pompey Cup, losing in the first round to Clydebank, we were in the running to win the second of the 'big' junior cup competitions, the West of Scotland Cup. We beat Dreghorn 6-1 away from home in the opening round and followed that with another big win, 5-1 on this occasion, against Saltcoats Victoria in round two. I was at centre-forward for that one but missed our next round encounter with Beith through injury. That ended 1-1 but I was back for the replay that saw us secure a narrow 1-0 win.

Newarthill Thistle succumbed 4-1 in the quarter final, which took us through to the last four where we were joined by Irvine Meadow, Parkhead and Clydebank. Baillieston drew Irvine Meadow who sat second in the Western League and we faced the Ayrshire side at Cathkin Park, the home of Third Lanark, on 2 June. I was inside-right on this occasion, but my fellow forwards and I couldn't conjure up a goal. I went close to opening the scoring with a thumping shot that was deflected for a corner, but a mistake from our goalkeeper allowed Hugh Drennan to give Meadow the lead. They doubled their advantage later in the game and went on to face Clydebank in the final.

There were semi-final defeats for us too in the Central League Cup – we went down to Blantyre Victoria at Celtic Park – and the Lanarkshire Challenge Cup, but Baillieston did pick up silverware in the shape of the Eastern Charity Cup. After a first round 'bye' we beat Shawfield 1-0 in the second round and then needed extra time to edge out Vale of Clyde by the odd goal in seven in the semi-final. Bridgeton Waverley were our opponents in the final and we claimed the cup with a fine 3-1 win at Greenfield Park.

I have to say it was all a bit hectic as the season typically ran to mid-June – as a comparison the final league fixture Rangers played that season was on 28 April – but I thoroughly enjoyed my two years at Baillieston. Although it was primarily about getting game time and showing the powers-that-be at Rangers that I was the real deal, I also developed as a player when I was there.

Mr Symon thought highly of the junior game and was quoted as saying that it was pointless calling players like myself back from the juniors if there wasn't a regular place for me in the Rangers reserve team. For season 1956/57, however, it looked like there would be a place in that team for D. Wilson as I got the call towards the end of April 1956 that I was to report to Ibrox in July for training ahead of the new season.

My journey was about to begin.

CHAPTER 2

PLAYING FOR RANGERS

I WAS brought back to Ibrox and signed as a professional ahead of season 1956/57. It was a great thrill for me to see my name among the 33 on the 'Rangers Roster' when it was published in the *Evening Times* on 21 July 1956.

Fellow signings that summer were Jock Dodds (Dalkeith Thistle), Willie Logie (Cambuslang Rangers) and Stewart McCorquodale (Blantyre Victoria). They all came, like me, from the junior ranks and this would also be the first full season at Ibrox for Bobby Shearer, who had been recruited from Hamilton Accies the previous December.

It was Bobby who took me in to Ibrox each day. I was still staying with my mother and father, although by now we had moved to Cairnswell Avenue in Halfway so Bobby said if I could get to Cambuslang he would pick me up at the bus stop. He would get me there every morning then drop me off again after training. He was a real Ranger – Captain Cutlass they called him – and he is in the select band of players who have had the honour of captaining Rangers to the domestic treble.

In that same issue of the *Evening Times* that published our squad list, Peter Hendry was asking where the up-and-coming outside-lefts were. The only one listed for Rangers was the South African Johnny Hubbard, so Peter felt that our scouts should be on the lookout for talent to provide competition for wee Johnny. In the end they didn't need to bother as they had a new wee blond-haired recruit that would very soon be fulfilling that role.

I went in to the reserves initially and they were coached by the legendary Rangers forward, Bob McPhail. And if one Rangers legend, Jock 'Tiger' Shaw, is to be credited for turning me into a right-winger then it was Mr McPhail who can take the recognition for suggesting I could have just as much impact playing on the other wing. Bob recognised that I was comfortable using both feet so he suggested I could play at outside-left too. Thus, Peter Hendry's point about the paucity of left-wingers was now a moot one as I emerged as the man who would don the number-11 jersey on the occasions that Johnny Hubbard was absent.

The fact I was comfortable using both feet was thanks to the Wee Blue Devil himself, Alan Morton. An outstanding outside-left in his heyday – he had been Bill Struth's first signing back in 1920 and had terrorised the England defence when the 'Wembley Wizards' beat the Auld Enemy 5-1 in 1928 – I met Mr Morton when I first went to Ibrox. He was on the board of directors and, noticing I favoured my right foot, he suggested training with a football boot on my left and a sandshoe on my right. That encouraged me to develop my left foot as the heavy balls back then meant consistent kicking with the foot I wore the sandshoe on would have been painful. Becoming two-footed would prove hugely beneficial, so Mr Morton's advice stood me in good stead throughout my career.

But I was going to be hard pressed to regularly grab the number-11 jersey ahead of wee Johnny. He had arrived from South Africa in 1949 and had taken over from Eddie Rutherford on the left wing. In season 1954/55 he hit a hat-trick in a 4-1 win over Celtic and, unsurprisingly, one of Johnny's goals came from the penalty spot. He was dubbed 'The Penalty King' as he almost never failed to score a penalty kick. I had so much respect for the man and he was great with me when I joined. Although he was full time and trained during the day, he would always take time out to speak to me when I attended games at Ibrox on a Saturday. And when I eventually took his place in the team there was no bitterness.

We were different types of winger. Johnny was like Willie Henderson in the respect he liked to beat his man, get to the byline and cross the ball in to the box. I, on the other hand, preferred to cut inside on to my stronger right foot before either having a shot or picking out a team-mate. Nonetheless, Johnny would always be there to talk to and share his experiences with me.

There were some excellent players in that Rangers reserve team, a blend of youngsters like myself and older, more experienced players. In goal was Billy Ritchie. Billy had signed from Bathgate Thistle in August 1954 as understudy to George Niven. He would eventually supplant George and claim the number-one jersey, going on to play over 300 games for the first team.

In front of him were the likes of Willie Moles, Alan Austin and Willie Logie. George Young was in the twilight years of his career and these chaps would all be tried at first-team level as his potential replacement at centre-half. Alan, who signed from Irvine Meadow, would make his first-team debut against Celtic in September 1957, but Willie Logie made the step up sooner. Indeed, Willie made quite an impact when he broke into the first team. He made his debut in a 1-0 defeat against Kilmarnock and, in November 1956, he was in the side when Rangers played in European competition for the first time. But he fell foul of officialdom in the second leg against the French side OGC Nice when he was ordered off six minutes from the end. He eventually lost his place to Harry Davis.

In our forward line we had Derek Grierson and the burly South African Don 'The Rhino' Kichenbrand. Derek had made over 100 first-team appearances after signing from Queen's Park in 1952 and had scored 23 league goals in his first season at Ibrox. And Don had bulldozed his way through defences to be Rangers' top scorer in season 1955/56. Alas, the arrival of Billy Simpson and Max Murray limited their first-team opportunities, but it was great for me to have someone with their experience alongside me in the second team.

Like Bobby Brown, Derek was a school teacher, and I got to know him particularly well as he would always be training at night. He would always make himself available for a pass and rather than mope around the place because he wasn't playing for the first team, he always went out and put a shift in.

The prolific Harry Melrose, who, like me, had been in the junior ranks, having been farmed out to Dalkeith Thistle, and Jimmy Walker were also prominent at that time, although neither made significant inroads in the first team.

Like the first team, the reserves started the season with the League Cup and our section mirrored that of our first-team counterparts. Rangers were bracketed with Aberdeen, East Fife and Celtic in Section Two. We lost our opening match away at East Fife 1-0 but followed that with a win over Celtic. I drew praise for my performance in that one, with Percy Huggins in the *Evening Times* saying that I had shown the potential to become the next Johnny Hubbard. We won the game 3-1 and I was involved in the move that created our second goal for Ralph Brand before I grabbed a goal myself.

It was a terrific way to start my time at Rangers, but we lost our next tie, 3-2 at home against Aberdeen. We then edged out East Fife 5-3 at home – John Prentice scoring a hat-trick – and on the same day our rivals Celtic lost 5-0 at Pittodrie to register their fourth successive defeat. However, they arrested their decline when they beat us at Parkhead and a 5-1 thrashing against Aberdeen four days later ended Rangers' interest in the competition.

In the Reserve League we opened with a 3-0 drubbing by Dundee at Dens Park on 15 September, and six days later we lost 2-1 against Celtic at Ibrox. That match was played on the day that arguably the club's greatest-ever manager, Bill Struth, passed away. He was laid to rest in Craigton cemetery. In front of his grave was a tree and it was promptly chopped down as it obscured the view of Ibrox, thus giving him the chance to still see the place he called home on a daily basis.

I tasted victory in a Reserve League match for the first time at the end of September when we came from behind to beat Ayr United at Somerset Park. And emphatic wins over Dunfermline (5-2) and Queen's Park Strollers (8-1) shot us up to seventh in the league, six points behind leaders Hearts but with two games in hand.

The reserve games were an excellent education for a young lad like me. They were high-scoring games, so as a forward I was always involved. As if to prove that point, we faced Motherwell Reserves at Fir Park on 10 November and won 5-4, with Jimmy Walker scoring four goals for Rangers.

At the end of November we matched the first team by beating Aberdeen 3-1, and as we headed towards Christmas my form for the reserves was such that I was being touted for a call-up to the first team. And when Mr Symon picked a first-team squad of 13 players to face the British Army at Ibrox on 18 December I was among those selected. I was joined by some of my pals from the reserve team too, as Willie Moles, Harry Melrose and Jimmy Walker were also included.

I had been making a name for myself in the press, with Percy Huggins of the *Evening Times* effusive in his praise of me, and he was at it again following the match against the Army. Under the headline 'This David can be a Goliath', Mr Huggins stated he had seen me play for the reserves earlier in the season but now, four months later, felt I was more polished and precise and had more guile.

In truth, Mr Symon fielded largely a reserve team that night, with only Bobby Shearer, Sammy Baird and Ian McColl retained from the team that had beaten Hearts in the league the previous weekend. The Army XI contained four players from Manchester United – Duncan Edwards, Bobby Charlton, Eddie Colman and Bill Foulkes – and it was the latter who was my direct opponent. He was a big lump of a man and a fine full-back but I wasn't overawed.

I thought I played well and linked up successfully with Sammy, who was playing inside-left. And I wasn't just consigned to the wing either; on occasion I would make my way into the middle and, on one of those forays, I scored what would prove to be our only goal of the match. That came six minutes into the second half, two minutes after the Newcastle United centre-forward, Bill Curry, had put the Army 2-0 ahead. We had trailed 1-0 at the interval after our left-back, John Little, had scored an own goal and the game ended 3-1 in favour of the Army when Curry scored again in the final minute of the match. Incidentally, the beaten Army goalkeeper was Alan Hodgkinson of Sheffield United and he would have a Rangers connection almost 40 years later when he coached Andy Goram.

A few weeks later I made my league debut against Dundee at Dens Park. I could actually have been lining up against Rangers that day. Willie Thornton was the Dundee manager, the former Rangers player having taken over from George Anderson in July 1954. Not long after I had agreed to go to Rangers, Mr Thornton approached me and offered me the chance to sign for Dundee. Although I was still young, he said I would go straight into the first team, but by then I had committed myself to Rangers so I politely declined the opportunity.

That wasn't the only time I was approached to sign for a club. I was a member of 194th Glasgow Boys' Brigade Company and we used to go through to Arbroath for our camp. I was playing at Gayfield, Arbroath's home ground, one day when one of the club officials came on to the park and asked if I would sign for them. Once again my commitment was to Rangers so I rejected this chance too.

Incidentally, I loved my time in the Boys' Brigade. It's a fantastic youth organisation which instilled in me discipline and core values that I have used throughout my life. Under the guidance of our captain, Mr Price, I started as a Life Boy and progressed all the way to the rank of staff-sergeant, an honour that was bestowed on me on 25 March 1955. I am also proud to have achieved the Queen's Badge, the highest award that may be gained by a member of the Boys' Brigade.

It was commonplace in those days to play a number of games over the festive period, and the game at Dens Park was our third in just four days. Doubles from Billy Simpson and Max Murray had given us a 4-0 home win over Queen of the South on 29 December and we were back at Ibrox three days later for the traditional Ne'erday Old Firm clash. I had played for the reserves 24 hours earlier, scoring our second goal in a 3-0 win over Celtic Reserves at Parkhead, but was in the stands to watch Rangers dominate the first-team fixture. Murray and Simpson were on the scoresheet again but the 2-0 victory barely reflected our superiority.

The third of our matches was on 2 January against Dundee, and this time I was involved. Just eight days short of my 20th birthday, I travelled through to Dundee from Ibrox on the team bus and we went to a local hotel where we had dressed fish for lunch. That was about midday and after that Mr Symon named the team, and I was one of two changes from the XI that outclassed Celtic. Johnny Hubbard was rested so I came in at outside-left and Harry Davis returned from injury to replace Willie Logie at left-half.

Although delighted to get the opportunity to make my league debut, I was really nervous after Mr Symon told me I was playing. But our captain, George Young, was superb at keeping me calm. He told me just to keep it simple and play my own game and after that I was raring to go.

The big man was a stickler for standards, though, as I found out to my cost just before we took to the field. I was his boot boy and, noticing a speck of dirt on one of his boots, he told me to bend over and he promptly kicked me up the arse! When I asked what he had done that for he said that as he was leading the team out, he would be the first one the photographers would take a picture of. As Rangers captain he expected to look immaculate in any such picture and after that I made sure his boots were sparkling for every game he played in.

Geordie's boots were the old school football boots – size 12 – and we all wore similar footwear until the early 60s. And I was one of the trailblazers when the new boots were introduced. Denis Law had gone to Italy to sign for Torino and he sent me six pairs of the new, modern, lightweight boots they were using over there. He did it because he was my 'neighbour' in the national team as he played inside-left while I played outside-left.

Dundee were unbeaten at home prior to facing us, but we comprehensively ended that record. I was up against the Dundee right-back, Hugh Reid, and it was certainly a big difference from playing with the reserves. The main difference was the pace of the game but I was lucky in that respect as I was always quick and I had an electrifying start to the game. Twice inside the opening seven minutes, I set up goals for Alex Scott and Billy Simpson, and the great Gair Henderson in the *Evening Times* compared my running to that of Alan Morton. Lofty praise indeed! It wasn't the last time I would be compared to Mr Morton and, if I'm honest, the comparison made me feel uncomfortable. Alan had been a top-class player in his heyday and, although I wasn't short of confidence in my ability, it was rather overwhelming to be mentioned in the same sentence as one of the game's greatest-ever players.

George O'Hara halved the deficit after 57 minutes, when he netted after Bobby Shearer had cleared a Jimmy Chalmers shot off the line. But George Young secured a 3-1 win when he scored a penalty two minutes from time. The victory meant we were the only team in the First Division to win all of our matches over the festive period.

Johnny was back in the team again the following week – indeed, the Dundee fixture was the only league match he missed all season – and I was back at outside-left for the reserves. And on 19 January, when we faced St Mirren Reserves at Love Street, I was joined on the pitch by Jimmy Millar. Jimmy, a wing-half then, had only just returned from National Service where he served in the Troodos mountains in Cyprus. He had also spent time in Port Said and this was him now demobbed and back at Ibrox. He wore the number-four jersey that day in Paisley but once he was converted to a centre-forward he and I, aided and abetted by Ralphie Brand, would wreak havoc on defences throughout the early part of the 1960s.

I managed five more appearances for the first team before the season finished. These were all at outside-right in place of Alex Scott, with the first being a 3-3 draw against Queen's Park at Ibrox on 23 February. I remember the weather that day as much as anything as the blizzard that engulfed the stadium meant the gates were kept locked until 35 minutes before kick-off. As you can imagine, the pitch was covered in snow but I adapted well to the conditions, creating the opening goal of the game after just four minutes. With my first touch of the ball I cut inside on to my left foot and my cross was clinically despatched by the head of Max Murray. Incidentally, the beaten goalkeeper was Bob Crampsey, who went on to become one of the country's most respected football journalists when he finished playing.

On my inside that day was Billy Simpson and we spent much of the match interchanging positions. Billy was a lovely guy. We sadly lost him in January 2017 at the age of 87 after a long battle against dementia, but in the years prior to his passing he and his wife stayed just down the road from us in Newlands. We would often meet at the corner of the street for a chat, with Billy usually set for a trip to the greyhounds at Shawfield, one of his favourite pastimes. Back when I was breaking through at Ibrox, though, he was a rampaging centre-forward, although he was also picked to play at inside-right on occasion too. Playing alongside guys like Billy was fantastic for my development and I recall creating a few goals for the big man before he left to join Stirling Albion in 1959.

Billy wasn't on the scoresheet in the 3-3 draw against Queen's Park but he played his part in a thrilling match. We trailed 2-1 at one stage and then, after Bobby Morrison equalised, we fell behind again to a bizarre goal. It was scored by the Queen's right-back Ian Harnett and was one to forget for our goalkeeper, George Niven. Harnett, standing some 60 yards from our goal, hoofed the ball clear and when the ball dropped out of the leaden sky it skidded on the 18-yard line towards Niven. George, anticipating an easy save, bent down to pick the ball up, only for it to squirm out of his grasp and over the line. A shock defeat was on the cards until Willie Hastie took me out inside the box. Hubbard scored from the spot with consummate ease.

I kept the number-seven shirt the following week when we came back from 2-0 down to beat Hibernian 3-2 at Easter Road, and seven days later I scored my first league goal in a 5-2 win over Motherwell at Fir Park on 9 March. Max Murray put us 1-0 ahead with a goal that brought about vehement protests from the Motherwell players. His header came off the underside of the bar and bounced behind the Motherwell goalkeeper, Hastie Weir. The referee, Mr Davidson, ruled the ball had crossed the line and was immediately surrounded by Motherwell players who were adamant he had made a mistake. The goal stood but what they perceived to be an injustice spurred Motherwell on and they scored twice before the interval to lead 2-1.

But we restored parity in the 64th minute through Bobby Morrison. Bobby, an inside-forward, had joined us in January from Falkirk in exchange for Derek Grierson and scored three goals in his first four games, with his dramatic late winner earning us the two points in our come-from-behind win over Hibernian.

Hubbard then gave us the lead with a goal straight from a corner kick and I extended our advantage in the 79th minute when, in the midst of a goalmouth scramble, I managed to poke the ball under Weir. Max Murray completed the scoring at 5-2 when Johnny and I combined to set up his second goal of the game.

I made a further two league appearances after that before Alex was restored to the right wing against Aberdeen towards the end of March. And he was instrumental in a run of nine straight wins that helped overhaul Hearts and clinch the league title. The win over Motherwell in early March left us seven points adrift of our Edinburgh rivals, although they had played three games more than us. A key win came at Tynecastle on 13 April – Billy Simpson scored the only goal of the game – and a 4-3 win over Dunfermline on the final day of the season sealed the deal.

I ended my debut season having made six appearances in the league – not enough to get a league medal – but I did pocket some silverware when I played in the 2-1 win over Queen's Park in the Glasgow Merchant's Charity Cup. Alex Scott was at outside-right for the opening-round victory over Celtic and again for the 2-0 semi-final win over Clyde. But I was handed the number-seven jersey for the final on 6 May at Ibrox as Alex was part of the Scotland squad due to face Spain at Hampden two days later. Bobby Morrison fired us in front but Andy 'Dandy' McEwan levelled for a Queen's side looking for their first Charity Cup success since 1891. But I played a pivotal part in our winning goal in the 70th minute, crossing in to the box for big Don Kichenbrand to head beyond Jim Ferguson in the Queen's goal.

Incidentally, it wasn't just the forward line I played in for Rangers. I played in every position apart from centre-half, including a game where I had to take over in goal. There were no substitutes for outfield players back then, far less goalkeepers, so when the Rangers goalkeeper, Norrie Martin, fractured his skull up at Pittodrie in a League Cup sectional tie in August 1965, yours truly went between the sticks. I was captain that day too – Eric Caldow was absent through injury – so I made the call to take the gloves when Norrie was carried from the field after 65 minutes following a clash with Ernie Winchester.

It was 0-0 at that stage and I was soon in the thick of the action, saving a shot from Billy Little and fearlessly jumping in to a ruck of players to punch clear a cross from Ian Burns. We looked set to hold on for a point but we couldn't keep the Dons at bay and they scored twice in the last three minutes. I acquitted myself well in the circumstances, but the situation certainly added weight to the argument that Scotland should have joined our English counterparts in introducing substitutes. On that same day a chap called Keith Peacock of Charlton Athletic went in to the history books as the first-ever in-game substitute in English football when, ironically, he was introduced when goalkeeper Mike Rose was injured.

The Aberdeen game was one of five in which I was between the sticks. The others were all when I was at Dundee United, once in the first team and three times with the reserves. One of the reserve games was against Airdrie at Broomfield and I was in the crowd when an announcement came over the tannoy system asking me to report to the dressing room, which was located in the old pavilion there. When I got there I saw our goalkeeper had dislocated a finger so I was asked to replace him in goals. And I kept a clean sheet in a 4-0 win.

In addition to the Charity Cup, I added the Reserve League title to my roll of honour. The race for the title was enthralling, with ourselves, Hearts, Aberdeen and Motherwell all in the hunt as the season reached its conclusion. We had trailed in seventh place in February but by early April we were only three points adrift of pacesetters Hearts.

But thanks in no small part to the goals of Kichenbrand – he scored four in a win over East Fife and another in a 3-0 win over Raith Rovers – we cut the gap to a single point on 13 April with a remarkable 3-2 win over our Edinburgh rivals at Ibrox. We were 2-0 down at the interval but a stirring second-half fightback kept us in contention. On the same day Hibernian battered St Mirren 8-1 to take over from their city rivals at the summit, but crucially we had two games in hand over the Easter Road side.

Those games turned out to be away victories over Dunfermline (1-0) and Kilmarnock (3-2) and when we beat Kilmarnock 4-1 at Ibrox – notching up our 100th league goal of the season in the process – we were the title favourites. A 2-0 home win over Queen of the South in our penultimate fixture meant we would be champions if we won our last game.

But we almost contrived to throw it all away. Our last match was against Airdrie at Ibrox and we drew 3-3 to finish on 49 points, the same total as Hearts and Aberdeen. That ended a run of seven wins in a row, but we were still ahead on goal average. Motherwell, a point behind us, still had a game to play against Falkirk but they lost 3-2 and I had a Reserve League medal by the margin of 0.184 of a goal!

I was still Johnny's understudy in season 1957/58, although I started the campaign in the team as Hubby was out with an ankle injury. I was in the first XI in the annual 'trial' match at Ibrox that pitted the first team against the reserves, opening the scoring in what would be a 6-0 win for the top team. And I started in our opening two League Cup ties as well, creating the opening goal for Max Murray in our 6-0 win over St Mirren – Maxie and Billy Simpson both scored hat-tricks that day – and making another positive impact four days later when a Sammy Baird goal gave us a 1-0 win over Partick Thistle at Firhill.

Johnny was back in action for our next outing, a 4-3 win over Raith Rovers, but I took great heart from the positive reviews I received in the media. Journalists were commenting that it must have been a tough decision for Mr Symon to take me out of the team when Johnny declared himself fit, and that was a fantastic boost to my confidence.

I went back to the reserves but as I was fortunate I could play in any position along the forward line, there was always a good chance of getting called up to the first team. For example, I was selected a number of times at inside-left in 57/58 but I was on the wing when I made my European debut in September. This was our second successive season in the European Champions Cup, a tournament that had been devised by former French international footballer Gabriel Hanot and Jacques Ferran, who worked with Hanot at the French newspaper *L'Equipe*.

Ironically, it was a French team I made my debut against, St Etienne. I didn't play in the first leg at Ibrox – a match we won 3-1 – but was drafted in for the return leg in the Stade Geoffroy-Guichard. Hubby was ruled out with flu so I came in at outside-left, while Jimmy Millar replaced Alan Austin at right-half. Austin had made his debut the previous weekend against Celtic at Ibrox, but it was an inauspicious one; we lost 3-2, the first time Celtic had won at our stadium since season 1935/36.

That league defeat left us in 11th place in the First Division and we were faced with an arduous trip to get to our destination. It was not as easy and comfortable as it is for players nowadays. We had to fly from Renfrew Airport to Monaco then board a bus to take us to Saint-Etienne. It was stifling in a glass-topped bus which had no air conditioning and that undoubtedly contributed to Johnny Little, Don Kichenbrand and Alex Scott feeling unwell on the morning of the match.

Big Don and Scotty had scored at Ibrox – Billy Simpson got the other goal – and we should have won the first game more comfortably. Their goalkeeper, Claude Abbes, had been magnificent and the tie was back in the melting pot when the chap Oleksik scored for St Etienne after 11 minutes of the second leg.

What struck me was that the game was played at a much faster pace than the domestic matches and the opposition moved the ball a lot quicker. But we could hold our own and we refused to be beaten that night. We lost Billy Simpson for a period of the game when he suffered a bad cut to his forehead that required three stitches. And our centre-half, John Valentine, was in the wars too; his eyebrow was split open after he was accidentally kicked in the head.

Under such circumstances a lesser team may have folded, but we stood strong and I equalised on the hour mark with a diving header to restore our two-goal aggregate advantage. We should have sealed our place in the next round 15 minutes from time when I was fouled by Francois Weikhart and the referee awarded a penalty. Ian McColl took it, but Abbes, who would play for France at the 1958 World Cup finals, saved his effort. A late goal from the hosts made for an uncomfortable end, but we made it through to the next round.

We made history that night. When we took our first bow in this arena in season 1956/57 we were eliminated by OGC Nice after a play-off, so I was part of the first Rangers side to win a European tie over two legs. The match was also a highlight for a gift we were presented with by St Etienne. As I trooped wearily off the field at full time, one of their officials approached me with a racing bike. He indicated that this was a gift for Rangers but my immediate concern was how we were going to fit it on the aircraft that was flying us home! In the end we solved that problem and you can still view that racing bike today if you undertake a tour of Ibrox, for it sits proudly at the back of the Trophy Room beneath the portrait of Bill Struth.

My trip to France was soon followed by a journey to Italy as we drew AC Milan in the second round. I had gone back into the reserve team so I missed the first leg at Ibrox but was selected for the return match. By then, however, the tie was all but over. We were 1-0 up at half-time at Ibrox – Max Murray scored – and were wasteful in our finishing thereafter. We were duly punished for that in the final 16 minutes by a side who had qualified for the second round by defeating Rapid Vienna 10-8 on aggregate. Two goals from Ernesto Grillo, one for Dario Baruffi and another from Gastone Bean, made it 4-1 on the night to effectively knock us out.

As a team, Rangers were still making their way up the learning curve in European competition but, for me, it was good to get the experience of another European tie under my belt. Once again we had to take a circuitous route to get to Milan, thick fog meaning our flight was diverted to Turin, which necessitated a four-hour, 70-mile bus journey to reach our destination. Once there we found the tie had been switched from the San Siro to a smaller ground and we ended up losing 2-0 on a night when the rain came down in torrents. There was no great shame losing out to that Milan side, though. Inspired by the Uruguayan forward Juan Schiaffino, they beat Borussia Dortmund and Manchester United en route to the final against

Real Madrid. They took Puskas, di Stefano et al to extra time before going down 3-2.

That season is also infamous for one of the worst results in Rangers' history. I supplemented my two earlier appearances in the League Cup when I deputised for Alex Scott in the 4-0 win over Brechin City in the semi-final at Hampden, but Alex and Hubby were on the wings when we took the field for the final in the Hampden sunshine against Celtic. But I, and the masses of Rangers followers, watched in horror from the stand and the terraces as we were walloped 7-1, with our young centre-back John Valentine having a torrid time. He never played again for the first team after that – Mr Symon brought in big Willie Telfer from St Mirren in the wake of the defeat – but it was a terrible day for everyone associated with Rangers.

We suffered a horrible hangover from that defeat and ended up runners-up in the league, a mammoth 13 points behind Hearts. The Edinburgh side beat us 3-2 at Ibrox the week after the League Cup Final, and we also contrived to lose 4-3 at home to Kilmarnock. Hubby was still the main man at outside-left as proven by his four goals in the 4-0 win over Falkirk at Brockville, but I replaced him on the wing four days before Christmas, scoring our third goal in a 5-1 win over Third Lanark. I played in the next six league matches after that, including the 1-0 win over Celtic on New Year's Day. But just 21 days later my services were called upon elsewhere.

CHAPTER 3

IN THE ARMY

1958 WAS a big year for me as I was now eligible for National
Service. This had been introduced back in 1947 to resolve the
shortage of military personnel after the conclusion of World
War Two. People of military age were called up and I was one
of over two million people who were conscripted. Initially
conscripts were to serve for 18 months but during the Korean
War this was increased to two years.

I joined the Corps of Royal Engineers, who were usually
referred to as the Sappers. This comes from the French word
sappe which means spadework or trench. We provided military
engineering and technical support to the Armed Forces. My
army number was 23448393 and I went to Aldershot and
passed my medical before going through six weeks of basic
training. During that time you weren't allowed to go home and
they really put us through our paces. Fortunately I was really
fit, which helped, but it was still tough going.

I was then posted in barracks at Farnborough and they
weren't as bad as some may think. We each had a steel bed

that had to be made a certain way each day ahead of a daily inspection. And we had to be up and out early too, which led to a touch of embarrassment for one of the other lads one day. This fellow had been away playing football for Blackburn Rovers and had got back late the previous evening. As a result, he hadn't risen when he was supposed to but, rather than wake him, it was arranged for his bed to be pushed out on to the parade ring and we proceeded to do drills round about his bed.

Johnny Lawlor and I were the only Scots in the regiment. Johnny, who played football for, among others, Kilmarnock, Aldershot, Stirling Albion and Dumbarton, would come back to my mother and father's house with me when I came back home. And on one of those occasions he was the victim of a prank by my father. As we were getting packed up to return to barracks, my mother gave us what looked like biscuits from the Gray Dunn factory my father worked in. Unbeknown to us, my father had cut wood to the same size as the biscuits and then wrapped the wood up to look like it was a biscuit. You can imagine Johnny's reaction when, soon after we left, he hankered after a biscuit only to remove the wrapper and find a piece of wood!

The head man at the barracks was a Colonel Brown, and I made an early impression on him when he carried out an inspection of our billets. I had placed a board on the wall with nails in it and from the nails I hung my boots. That was what we did at Ibrox as we could easily see if our boots were short of a stud or two. The staff sergeant didn't think I would be allowed to do it yet, during the inspection, Colonel Brown came over and was so taken with my board that he insisted everyone in the barracks also got one for above their respective beds.

There were plenty of things to do on top of our daily duties, and by the time National Service ended for me I had collected medals for boxing, shooting and jumping. And, naturally, I played football, turning out for the British Army team, the same one I had made my debut for Rangers against, and also my regiment.

The Army team I played in was festooned with top international players. We played numerous matches and also played in a tournament called the Kentish Cup. Named after Brigadier General R. J. Kentish and first contested back in 1921, it involved the British Army, the French Army and the Belgian Army. We lost 2-1 to the French Army in Paris in December 1958 before we defeated the Belgians 3-2 at Stamford Bridge in London. Playing alongside me in that one were Falkirk's goalkeeper, Bert Slater, who was serving with the Royal Signals, his team-mate, Alex Parker, who was with the Royal Highland Fusiliers and Jackie Plenderleith of Hibernian and the Royal Army Service Corps.

A number of my appearances for the Army team were back on home soil and I scored the second goal in a 2-1 win over Aberdeen at Pittodrie in September 1958. We trailed 1-0 until Gerry Hitchens of Aston Villa equalised with six minutes left. Three minutes later it was down to me to secure victory. I even played against Rangers as I was part of the team that won 1-0 at Ibrox six days prior to our victory against the Dons. Peter Dobing, who was a lance corporal in the Lancashire regiment and played for Blackburn Rovers, scored the only goal of the game in front of a crowd of around 20,000.

Those wins were certainly memorable, but there was a chastening experience too when the Army XI went to Tynecastle to play Hearts in August 1959. We had lost 3-1 in Edinburgh back in April 1958, the Army's first defeat on Scottish soil, and we lost out again on this occasion. I got myself another goal just after the half-hour mark but that only temporarily stemmed the flow of goals at the other end. By the time the referee, Mr W. L. Fyfe from Edinburgh, blew the final whistle, the Army goalkeeper, Tony Godfrey of Southampton, had conceded EIGHT goals! This was a Hearts side that would go on to win the league and League Cup in Scotland in the season that followed, but it was still a sore one to take.

In addition to our matches in the Kentish Cup and against club sides – I can vaguely recall an encounter with Plymouth Argyle too – the Army side would take on XIs selected by the Football Associations of England and Ireland.

We faced the Irish at Windsor Park in Belfast on 11 March 1959 and the match was memorable for Peter Dobing as he scored all our goals in a 4-2 win. And it was notable for me too as I had an opportunity to play against one of the game's greatest players; Danny Blanchflower was the right-half for the Irish side that evening.

Facing the English FA was a less memorable occasion for yours truly though. The match was played at St James' Park in Newcastle just over six months after our win in Belfast and, in fairness, the Army hadn't fared too well in the fixture in recent years. In 1957 Brian Clough had scored five times in a 6-3 win for the FA and added a brace of goals the following year in a 4-1 win.

Clough had by now graduated to the full England XI but his attacking prowess had been replaced by someone I was all too familiar with, Joe Baker. Both Joe and his brother Gerry were plying their trade in Scotland. Gerry was part of the first team picture at St Mirren and Joe was with Hibernian. Joe, in particular, was starting to make a name for himself and in season 1958/59 he was top goalscorer in the top division, netting on 25 occasions. A remarkable 42 league goals were bagged the following season and Joe's goalscoring form eventually won him a move to Torino and from there he went to Arsenal for a club record £70,000.

The Army's front five that night in the North East had a Scottish flavour. I was outside-right and was joined by John White of Tottenham Hotspur, Alec Young of Hearts and George Mulhall of Aberdeen. It was George who netted the Army's only goal of the evening after 55 minutes, equalising the game's opening goal that was scored by, you've guessed it, Joe Baker. Two goals in the last ten minutes won the match for the English and my night was summed up when the Hearts goalkeeper, Gordon Marshall, saved my penalty kick.

The matches for my regiment were usually on a Wednesday and we travelled all over Europe. We remained undefeated in my time as a sapper and won the Army Cup. In one of those matches I was up against a major and he defiantly told me before kick-off that not only would I not get past him, he was going to kick me off the park. He didn't manage to succeed with either of his predictions, though, for I gave him a torrid time and scored a hat-trick!

Although I was based in England I would still try and get back to Glasgow when I could to play for Rangers. I would usually leave the barracks on the Friday to fly back to Glasgow then I would fly back on the Sunday. Arrangements would be made for me to leave, but one day I got caught trying to sneak out early. I was supposed to be leaving at 3pm but decided to go half an hour early by crawling under the barbed wire perimeter fence. But my uniform got caught and no matter what I did I couldn't free myself. I then felt a hand on my shoulder and when I looked round, I was horrified to see Colonel Brown standing over me. I thought I was for it but rather than bollock me he helped free me from the wire and wished me well on my homeward journey.

Such was my form with the Army team – I scored over 200 goals in the two years I served as a sapper – I would often be excused from sorties and one such exemption came when we were due to go to Christmas Island in the Pacific Ocean. That was where Operation Grapple was taking place. A total of nine nuclear explosions were carried out but I didn't have to go as the guy that ran the football team spoke to the colonel and told him I needed to stay at home to play for the football team.

Mr Symon thought that all the travelling was tiring for me so he didn't play me as often as I would have liked. My first appearance for Rangers as a sapper was on 8 March 1958 in a league match against Clyde at Shawfield, but I did not play again in the league until we lost 2-1 to Hearts at Tynecastle on 30 April. I got my second goal of the season in the penultimate league match of the campaign, a 2-1 win at Firhill against Partick Thistle, and I also played in the quarter-final and semi-final of the Scottish Cup.

The latter matches against Hibernian were controversial. We drew the first match at Hampden 2-2 but were 2-0 down just after half-time in the replay four days later. Sammy Baird reduced the arrears with a 54th-minute penalty and, with two minutes remaining, we thought we had equalised.

Ian McColl's cross was turned in by Max Murray but, after consulting with his linesman, the referee disallowed the goal for what was perceived to be a foul on the Hibernian goalkeeper, Lawrie Leslie.

I was praised in the press for my performance against Hibernian and I continued to get back up to Scotland when I could in season 1958/59. I managed a total of 15 appearances in the league and scored two goals. We had signed Andy Matthew from East Fife for £4,500 and he would spend most of the campaign competing with Johnny Hubbard for the number-11 jersey.

In truth we didn't start the season too well. We opened with a fine 3-0 win over Hearts at Ibrox in the League Cup – I opened the scoring after only five minutes – but then contrived to lose 3-1 to Raith Rovers at Starks Park, draw 2-2 with Third Lanark and go down 2-1 against Hearts at Tynecastle. We eventually finished second behind our Edinburgh rivals to exit the competition.

Our attempt to regain the league title started poorly too. We won only three of our first nine games, which left us seventh, four points adrift of Hearts who had a game in hand. I started the first five games, including the 2-2 draw with Celtic at Parkhead. We fell behind when Bobby Collins scored after 28 minutes but Hubby levelled the scores from the penalty spot four minutes before half-time.

There was a bit of dubiety over the award of the spot kick. Billy McNeill slid in to challenge me and some observers felt he won the ball cleanly. The Celtic players' protests were long and loud and their supporters voiced their displeasure too, and bottles came raining down from the terraces. This was commonplace in those days and used to happen a lot at Ibrox too.

Nonetheless, Hubby kept cool and scored and Ralph Brand earned us a draw in the second half when he equalised. The referee, Mr Harvie from Dalry, did not have the best of games and we were a wee bit irked that he allowed Celtic's second goal to stand. Their outside-right, Eric Smith, clipped the ball in to the net but Mr Harvie signalled there had been an infringement. However, after being encouraged by the Celtic players to consult with his linesman, he awarded the goal. Even back then the job of being the Old Firm referee was a challenging one!

We won, unconvincingly, at home to Partick Thistle a week later and then lost back-to-back to Airdrie (4-5) and Dundee (1-2). We were struggling to find a centre-forward and when I donned the number-nine jersey against Dundee, I was the fourth different player to wear it in this, our fifth league game. Max Murray found his shooting boots eventually and the 17 goals he scored in the last 20 league games went a long way to securing Rangers the title.

Our fans let their frustrations be known at the end of the Dundee game. They were less than enamoured with our forward line – such were our injury worries, Johnny Hubbard was selected at inside-right, with Andy Matthew on the left wing – and they voiced that displeasure when the game ended. I had had a tough time against the Dundee centre-half, Jimmy Gabriel, and eventually Mr Symon switched me with Johnny. We were 2-0 down by that time and Sammy Baird's goal two minutes from time was too little, too late.

The game against Dundee would be my last for a while in the first team. I played in only four of the next 22 league games – one of them was a thumping 5-0 win over title rivals Hearts in which Maxie scored a hat-trick – and also appeared at inside-left when we exited the Scottish Cup in February.

Having beaten Forfar Athletic and Hearts we drew Celtic away in the third round. I had played, and scored, a week earlier in a 3-0 win over Stirling Albion in the league, and Mr Symon put his faith in me again at Parkhead. But we were outplayed by Celtic on the day. Johnny Divers put the home side ahead on the stroke of half-time and, a couple of minutes after the restart, Matthew McVittie doubled their lead. We rallied and Maxie drew a wonderful save from Frank Haffey after 79 minutes, but he had to wait until stoppage time to score. By then it was too late and we were out.

My absence from the first XI did not mean I was confined to barracks and out of a Rangers jersey come the weekend. I would often come back up the road to play for the reserves too. A couple of weeks after the Dundee defeat I was among the goals as we beat St Mirren Reserves 4-1 at Love Street, and on successive Saturdays at the start of November I played inside-left against Hibernian Reserves at Easter Road and Clyde Reserves at Ibrox.

The Clyde match, which ended 1-1, came three days before a glamorous floodlit first-team friendly against the Italian side Napoli at Ibrox. Hearts' title win in season 1957/58 meant there was no European competition for Rangers to play in but that didn't stop us crossing swords with teams from the continent. And with Alex Scott due to play for the British Army the following night against Scotland, I was called up from Farnborough to play at outside-right for the Napoli match.

On a cold and wet night under the lights, we found ourselves 2-0 down after just 23 minutes but bounced back emphatically to win 5-2, and I was fortunate enough to score two goals. My first came 11 minutes before half-time and I restored parity at 2-2, ten minutes after the restart. We were excellent in that second half and only the form of Ottavio Bugatti in the Napoli goal stopped us racking up goals galore. As it was, Harry Davis, Max Murray and Andy Matthew, from the penalty spot, scored to secure a comfortable win.

There was a bit of hilarity before the game when our visitors arrived in the country without their mascot. Napoli were nicknamed *I ciucciarelli,* which means 'the little donkeys' in the local dialect. They had carried this moniker since the late 1920s after a dismal season that saw them gather just a single point from 18 league games. It was meant to be an insult since the Neapolitan symbol is a rampant black horse, but Napoli instead elected to adopt the donkey as their mascot and he was named *O Ciuccio.*

Unfortunately their famous four-legged mascot couldn't make it to Glasgow so the *Evening Times* stepped in and recruited Sammy, who was the donkey mascot for Yoker Athletic. The Italians were delighted at the gesture but us Rangers boys were just pleased we didn't make an ass of ourselves when we eventually took to the field of play.

After the game I was lauded for my performance but a return to barracks and an SFA suspension – more on that later – meant I missed out a fortnight later when we beat Grasshoppers from Switzerland 3-0. In the interim I deputised for the injured Andy Matthew when we faced Kilmarnock at Rugby Park on 22 November and took just three minutes to open the scoring in our 3-0 win with a left-foot shot.

I was still finding my feet as a Rangers player, though, and I was in and out the first team for the rest of the season. I came back from suspension to play a part in an epic 6-3 win over Queen of the South in early December, but by the time we faced Celtic in the traditional New Year Old Firm fixture, Andy Matthew had recovered from his knee injury to return to the first XI.

If I'm being honest, though, that was one game I was glad to miss as the weather was horrendous. The wind howled and swirled around the stadium with such force that the goalkeepers, George Niven and Dick Beattie, often had to grab hold of the post to keep them on their feet. On top of that there was rain, hail and sleet which turned the pitch into a quagmire. Rangers won 2-1 but the conditions were summed up when, with six minutes remaining, Celtic were awarded a penalty and, with it, a chance to equalise.

A few minutes earlier the talk had been of abandonment – the goal-lines were no longer visible – but play went on and when Willie Telfer fouled Divers, Jack Mowat, the referee, pointed to the penalty spot. Well, he pointed to where he thought the penalty spot was for when wee Bertie Auld picked up the ball to take the penalty he couldn't find the mark! I felt for the wee man as he had little option but to shoot high given the ankle-deep mud and surface water. The result was the ball thudded off the bar and the two points stayed at Ibrox to keep us on course for the league title.

I had no issues flitting in and out of the first team as my time in the reserves was excellent for my football education. At various times throughout the season I would be joined in the forward line by the likes of Max Murray, Sammy Baird,

Billy Simpson and Johnny Hubbard and playing alongside chaps that had played at the very top level for the club was invaluable.

The win over Celtic was our fifth in succession but we lost for the first time since late September when Partick Thistle won 2-0 at an icy Firhill on 3 January. Such was the extent of the freezing conditions, the corresponding reserve fixture at Ibrox that I was due to play in was postponed and it would be 21 January before the first team took to the field again.

I saw action in that period, though. Although the first team game fell foul of the weather, the reserves faced Airdrie Reserves at Broomfield on 10 January. And the match would feature a rarity, a missed penalty from Johnny Hubbard, the wee man hitting the crossbar with his effort just before the end of a goalless first half. I was playing centre-forward and had struck the woodwork too early in the match, but we eventually found a way through after the interval and won 2-0 to sit top of the Reserve League table, a point ahead of Clyde.

We weren't so fortunate the following week, with both the first team and the reserves inactive. It wasn't the cold snap that caused the postponements this time around, though. A thaw had set in and pitches that were playable on the Friday were suddenly unplayable 24 hours later. It was a day of call-offs all over the country in fact, with a total of 38 senior football matches postponed.

When the first team eventually resumed active service with a 2-1 win over Airdrie at Ibrox, I wasn't involved. Harry Davis and Ian McMillan got the goals and the victory kick-started a run of 12 games unbeaten that all but sealed the league title. I came back in to the team just over halfway through the sequence, replacing Andy Matthew at outside-left for a 3-1 win over Clyde at Ibrox on 7 March.

It was a late call from the manager, but a groin injury counted Andy out and Mr Symon handed me the number-11 jersey. Although I didn't score, I did provide the pass for Ian McMillan to bring us level at 1-1 against a Clyde side fighting for their lives at the bottom of the league. Alex Scott and Max Murray sealed the win in the second half and that was the start of a run of six straight games for me in the first team.

And the second game of the sequence was an epic. We travelled to face Falkirk at Brockville and our opponents were on the fringes of the relegation dogfight so therefore hungry for points. Scott, McMillan, Murray, Brand and Wilson was again the selected forward line, but we got off to an awful start and found ourselves 2-0 behind after just 16 minutes. I had been denied a goal by Bert Slater in that time period, but I turned provider when we pulled a goal back within a minute of going two down, my run and subsequent cross being clinically despatched by Max Murray.

The action really was frenetic and by the time the clock ticked on to the 30-minute mark, we were 4-2 behind. I claimed another assist for our goal in that period – Maxie was again the scorer – and came within a whisker of getting on the scoresheet myself before the break when I cut in and struck a shot that beat Slater but thudded against his right hand post.

Half-time gave everyone a chance to catch their breath but it was only a temporary reprieve as the second half was just as frantic as the first. We were first to strike when, after I was fouled by Jim Richmond, Eric Caldow despatched a penalty kick. And we were back on level terms with less than ten minutes of the second half gone when Ralphie made it 4-4. There would be another goal for each side before the final whistle sounded – Ian McMillan the scorer for Rangers – and at the end the spoils were shared at 5-5. I had not managed to add to my two league goals – I had doubled my season's tally a month earlier with a goal in a 3-0 home win over Stirling Albion – but just over three years later at the same venue I would more than make up for that.

Three successive wins followed the draw at Brockville, which meant, with two games to play, Rangers only needed a single point to win the title. We drew a blank in the first of those games, losing 2-0 to our nearest challengers, Hearts, at Tynecastle, but all and sundry expected we would finish the job in our last match at home to an Aberdeen team that were staring into a relegation abyss.

The visit of the Dons to Ibrox saw the end of my run of games in the team. Mr Symon recalled Andy Matthew at outside-left and I had to content myself with a place on the left wing for the reserves at Pittodrie. We lost 1-0, but when we trooped off all we wanted to know was the score from Ibrox. Had the lads secured the single point we needed to win the Division One title? Remarkably the first team had, like ourselves, lost. Ralph Brand had scored to make it 1-0 but the Dons were level by the interval and a second-half goal from Norrie Davidson secured the win.

Now attention shifted to Parkhead where Hearts were taking on Celtic. A draw for Hearts would have been enough to pip us at the post on goal average. But they contrived to lose 2-1 too and for one of the few occasions in the history of

Scottish football, everyone at Rangers was delighted with a Celtic victory!

With the title secured, the squad embarked on a two-match post-season tour of Denmark. I wasn't involved but this would be a landmark trip for Jimmy Millar. He had come from Dunfermline Athletic as a half-back, but Mr Symon brought him on to replace Maxie at centre-forward in the first match against Frem, and Jimmy promptly scored all four goals in a 4-0 win over Staevnet. The trip was rounded off with a 2-2 draw with Vejle, with Jimmy again on the scoresheet, and Mr Symon now had the number nine he craved. Over the next four seasons Jimmy would make the centre-forward position his own and establish himself as one of the finest forwards ever to play for Rangers.

Season 1959/60 commenced on 3 August with our annual 'trial' match at Ibrox. I joined the likes of Sammy Baird, Ian McColl and Maxie Murray in the reserves line-up, but we were torn apart in front of a crowd of 12,000. We shipped NINE goals and the star man was the man who had been in possession of the number-11 jersey for the majority of the previous season, Andy Matthew. He scored two goals, as did Jimmy Millar and Alex Scott. Brand, Caldow and Ian McMillan got the others to leave us reserves with faces as scarlet as the jerseys we were wearing that night.

It was no surprise, therefore, when Mr Symon picked the same front five when the competitive action got underway with an emphatic 6-1 win over Hibernian at Easter Road in the League Cup. Andy impressed again, grabbing one of the goals, but the star of the show was Ralph Brand who scored four times. Ralphie was an up-and-coming inside-forward and a smashing finisher who had been our top scorer in 1957/58 with 21 league goals.

Ralph and I would very soon strike up an almost telepathic understanding but, in the meantime, as he was making a name for himself in the first team, I was seeing action at outside-left for the reserves, opening the scoring in our 2-1 win over Hibernian in the Reserve League Cup. With Johnny Hubbard transferred to Bury, it looked like it was between myself and Matthew for the left-wing slot in the first team.

I travelled back to barracks as I always did after a match, but I was back up the road four days later when I got the call to replace Matthew for the next first-team outing against Motherwell at Ibrox. Andy had hurt his ankle so I was selected. But we didn't play very well and when Ian St John scored late in the game the Fir Park side secured a 2-1 win.

I was still in the team when we returned to the stadium on the Saturday to face Dundee. And this time I fared better. After Jimmy Millar had a goal ruled out, Ralphie put us in front after 20 minutes and we were 2-0 ahead at the interval after I drove an unstoppable shot past John Horsbrough in the Dundee goal with my right foot.

That's how it finished, and I was back among the goals when the league action started on 19 August. We faced Stirling Albion away from home and should have won comfortably but got a real fright before edging the game by three goals to two. Jimmy Millar headed us in front after only seven minutes – I provided the cross that created the goal – and the big man doubled his and our tally 13 minutes before half-time with a fine goal. When I made it 3-0 after 62 minutes we should have coasted to victory, but two late goals – one of them an own goal from Eric Caldow – meant a nervy ending before the points were finally secured.

I was enjoying my wee run in the first team, scoring and creating goals, but it looked to be over three days after our win over Stirling Albion when Andy Matthew was declared fit to face Hibernian in the League Cup at Ibrox. But on this occasion I wasn't demoted to the reserves, instead I moved to inside-right to fill in for Ian McMillan. And I kept my scoring streak going, scoring twice as we kept the pressure on Motherwell at the top of Section Four with a 5-1 win.

But the Steelmen secured their place in the last eight just four days later when they beat us 2-1 at Fir Park. There was no shame in losing out to Motherwell – they were the only team across the four sections to win all six games they played – and they would end the season fifth in the Division One table.

The defeat made our final fixture at Dens Park against Dundee academic, but we won 3-2 and I made it five goals in six games with a goal in that one. And it would soon be six goals in seven outings when I opened Rangers' account when we beat Celtic in the season's first Old Firm game on 5 September. I was still deputising for McMillan at inside-right and took just nine minutes to put us in front with a diving header. We led by my goal at the interval but managed to net a further two goals in the second half – Scott and Millar were the marksmen – to secure a 3-1 victory.

I was back in the reserves a couple of weeks later, though. With McMillan fit again he was restored to the starting XI when we faced Ayr United at Ibrox. I was joined in the second XI by Eric Caldow, who had lost his place at left-back to Johnny Little. And Eric and I were both glad to have been in

Ayrshire for we avoided the backlash that followed the first team's embarrassing 3-0 loss. For the record, the reserves won 4-2 but the capitulation at Ibrox to the newly promoted side understandably hogged the headlines.

A return to first-team action followed the week after the Ayr debacle. I replaced Jimmy Millar at centre-forward in a 3-0 win over Partick Thistle at Firhill, but after pulling on the number-ten shirt a week later in a 4-1 home win over Dunfermline Athletic, I missed the next four games, the last of which was a defeat at home to Hearts.

Thereafter, I was rarely out of the first team for the next three seasons. There's no doubt my demobbing in February 1960 when I completed National Service helped and the name 'Wilson' was typed on to the teamsheet at Rangers with more regularity. Between 7 November 1959 and 7 May 1960 I missed just two matches. I was injured when we drew 1-1 with Hibernian at Ibrox on 2 January and was absent again on 27 April when we went down 4-1 against Clyde at Shawfield. I should have missed out against Dundee at Ibrox too, as I was in Anderlecht with the British Army to face the Belgian Army when the game was originally scheduled for 6 February. However, dense fog forced a postponement and I was back in blue for the rearranged fixture which ended in a no-score draw.

As I alluded to earlier, I spent the opening spell of the season deputising for Matthew, McMillan and Millar at outside-left, inside-right and centre-forward respectively. But I was on the left-hand side of the forward line from November onwards, either playing inside-left or on the left wing. In that glut of games I scored six league goals, including our last league goal of the season in a 2-1 final-day defeat at home to Third Lanark.

Believe it or not, Celtic were not our main rivals for the league in those days. They won the title in 1953/54 but since then it had mostly been Hearts that had fought with us for the big prize. They had some smashing players in that era, like Alfie Conn Senior, father of future Ranger and Barcelona Bear, Alfie, Willie Bauld, Jimmy Wardhaugh, Dave Mackay and Alex Young.

Jimmy, Willie and Alfie were dubbed 'The Terrible Trio', and I remember Jimmy coming up to me after one game early in my Rangers career. He shook my hand and told me that he had no doubt I would have a successful career. To get praise like that from a guy who was an established forward in the Scottish League so early in my career was a terrific boost.

The Tynecastle side would add to their title win of season 1957/58 in 1959/60. They beat us home and away – both by two goals to nil – and eventually finished 12 points ahead of Rangers, who finished third. But it was the Rangers that got their hands on the Scottish Cup. I played in all seven of the cup ties and grabbed a hat-trick in the opening-round win over Berwick Rangers. That game at Shielfield Park was memorable for a number of reasons.

It was a freezing cold day for this, the first-ever Scottish Cup tie Rangers had played in England. There was a biting wind and the sleet that was falling resulted in a pitch covered in snow and ice. And we played into the blizzard in the first half when our skipper, Eric Caldow, lost the toss.

Our opponents more than held their own in the opening exchanges, with George Niven pulling off a couple of fine saves. But I scored my first goal ten minutes before half-time to settle our nerves. Alex Scott won a corner and, from the ensuing kick,

Bobby Hume picked out Jimmy Millar. His header landed at my feet and I swiftly despatched the ball behind the home goalkeeper, Tom McQueen.

Jimmy almost doubled our lead a couple of minutes later, but his shot thudded against the post. We looked all set to canter to a comfortable victory but, just before half-time, Berwick were level. Ian Whitelaw lobbed the ball into our penalty area and there was an almighty stramash. The ball eventually emerged at the feet of Whitelaw and his shot beat Niven.

The goal was a bit of a shock to the system and we weathered a wee bit of a storm afterwards. However, I almost took us in at the interval in front but my header cleared the crossbar by a matter of inches. But I wasn't to be denied, and in the second half I scored another two goals to complete my first hat-trick for Rangers. After another header of mine grazed the post, I picked up a pass from Bobby Hume and beat two players before shooting past the goalkeeper from close range. That was in the 62nd minute and I completed the treble three minutes from time when I found the net after a scramble in the goalmouth.

All in all a very satisfying day at the office, so I was looking forward to a nice, warm shower when we got back to the dressing room. As you can imagine the playing conditions were such that as we trooped off the field we were caked with mud and frozen so there was understandably a great deal of consternation when it transpired the powers-that-be at Berwick had turned the hot water off! As a result nobody had a shower. We just put our clothes on over the mud that was encrusted on our legs and got on the bus back to Ibrox!

I seemed to like playing in the Scottish Cup that year. After creating the opening goal for Jimmy Millar, I scored our third goal against Stenhousemuir in the third round. And I was in among the goals again when we faced Hibernian in the quarter-final at Ibrox. An early handball by our centre-half, Bill Paterson, was punished when Bobby Johnstone fired the visitors ahead from the penalty spot, but we were back on level terms by the interval when Sammy Baird got himself on the end of my in-swinging corner kick to divert the ball into the net. And when I bent another ball towards goal 12 minutes after the restart I claimed my fifth Scottish Cup goal of the season. Jimmy was fouled by Jackie Plenderleith on the left wing and when I swung the free kick in it curled beautifully beyond the outstretched fingers of Willie Muirhead in the Hibernian goal. If I'm being honest I thought I had made a bit of a mess of the delivery – I hadn't intended to shoot for goal – but nonetheless I was delighted with the final outcome!

However, Hibernian were a better side now than the one we had scored 11 goals against over two League Cup ties earlier in the season and they equalised within three minutes. I was then guilty of passing up several glorious chances to restore our lead – writing in the *Glasgow Herald*, a 'special correspondent' noted that, collectively, our finishing had been 'incredibly bad' but identified me as the chief sinner in front of goal – but I made amends when, after 73 minutes, my low cross from the left wing was rocketed in to the roof of the net by Jimmy Millar.

The victory over Hibernian took us through to the last four where we faced Celtic. They had a dreadful season in the league, finishing ninth, 21 points behind Rangers, so the cup was their last chance of snaring one of the big three domestic trophies.

We were hampered by the swirling wind at Hampden in the first half, and slack marking allowed Stevie Chalmers to give Celtic a half-time lead. But we were the superior side in the second half and should have scored more than the one goal we got. That inevitably came from Jimmy Millar and it was a splendid goal. I picked up the ball on the left and arrowed a cross in to the penalty area. It was about chest height and Jimmy stooped 15 yards from goal to head the ball magnificently beyond Haffey.

In the replay four days later, we found the goals that had eluded us in the second half of the first game. I opened the scoring after 28 minutes, when Duncan MacKay was indecisive in dealing with a free-kick from Sammy Baird. I think Duncan expected Frank Haffey to come for the ball, but I pounced as he dilly-dallied and we were ahead. Neilly Mochan levelled the score six minutes later and, with the wind at their backs, Celtic must have fancied their chances after the interval.

But within four minutes of the restart Jimmy had us in front, and with 19 minutes to go the guy who was too wee for Cambuslang Rangers scored with a header for the Rangers to edge us towards the final. As the Celtic defence stood still, I got on the end of a cross from Alex Scott to beat Haffey. Thereafter, we contained Celtic as we were reduced to ten men after Harry Davis was taken off on a stretcher. Celtic tried to breach our defence but couldn't, and the next goal in the game was the icing on the cake for Rangers, another header from the magnificent Millar in the 79th minute.

We faced Kilmarnock in the final and I was able to secure us a wee advantage in the week leading up to the game. I was on a training course with the Kilmarnock goalkeeper, Jimmy

Brown, and found out he had damaged his left collarbone. This meant he couldn't fully extend his left arm so when I got the ball out wide at Hampden, I slung over crosses towards Jimmy that I knew Billy would either not be able to reach or have to be unorthodox and use his right hand to try and field them.

It was from one of those crosses that we hit the front after 22 minutes. I beat their right-back, Jim Richmond, and hung the ball up above Brown. He was unable to reach it and Jimmy seemed certain to score. However, he contrived to head the ball up into the air but fortunately got his head on the ball again before Billy could recover. Although Eric missed a penalty shortly after half-time, Jimmy scored again in the 68th minute and the cup was ours.

Rangers also made the semi-final of the European Cup that year, and there were several memorable matches in that run. After seeing off Anderlecht 7-2 on aggregate in the opening round we were drawn against Red Star Bratislava. The first leg at Ibrox was a tempestuous affair. Just before the interval we were trailing 2-1 when I embarked on a mazy dribble. I crossed into the box and big Sammy Baird rose to meet the ball. Their goalkeeper, Frantisek Hlavaty, also came out to claim my cross and the pair collided. With Hlavaty lying prone, Alex Scott netted to make it 2-2. Mayhem ensued as our visitors felt Sammy had fouled the goalkeeper and their protestations resulted in Stefan Matlak being ordered off.

With Hlavaty carried off on a stretcher, they had to play out the remaining minutes of the first half with nine men. With the goalkeeper back in position, we fell 3-2 behind after 68 minutes then spurned a chance to equalise when Eric missed a penalty. Barely a minute later, though, we were level when yours truly got himself on the end of an Alex Scott cross to make it 3-3. Jimmy Millar's goal in the final minute secured a 4-3 win in what was a breath-taking match. The return leg was tousy too. Jimmy was ordered off for retaliation but I set up Alex for a goal after 70 minutes, and although they equalised in the last minute we held out to progress to the quarter-finals.

We drew Sparta Rotterdam at that stage and, for the first time ever, Rangers played the first leg away from home. We faced a Sparta side that contained the controversial Johnny Crossan. He had been banned from playing football worldwide due to alleged financial misdemeanours, although this was later reduced to a ban that only covered football in the UK. He would face us again – with more success – in 1962 when we played Standard Liege, but this time around he could only watch as I continued my fine European form by putting us 1-0 up after just four minutes.

Sammy Baird doubled our lead ten minutes before half-time, and although the home side halved the deficit before half-time, Max Murray had us 3-1 ahead after 63 minutes. A goal in the dying seconds made it 3-2 and the return leg at Ibrox now seemed like it would be a formality. 'Twas not the case, though, as despite relentless Rangers pressure a goal from Tony van Ede seven minutes from the end meant a 3-3 aggregate and a play-off at Highbury in London.

Younger readers may be asking why Rangers didn't progress as our three goals in Holland meant we should have gone through on the 'away' goals rule. But this rule wasn't in place yet so we ventured south in a bid to make the semi-finals. And that's exactly what we did. We were 1-0 down after just seven minutes but my free kick teed up Sammy to make it 1-1 at half-time. I got another assist for our second goal, picking up a headed clearance and setting up Sammy for his second, this one being a rasping drive from 25 yards. Jimmy Millar made it 3-1 after 70 minutes and we survived a late onslaught after the Dutch had scored a penalty to progress to the last four.

There we were, joined by Real Madrid, Barcelona and Eintracht Frankfurt. We drew the West Germans but we came a cropper, losing 6-1 in West Germany and shipping a further six goals at Ibrox to lose 12-4 on aggregate. Although they dominated the first half of the first leg and missed an early penalty, we were level at 1-1 at half-time thanks to a penalty of our own which Eric converted. But it was then that our tactical naivety kicked in. Rather than play it tight in the second half, we played exactly the same as we would have had we been playing a league or cup match in Scotland. The result was the concession of five goals to all but end our hopes of making the final at Hampden.

Ironically, a couple of years later we played Eintracht again to mark the official opening of the Hampden floodlights. There were 104,679 people there to watch us and we looked set for another hiding when we were 3-0 behind after 49 minutes. But clearly we were becoming a bit more streetwise as we pegged them back to 3-2 thanks to a rare double from Harry Davis. We should probably have won the game too, but Ralphie missed a penalty and Jimmy Millar, Alex Scott and me all struck the crossbar during a barrage of attacks in the second half.

We had a couple of other games at Hampden that season, defeating Partick Thistle on both occasions to win the Glasgow Cup and the Charity Cup. We reached the Charity Cup Final by beating Celtic at Ibrox. A fine goal from Paddy Crerand six minutes from time equalised an earlier strike from Ralphie and the outcome was decided by the toss of a coin. Can you imagine an Old Firm cup semi-final being decided in that manner these days? But that was the norm back then, and when the referee, Mr W. Brittle, called the two captains, Eric Caldow and Bertie Peacock, together it was Eric who called it right and we were through to the final. A dose of Millar and Brand two days later secured the silverware in a low-key match against a Thistle side that had finished mid-table in the league.

However, the abiding memory from that 1959/60 season wasn't the European run or our success in the cup competitions, it was of the performance of a young lad called James Curran Baxter in a league match against us on 21 November 1959. Playing at left-half, Jimmy ran the show for Raith Rovers who came to Ibrox and won 3-2. We started the game well and I scored with another header after just two minutes. The architect of the goal was Alex Scott and, when he found the net 11 minutes later, we looked to be coasting to victory. But Baxter brilliantly turned the game around. His breath-taking individual goal after 17 minutes was sandwiched by two goals from Jim Kerray but after the game all the talk was about how Jimmy had played.

And he made a lasting impression as, in the summer of 1960, Mr Symon signed him for Rangers. The final piece of the jigsaw had been put in place.

CHAPTER 4

THE BIRTH OF THE GREATEST-EVER TEAM

JIM BAXTER had already made an impression on the players at Ibrox even before he signed for Rangers. We had faced Raith at Stark's Park and were getting off the team bus when we heard the thrum of a motorbike engine. It got louder and louder the closer the motorbike got, and it sped past us and the rider parked up in a space that would normally be reserved for a car. The rider was, of course, Jimmy, and I was quick to tell him that he wouldn't get away with riding a motorbike once he joined Rangers. He didn't listen, and on his first day revved up to the ground on the same motorbike. He was subsequently summoned to see Mr Symon and was promptly told he would be getting the bus back home to Fife and would no longer have use of his motorbike!

Not that that was going to be an issue for Jimmy. The two wheels were soon substituted for four and Baxter was arriving at Ibrox in a 1958 Jaguar. I was also behind the wheel by then, having passed my driving test while on National Service.

My choice of car was a little more understated than Jimmy, with one of my first being a 1961 Ford Classic. I did go a bit unconventional with the colour, though, my car gliding through the streets of Glasgow with a rather snazzy yellow paint job!

Jimmy was some player. Alongside Willie Henderson, he's the best player I played with at Rangers. He had a wonderful left foot and a lot of the goals I scored came from either his precise passes or the space he created for me. I was very lucky as I had Jimmy behind me most of the time I played outside-left, and when I was moved to the other wing, on occasion, I had Ian McMillan playing at inside-right. He was an exceptional player too.

Off the park Jimmy was always full of fun, but I got my own back on him for one of his japes one day. I was due to meet a journalist to do an interview after a game one Saturday so I quickly got changed into my suit and most of the boys, including Jimmy, were still in the big, communal bath when I was ready to leave. I went in to say my goodbyes and the next thing I knew Jimmy was splashing me with water until I was soaked through. I wasn't best pleased. But Jimmy and I changed next to each other so the next chance I got I came into the dressing room before him and put on his suit jacket and flannels.

He was due to go to the dancing that night so, as he was in the bath getting spruced up, I went in to see him. The same thing happened as had done previously. After commenting that my clothes were a bit ill-fitting, he proceeded to douse me with bath water again. However, this time I decided to dive full length into the bath. I resurfaced and reached into the inside pocket of the jacket and pulled out Jimmy's wallet. You can imagine the look on his face when he realised I was wearing his suit! He was raging as, unlike me, who stayed locally in Cambuslang, Jimmy had to go all the way back to Fife to get new gear before he could enjoy his night on the tiles.

There's another infamous story involving the great cricketer, Sir Garfield Sobers. Jimmy was at Nottingham Forest and he and the team went to the County Ground to watch the cricket. Sobers left his bank card with Jimmy and told him to buy himself a drink, but he didn't know the full team were there. When he came back from the crease he was faced with a bar bill of around £2,000, Jimmy having treated himself and his pals to copious amounts of alcohol from the bar!

Everyone knows Jimmy was fond of a drink, but I never indulged. My mother and father were teetotal and I have never touched a drop of alcohol. I haven't smoked either, even though smoking was widespread among my team-mates. For example, Max Murray would often come in at half-time, take a cigarette out of his pocket then go and smoke it in the toilets. He would then go out and more often than not get himself a goal or two in the second half.

Jimmy was in the midst of his National Service with Black Watch when he signed, so he did not play in every game in 1960/61. But when he did he was magnificent, and he was one of the main reasons why we reclaimed the league title that year.

It was Jimmy who stole the show in the Ibrox trial match in early August. He strutted his stuff for the 90-minute match that saw the first team face the reserves for an hour then the third team for the last half hour. A year earlier I had been in the reserve XI but this time I was the outside-left for the boys in blue. Baxter was listed at inside-left, with Willie Stevenson at left-half. As an illustration of how strong our squad was, there was no place in the first team for Brand or Shearer and the reserve XI was also fortified by the presence of McColl, Baird, Murray and Matthew. The match finished 4-4, with the hour-long game with the reserves finishing 3-3 and the 30 minutes against the third team ending 1-1.

Although I didn't get a goal in the trial match, I was delighted to now be considered a first-team fixture and I'd like to think I repaid the manager for the faith he showed in me for I started the season in fine fettle. My team-mates and I were rampant in our first two league matches, with victories over Partick Thistle (6-3) and Celtic (5-1). I was on the scoresheet in both matches, with a double against Thistle followed by a strike in our thrilling Old Firm win at Parkhead.

It was nip and tuck for an hour, with Rangers leading thanks to Alex Scott's goal after two minutes. But once Jimmy Millar scored our second after 65 minutes, we found top gear. Sean Fallon in the Celtic goal had an uncomfortable match, and it was his fumble that presented Ralphie with the chance to put us 3-0 ahead 12 minutes from time. I got in on the act six minutes later, despatching a pass from Ralphie into the net. Harry Davis made it 5-0 with a header before Stevie Chalmers netted what was a mere consolation goal for Celtic in the last minute.

I was on the mark again seven days later, taking my league tally to five in three games with a double in a 3-0 home win over Airdrie, and we looked set to be out of sight in the race for the title given our scintillating form. But a goal from Dundee's Alan Cousin inflicted upon us our first defeat of the season on

8 October at Ibrox. And he would be on the mark again when we lost 4-2 at Dens Park in February.

Despite the setback of losing at home, we were still leading from the front and won eight of our next ten league matches. I was on the scoresheet in three successive matches in that run, netting against Aberdeen, Hibernian and St Mirren. The 2-1 win over Hibernian at Easter Road was significant, not just because we picked up two precious points but for the fact that Hibernian's goal was scored by an old team-mate, Sammy Baird.

Sammy had made his last appearance for the Rangers first team back in August when we lost 3-2 at home to Celtic in the League Cup, replacing the injured Ian McMillan at inside-right. A couple of months later, after St Mirren apparently baulked at the transfer fee Rangers wanted, Sammy signed for Hibernian. I was sad to see the big man go as he was a good player who had been a huge influence in my early days at Ibrox.

Sammy had played under Scot Symon at Preston North End but hadn't enjoyed English football, so when Mr Symon became Rangers manager, he brought Sammy back up north. He was a half-back who could also play as an inside-forward and he much preferred a long pass to a short one. That prompted Johnny Hubbard one day to joke that by the time he got on the end of one of Sammy's raking passes he was in the middle of the terraces! But all joking aside, Sammy was a fine player and a vital part of that successful era for Rangers.

It was yours truly who opened the scoring in Edinburgh, pouncing after only ten minutes to shoot past Ronnie Simpson in the home goal. It was a typical Wilson goal too as I took a pass from Ralphie, beat the full-back and shot home with alacrity. Ralphie made it 2-0 before Sammy reduced the arrears with a penalty kick. Ralphie then spurned the chance to make the closing minutes more comfortable for us when he missed from the penalty spot. I won the spot kick when I was upended by Jim Easton, but big Ronnie was equal to Ralph's effort.

That wasn't my only run of successive games scoring that season as I did it again over the festive period. Goals against Partick Thistle and Airdrie supplemented another Old Firm goal when we played Celtic at Ibrox on 2 January. Some dilly-dallying by Baxter saw us a goal down after 28 minutes, but Ralphie got us level in the second half before I profited from an error from Frank Haffey to head the winner with ten minutes left.

The Airdrie game – our 20th league match – was remarkable as it was our first drawn league game of the campaign. But rather than viewing the 1-1 draw as a point dropped, the result actually edged us further ahead of our nearest challengers, Aberdeen and Kilmarnock. While my goal secured a share of the spoils at Broomfield, Kilmarnock were losing 4-0 against Hibernian and Aberdeen were on the end of a 2-1 defeat at the hands of St Johnstone.

Rangers were now eight points clear but maybe we got complacent after building such a healthy lead, for we only won five of our next 13 league fixtures. That wretched run let Kilmarnock, managed by the former Rangers winger Willie Waddell, back into the title race. We had lost 3-2 against them at Ibrox on 26 November – I scored my ninth league goal of the season in this our 12th league game, but we contrived to throw away a 2-0 lead – and they did the double over us when they beat us 2-0 at Rugby Park on April Fool's Day. A week later we were humbled 6-1 by Aberdeen at Pittodrie and suddenly we were faced with the prospect of missing out on winning the league.

It went right down to the wire and we had to beat Ayr United at Ibrox on the final day of the season to ensure we were champions. Ayr, who had beaten us 1-0 at Somerset Park earlier in the season, were battling for top-flight survival, which made for an open and entertaining game. Willie Henderson had torn his ankle ligaments in our previous league match against Hibernian so I played outside-right, with Bobby Hume coming in at outside-left.

Ian McMillan was outstanding that day. He was the conductor of a Rangers orchestra that really hit the high notes. Alex Scott, playing at centre-forward, scored a brace to put us 2-0 ahead inside 25 minutes, before McMillan embarked on a fine run that ended with him setting me up for our third goal. Ralphie had us 4-0 up after 41 minutes and, although Ayr got a goal back, Scotty completed his hat-trick with a stunning free kick eight minutes after the restart. A fumble from Billy Ritchie allowed Ayr to score a second and offer a glimmer of hope, but that was extinguished when 'the wee Prime Minister', McMillan, crossed for me to head in my second and Rangers' sixth of the afternoon. Jim Christie, who would sign for Rangers less than a month later, chalked up the ninth goal of the game to make it 6-3, but Ralphie grabbed league goal number 24 of the season after 88 minutes to round off the scoring at 7-3.

Although I had played a part in our league wins in 1956/57 and 1958/59, this was the first title win that I felt I had made a significant contribution to. I managed 19 goals in 34 league games and I added a goal in the League Cup run too. That was a vital strike at Dens Park in the second leg of the quarter-final.

We won a titanic match 4-3 to clinch a 5-3 aggregate success and progress to the last four.

I put us 1-0 up after 21 minutes at Dens but, almost immediately, Dundee had a chance to equalise when Harry Davis was penalised for punching away a shot from Hugh Robertson. But Billy Ritchie saved Alan Gilzean's weak penalty and we proceeded to double our lead on the night when Ian McMillan's shot was deflected into the net off Ian Ure six minutes before the break.

With Dundee seemingly in disarray – in addition to being 2-0 down, their centre-half, Billy Smith, was injured and now hobbling on the right wing – we looked set to comfortably progress to the last four of the competition. But within three minutes of the restart Alan Cousin, who had passed a late fitness test to take his place at inside-right, scored with a header from a Bobby Seith cross and he used his head again 12 minutes later to equalise on the night. Then remarkably, with 15 minutes left, Dundee were awarded another penalty. Andy Penman took this one and scored and, all of a sudden, the tie was level at 3-3 on aggregate.

We were all set for a grandstand finish and, fortunately, Rangers came out on top. McMillan doubled his tally for the evening with ten minutes left and Ralphie got our fourth when he capitalised on a short backpass from Ure.

In the Hampden semi-final we defeated Queen of the South comprehensively 7-0. A double dose of 'M & B' and a goal from McMillan had us 5-0 up by half-time, and I was involved in Jimmy's second goal after 19 minutes. I embarked on a run that befuddled Jim Patterson – Jim is actually Queen of the South's all-time record goalscorer but was playing right-half that night – and a cheeky wee back-heel flick took me away from right-back Jim Kerr. I then lifted my head and rolled a pass into Jimmy's stride and he blasted the ball beyond former Scotland goalkeeper George Farm from the edge of the box.

In the final we faced Kilmarnock. And we had goalkeeping problems ahead of the game as just three days before facing them, when we had beaten Hearts 3-1 at Tynecastle – I was on the scoresheet, netting Rangers' third goal – we had had to play 83 minutes of the match with ten men. After just seven minutes Billy Ritchie collided with one of the Hearts forwards and had to be carried off. A trip to Edinburgh Royal Infirmary ended with his left ankle encased in plaster after it was discovered he had chipped a bone. Bobby Shearer took over between the sticks as we eased to victory, but we were fortunate for the final to have such a fine reserve goalkeeper, the evergreen George Niven. He had been supplanted by Billy earlier in the season but showed what a true professional he was by stepping in to the breach. He would remain our last line of defence until Billy was fit to play again in April.

We played against a swirling wind in the first half, but went in at half-time 1-0 ahead when Ralphie took a pass from Jimmy Millar, rounded Bill Brown in the Kilmarnock goal and struck the ball into the net. I almost made it 2-0 early in the second half, but my shot rose a fraction too high and struck the crossbar. But we secured the cup 16 minutes from time when Alex Scott whipped in what looked like a cross, but the ball eluded Brown, struck the post and then nestled in the net.

The Scottish Cup eluded us, though. After comfortably beating Dundee 5-1 away from home in the opening round, we drew 2-2 with Bobby Ancell's young Motherwell side at

Fir Park. They had a good, young side – they were nicknamed Ancell's Babes – but we fancied ourselves to win the replay at Ibrox. Motherwell had other ideas, though, going ahead through John McPhee. Goals from myself and Ian McMillan soon had us 2-1 in front, but Pat Delaney made it 2-2 before Bobby Roberts scored after an hour. We were now trailing 3-2 and, as we chased an equaliser, Ian St John, soon to be on his way to Bill Shankly's Liverpool, and Roberts scored again to make the final score 5-2. Our cause wasn't helped that day by the absence of Baxter. He had played in the draw at Fir Park but was called back to the Army so missed out on playing in the replay.

Unlike previous seasons when we didn't win the league, there was European competition on offer in 1960/61. Like the European Cup, the European Cup Winners' Cup was the brainchild of sports journalists and was to be contested by teams that had won the domestic cup competition. Our Scottish Cup win over Kilmarnock meant Rangers would represent Scotland in the inaugural tournament and, in the opening round, we drew Hungarian side Ferencvaros. But our future in the tournament looked to be in jeopardy when, after winning 4-2 at Ibrox, we were pegged back to 4-4 after 48 minutes of the second leg in Budapest. We needed a hero and found one in the shape of our wee blond-haired European talisman – yours truly – and I notched another European goal to put us through and set us on the road to the final.

We had travelled in style to the Hungarian capital. The aircraft we flew on had been used by Queen Elizabeth II and Prince Philip when they had flown to the USA in 1957. But when we arrived at the Nepstadion torrential rain had rendered the pitch almost unplayable. To ensure the game went ahead, a large sheet was placed over the playing surface, and when it was removed the pitch was deemed playable.

We started with Ralphie at inside-left, even though his car had struck a bus en route to Prestwick Airport for our flight. We came out the blocks quickly and Jimmy Millar almost put the tie to bed in the tenth minute when his shot struck the post. But goals in the 18th and 48th minutes for the hosts brought the aggregate scores level. The game now opened up, but after 63 minutes Rangers nicked what would prove a vital goal. Alex Scott lofted the ball forward only to see right-back Gyorgy Kiss beat me to it and play the ball back in the direction of his goalkeeper, Gryorgy Horvath. But his pass was under-hit and I nipped in ahead of the goalkeeper and rolled the ball into the net from 12 yards.

The European ties offered a refreshing change from domestic football. The players we faced were more technically gifted and we usually got more time on the ball. But some of the teams we faced would often resort to underhand tactics to knock us out of our rhythm and there were a number of occasions when games degenerated into physical battles when things were not going the way of our opponents.

Ahead of the second-round tie with Borussia Monchengladbach, we were in great form. Four days prior to going to Budapest we lost 1-0 against Dundee at Ibrox. But on our return we racked up five straight wins, scoring 16 goals and conceding just three. The former Celtic centre-forward and *Daily Record* columnist John McPhail commented that Rangers were playing their best football for ten years and we carried that form into the first leg in West Germany. After 26 minutes we were 2-0 up thanks to Jimmy Millar and Alex Scott and, for good measure, our goalkeeper George Niven saved a penalty kick.

We comprehensively outplayed our hosts and went further ahead when McMillan made it 3-0 on the hour mark. Clearly annoyed at our dominance, the home side decided to resort to playing the man rather than ball in response. I bore the brunt of the punishment and commented at the time that Borussia were the roughest and toughest team we had faced in European competition.

Noting that I was being subjected to some heavy tackling, Harry Davis instructed me to let the opponent go past me when the next opportunity arose. I did as I was asked and Harry whacked him so hard he relieved him of three teeth and fractured his jaw. I saw at first hand the damage my team-mate had done; Harry came up to me and showed me his hand, which was bloodied. Embedded in there were the teeth our West German opponent had lost!

The tie was dubbed 'The Battle of the Rhine'. There was brutality on the field and on the terraces too as skirmishes broke out between the British soldiers in attendance and the West German civilians.

In the return leg we blitzed Borussia. Baxter had us 1-0 ahead after only two minutes and we were 5-0 up at half-time. There were puddles all over the park but, like the rain, Rangers were relentless, scoring a further three goals after the break. It was a special night for Ralphie as he became the first Rangers player to score a hat-trick in a European tie. In contrast to the first leg, this match was played out in good spirits and, as testimony to that, Rangers were invited to take part in a friendly match to mark the opening of Borussia's new stadium, the Stadion Bokelberg, in July 1962.

Rangers were now through to a last four showdown with Wolverhampton Wanderers. Managed by Stan Cullis, Wolves were one of the top English sides of the era, having won the English First Division in 1953/54, 1957/58 and 1958/59. A 3-0 win over Blackburn Rovers had handed them the FA Cup in 1959/60 and they narrowly missed out on the double when Burnley pipped them to the title by a point.

We were handicapped by the loss of Jimmy Millar for the first leg at Ibrox. He had slipped a disc in his back against St Johnstone in January, so Doug Baillie was deployed at centre-forward to replace him. Ian McMillan was also missing – he had stretched a ligament in his right knee – so I played inside-right with young Bobby Hume at outside-left. There were further positional changes with the game just ten minutes old when Harry Davis overstretched and tweaked a thigh muscle. There were no substitutes in those days so Harry hobbled over to the right wing, Alex Scott went to inside-right and I went back to fill in at right-half. I told you I had played every position bar centre-half!

The changes knocked us out of our stride. We had started well and I drew a good save from Malcolm Finlayson with an early shot but Eric had to hack a goal-bound shot off the line and Jimmy Murray of Wolves rattled the woodwork with an effort. But we stabilised ourselves and took the lead after 33 minutes. I claimed the assist, my overhead kick falling to Alex Scott who outpaced Ron Flowers before blasting the ball beyond Finlayson from 20 yards.

The end-to-end action did not abate after half-time and the 79,229 supporters on the sloping terraces were enthralled by the spectacle. We looked to have doubled our lead after 52 minutes when Ralphie found the net, but he was denied by an offside flag. Thereafter, we had the returning Billy Ritchie to thank for keeping a clean sheet. This was Billy's first match since he had been carried off after seven minutes at Tynecastle back in October. And Billy was tremendous against Wolves, with his save from a Flowers effort the best of a clutch of outstanding stops on the night.

In the end we did manage to get a second goal, Ralphie scoring with six minutes left. He had been well policed by the Wolves defence, but when a wayward pass from Eddie Clamp fell in to his path he did what he did best, and we had a 2-0 lead to take to Molineux for the return leg

When we arrived in the Midlands on 19 April in the midst of a snow-covered winter wonderland, restoration of national pride was at stake. I will go into more detail on my international career later, but prior to the Wolves match England had beaten Scotland 9-3 at Wembley. I had played – and scored two goals – that day but it was a stinging defeat, making me more determined than ever to play well and help Rangers beat our English counterparts.

We knew it was not going to be easy, though. Earlier in the competition Wolves had welcomed Austria Vienna to Molineux after losing 2-0 in the first leg and promptly hammered them 5-0. And they started the game against us on the front foot on a real quagmire of a pitch. Ritchie was again in imperious form, making an early double save then denying their outside-left, Cliff Durandt. Remarkably, after Ritchie made that save, Jimmy Murray missed a gilt-edged opportunity to score when he fired the rebound wide of a gaping goal.

With McMillan back in action and Alex Scott at centre-forward, I was playing outside-right and I had a tremendous game. I was up against George Showell and gave him a torrid time and ended up being voted man of the match.

Despite being under pressure for much of the first half, we went in 1-0 up at the break thanks, in part, to a goal from Scotty, but predominantly because Billy Ritchie pulled off one of the best saves I've ever seen. Ron Flowers hit a screamer from around 30 yards but Billy somehow sprang across his goal and palmed the ball to safety.

Scotty's goal gave us some breathing space, and, although Peter Broadbent scored a fine goal after 65 minutes, we defended resolutely and booked our place in the club's first-ever European final.

Incidentally, Wolves weren't the only English side we faced that season. Arsenal were a regular opponent in that era, and when we welcomed them to Ibrox on 13 December this was the 12th time we had faced them. The financial gulf between English and Scottish sides was apparent even then, though, with our opponents boasting a side with a collective value of £250,000. For instance, their inside-right, George Eastham, had cost £47,500, which dwarfed the £10,000 Rangers had paid for his opposite number, Ian McMillan.

But while there may have been a chasm between the sides financially, we were more than a match for them when it came to football ability. And, as if to prove that point, Rangers, minus Baxter who was playing at Stamford Bridge for the British Army against the Belgian Army, almost blew the Gunners away in an explosive opening half hour. Three times in that period the ball found its way beyond Arsenal's Welsh international goalkeeper,

Jack Kelsey, courtesy of goals from the terrific attacking trident of Millar, Brand and Wilson. Ralphie scored again in the second half with a penalty and, although Scots David Herd and Jackie Henderson got on the scoresheet for Arsenal, we were worthy winners on the night.

The European Cup Winners' Cup Final was played over two legs and we would be facing Fiorentina. They were managed by one of the Magnificent Magyars, Nandor Hidegkuti, one of the first players to play as a deep-lying centre-forward. He had scored a hat-trick for Hungary against England in a 6-3 win at Wembley in 1953 and scored again when the Hungarians won the return match 7-1. And his Fiorentina team had a fine player at outside-right in Kurt Hamrin, who, like me, was fond of a goal or two from the wide areas and he was a constant threat to us over the two legs.

The first game was at Ibrox. We started well and I missed a good chance early in the game before Harry Davis was short with a pass-back, allowing Luigi Milan in to open the scoring. In truth, Fiorentina were an excellent side but a dirty one too. They spent most of the night blatantly fouling us, but the referee, Mr Steiner from Austria, turned a blind eye most of the time. But he did intervene after 18 minutes when their captain, Alberto Orzan, brought a fine run from McMillan to a premature conclusion resulting in a penalty for us.

It was down to our captain, Eric Caldow, to try and restore parity but his cause was hindered by the shenanigans of our visitors. Herr Steiner's decision did not find favour with the Italians and a posse of them surrounded him to protest. Even their assistant trainer came on to put his tuppence worth in.

It took about 90 seconds to restore calm before the Fiorentina goalkeeper, Santi Albertosi, started dancing about like a looney on his goal-line. That was not allowed back then and neither was coming off your line, but that is exactly what Albertosi did; when Eric struck the ball, he was almost at the edge of the six-yard box. In all the kerfuffle, Eric fired his left-foot shot wide of the target, but we thought nothing of it as we expected the referee would order a retake. Imagine our disbelief then when Herr Steiner awarded Fiorentina a goal kick! He later claimed his eyes had been fixed on Eric so he had not seen the advancing Albertosi. Had he done so, he said he would have ordered that the penalty be retaken.

We badly missed Jimmy Millar that night. He was still absent with a back injury, but he would have been handy to have when we changed our tactics shortly after I had had a close-range effort blocked by Albertosi. We had been unable to break down the stubborn and obdurate defence of Fiorentina so we decided to launch long balls forward, but they were simply gobbled up by the Italians. And when Hamrin released Milan in the closing minutes, he strode forward to net his second goal of the night and secure a 2-0 advantage for *I Viola*.

Jimmy returned in Florence ten days later but, on a pitch baked hard by the scorching sun, we lost 2-1 on the night and 4-1 on aggregate. Clearly the Italians had done their homework as they doubled up on Jimmy by deploying two men to mark him.

What had been a successful season for Rangers ended that night and it had also been an incredible campaign for me. In the days before squad rotation and players being rested, I was one of eight players who played in all our European ties and, over the course of the campaign, I played the full 90 minutes in every single match Rangers contested, making 70 appearances and scoring 23 goals. I had now made the outside-left position my own, with all but six of my appearances coming in the number-11 jersey. And to top it all off I had won my first full cap for Scotland too.

And I wasn't the only player in that team to almost ink his name indelibly on the teamsheet for the next few seasons. Save a couple of changes in the half-back line and the introduction of Willie Henderson at outside-right, the team that lost against Fiorentina would play almost week in, week out until it started to break up in 1965, becoming, in the process, one of the finest-ever teams in Rangers' history, with the names still tripping off the tongues of fans from that era to this day.

CHAPTER 5

SCOTLAND THE BRAVE

I AM a proud Scotsman and it was a great honour to represent my country. I first turned out in a dark-blue jersey on 10 December 1958 when I was selected for the Scotland U23 side that was due to face Wales at Tynecastle. Between 1955 and 1976 we had a team at this level and I was joined in the squad that travelled to Dunbar two days before the game by guys like Bert Slater of Dundee, Jimmy Baxter, then at Raith Rovers, and another future Ranger, Doug Baillie, who was at Airdrie and was also team captain.

I have to admit I was surprised I was selected as I was actually in the midst of a seven-day SFA-imposed suspension when the squad was announced. I didn't even do anything wrong! I had been cited for allegedly using 'unparliamentary language' to the referee in a league match for Rangers but it wasn't me who swore at the official. It was mistaken identity but I was summoned before the referee committee and a telegram was subsequently issued to Rangers to inform them I had been suspended.

To put my punishment into perspective, on the same day a lad from Third Lanark was up in front of the committee after being ordered off for the sixth time in his career. The big chap was worried as only four years earlier the Rangers centre-half Willie Woodburn had been suspended *sine die* for the fifth red card of his career. By now though the SFA were clearly not as draconian as they had been then; the lad got the same punishment as me for his misdemeanour, a seven-day suspension.

We lost out 1-0 to the Welsh but I remember it being a rather tempestuous encounter. There were numerous bad fouls and it's fair to say that our opponents indulged in a bit of play-acting. The only goal of the game was scored after 12 minutes by Birmingham City's Bryan Orritt, but that didn't reflect their behaviour that Cyril Horne, writing in the *Glasgow Herald*, described as 'unscrupulous'. As an example, in the second half I was scythed down by a wild challenge, but not content with taking me out the game, my opponent then thought it appropriate to slap me across the face! No action was taken by the referee either.

Despite the heavy treatment doled out, I did play well in the game, with Gair Henderson of the *Evening Times* saying that I 'showed ball control [and] plenty of determination in the face of intimidation'. I also drew a very good save from the Welsh goalkeeper, Vic Rouse of Crystal Palace.

I won that solitary U23 cap during my National Service and my time as a sapper meant it would be 1960 before I won my first full cap. That was against Wales at Ninian Park in Cardiff on 22 October 1960. I wasn't in the original pool chosen by the selectors, but when Motherwell's Andy Weir got injured I was called up. We lost 2-0 – Roy Vernon and Cliff Jones scored for Wales – in what was a Home Championship tie. That was an annual tournament that included ourselves, Wales, England and Northern Ireland. And my next cap the following month came against the Northern Irish at Hampden. We got back to winning ways in that one – Ralphie scored a double in a 5-2 win – which set us up nicely for the big one; England at Wembley on 15 April 1961.

Although they were the Auld Enemy, England had some side back then. Managed by Walter Winterbottom, their forward line included Jimmy Greaves, Johnny Haynes and Bobby Robson and they had my old adversary, Jimmy Armfield, in defence. The Scots had some quality players too; my good pal and team-mate Eric Caldow was our captain and joining me up front were Denis Law and Ian St John.

But on the day we were pulverised by England. A double from Greaves and a goal from Robson had the home side 3-0 ahead with less than half an hour on the clock. Dave Mackay reduced the arrears three minutes into the second half and it looked as if it was game on when I scored one the best goals of my career five minutes later.

Hibernian's John 'The Gangster' McLeod slung in a cross and I threw myself full length towards the ball to bullet a diving header beyond Ron Springett. Alas we couldn't muster an equaliser and our goalkeeper, Celtic's Frank Haffey, had an afternoon to forget. He shipped a further six goals which helped coin the phrase, 'What's the time? Nine past Haffey.' I told him after the game that he would have to move to Australia after a performance like that and eventually that's exactly what he did. He's still there all these years later!

There's also an infamous photograph from the time that was taken by the renowned photographer Eric Craig. He came back on the train with us from London and asked Frank if, on our return, he would mind posing for a picture at Platform 9. He duly obliged but I recall that he got a bit of stick from the players and the supporters as a result.

Incidentally, our third goal has been credited in some sources to Jimmy Quinn, but I'm adamant to this day that it should have been given to me. Barely a minute after England had gone 5-2 ahead I struck a shot towards goal that Jimmy dummied. That deceived Springett but Jimmy didn't make contact with the ball. However, although the SFA website and the match report in the *Glasgow Herald* credit me with the goal, there are still some who recognise Jimmy as the scorer.

I'm told that was our 213th international match against a team from the British Isles and was the first time we had shipped nine goals. We at least avoided double figures as a seven-goal margin would have equalled that registered against Uruguay in the 1954 World Cup when Scotland lost 7-0.

But that was the last time I would taste defeat against England. A year later we beat them at Hampden for the first time for 25 years in front of a crowd of 132,441. I scored the opening goal after 13 minutes. The *Evening Times* described it as 'one of the best goals scored at Hampden in many a long year'. Ian St John started it all off, robbing Ron Flowers in midfield and running at the English defence before passing the ball to Denis Law on the right. Denis proceeded to pick me out with a pass and I had time and space to take a touch to control the ball before sending it beyond Ron Springett from 14 yards. My namesake in the England team, Ray Wilson, made a desperate bid to stop the ball going in but he succeeded only in diverting the ball in to the roof of the net, albeit after it had crossed the line.

Scotland completely dominated and only the form of Springett prevented us moving further ahead. Ron denied me a second goal when he turned my goal-bound shot over the bar and he had some good fortune too as Ian St John rattled the crossbar with a header. Our relentless pursuit of a second goal continued after the interval, but it was not forthcoming. And we were almost punished for our profligacy. I had a shot blocked by the England defence and they immediately sprang to the other end. The ball reached Johnny Haynes and his shot thudded against the underside of the bar.

The game then threatened to boil over and Jimmy Greaves got my dander up when he brought me crashing to the turf outside the penalty area. It was a brutal tackle and I was raging. But the referee, Mr Horn from the Netherlands, defused the situation by giving Jimmy a stern lecture and encouraging me to calm down.

Scotland eventually got the second goal our play deserved when we were awarded a penalty. Sheffield Wednesday's Peter Swan handled the ball in the box and my Rangers team-mate, Eric Caldow, scored with consummate ease.

Eric was heavily involved the following year too when we went back to Wembley. He was the victim of a terrible tackle from Bobby Smith which resulted in him breaking his leg. We all heard the crack and knew it was a bad injury and Eric was never really the same player after that.

With no substitutes to call upon, manager Ian McColl had to reshuffle the team. He was going to move Dave Mackay to left-back but I told him I had played there before – I had done so for Rangers when Eric was injured against the East German side ASK Vorwaerts in our European Cup run in 1961/62 – so I was redeployed and had a great game. I even got the chance to exact some revenge on Smith by booting him a couple of times! I believe my performance impressed the home fans too as they dubbed me 'The Fizz Kid' after the match.

Scotland were excellent with ten men, and two goals from Jimmy Baxter, the second of which was a penalty awarded for a foul on wee Willie Henderson, earned us a 2-1 win. An abiding memory for me was in the dying moments, picking up the ball from our goalkeeper, Bill Brown, and going on a run down the left to the byline. Once I got there I simply turned and ran back with the ball and gave it back to Bill to eat up a few more seconds. The final whistle sounded soon after and the victory helped Scotland win the Home Championship that year for the first time since 1951.

That wasn't the last time I would play at left-back. Some three years later I was called upon again to play full-back in a Glasgow Cup tie against Celtic. We had some rough luck that day as Roger Hynd was carried off, the luckless Norrie Martin damaged his left hand and George McLean also hurt his hand. This was all before half-time, too. We resumed, down to ten men – McLean eventually returned to action after 61 minutes – with Norrie at right-back, Davie Provan in goal and me at left-back. Remarkably we held firm and even took the lead when I set up wee Willie Henderson in the 65th minute. But we couldn't keep Celtic at bay and Bertie Auld equalised before Stevie Chalmers slotted in a rebound after Tommy Gemmell's shot had hit the post.

My family were extremely proud that I played for my country too. My dad would go along to as many games as he could and my granny would sit with her pals with her Scotland flag listening on the radio. I was told the place would be in uproar every time I scored. My mother was too nervous to listen, though. Instead she would knit as I ploughed my usual left-flank furrow.

She did listen to a game once when I played for Rangers in Russia and it almost cost my father a fortune. She asked my sister, Grace, to get the radio from upstairs but when my father came home from work he went into a panic. For some reason he had placed his wallet in the back of the radio and when he removed it, it was red hot! Fortunately its contents were salvaged but it was a funny story nonetheless.

I was back at outside-left again for Scotland when England came to Hampden in April 1964. I wasn't long back from my leg break but, with Hampden bursting at the seams – there were 133,245 folk in attendance this time – I had a huge part to play in the only goal of the game. After 72 minutes we won a corner kick, which I took, and my delivery found big Alan Gilzean who promptly despatched the ball behind Gordon Banks.

I should have scored a couple of goals after that, missing good chances from just outside the six-yard box, but we had now beaten the English three times in a row, which was very sweet. The match was also a landmark moment for big Alan, for his goal was his first in Scotland colours.

By then I was a fully fledged international. There weren't as many internationals back then as there are now, but when they did take place, unless I was injured, I was first pick at outside-left. I had won 18 caps so clearly was a favourite of the selection committee. That's how international selection worked back in my day, it wasn't the manager who picked the team, it was a committee. And if you were in the squad you would receive a telegram from the SFA to let you know.

When I initially made the breakthrough at international level, Scotland were about to enter in to the qualifying campaign for the World Cup in Chile in 1962. We were in Group 8 with Czechoslovakia and the Republic of Ireland and our first match was against the Irish at Hampden on 11 May 1961. Our visitors had the precocious talents of Johnny Giles in their ranks but we were superior all over the park that evening.

I was involved in our first goal, winning a free kick from which Eric Caldow picked out Ralph Brand who netted with aplomb. And my Rangers team-mate doubled his and Scotland's tally in the 40th minute when he latched on to a flick from Manchester United's David Herd, advanced into the penalty area and despatched the ball beyond Noel Dwyer in the Irish goal.

An early goal in the second half pegged us back to 2-1, but Herd restored our two-goal lead within five minutes and scored our fourth goal two minutes from time when he pounced after Dwyer had parried my shot.

We faced the Irish again four days later at Dalymount Park in Dublin. Ahead of the game Ian McColl took us to the STV studios to watch a re-run of the Hampden match and it was a good opportunity to see how we could improve. Unsurprisingly we were unchanged, although I did have to get a bit of treatment on a minor knock to make sure I was fit to play.

This one wasn't a classic. We were met with a strong wind and a rock-hard playing surface but we made the best of it and were 2-0 up after just 15 minutes. Alex Young of Everton got both goals, his second coming after I harassed the Republic of Ireland full-back Phil Kelly on the byline and won the ball before picking out Alex with a perfect pass. We sealed the win five minutes from time when Ralphie scored at the end of another fine attacking move.

Next on the agenda was a trip to Bratislava to face Czechoslovakia. In truth we got a bit of a doing in the Slovan Stadium. Tomas Pospichal, who played with Banik Ostrava, put our hosts ahead after only six minutes and we were two down soon after that when Baxter handled in the penalty area. Andrej Kvasnak netted from the spot but that would not be the last time he was involved that evening.

Paddy Crerand was a brilliant player and had been in superb form in the games against the Irish. But he had a temper so when, after 35 minutes, he was impeded by Kvasnak, he opted to retaliate. The Austrian referee, Herr Steiner, took action and ordered both players off.

Admittedly we hadn't played well in the opening half hour but now, shorn of one of our best players, we were really up against it. We reshuffled and I was redeployed in Paddy's position of right-half and I battled well in there, with the 'special correspondent' in the *Glasgow Herald* stating that I 'proceeded to play with the usual fire [I] showed in emergency'. But my fire couldn't help get us back in the game and first Josef Kadraba then Pospichal (again) scored to consign us to a humiliating 4-0 defeat.

Remarkably my season wasn't over after that defeat. Just three days later I was back in a Rangers jersey and lining up against Fiorentina in the European Cup Winners' Cup Final.

Can you imagine that nowadays? A vital World Cup qualifier and a European final only days apart, there is no way that would be allowed to happen.

Our return match with the Czechs took place in September at Hampden. We simply had to win if we were to retain any hope of going to Chile. And win was exactly what we did, and we did so by displaying the traits that are synonymous with us Scots, courage and bravery.

Our old pal Kvasnak stung us again when he opened the scoring after six minutes but, unlike in Bratislava, we didn't fold this time. That we didn't was down in no small part to the fact we had the outstanding player on the field, Denis Law.

Denis was a great man and he's a friend to this day. He won 55 caps for Scotland and his tally of 30 goals is the joint best for our nation, Kenny Dalglish having scored the same albeit having done so in 102 appearances. Denis and I may have played for different clubs in different leagues and trained infrequently together, but we formed a terrific understanding. It came naturally to us and a number of the goals scored by Scotland at that time came about as a result of the relationship Denis and I had.

It wasn't Denis who restored parity, though. That honour fell to Ian St John in the 20th minute, but we were behind again six minutes after half-time when Adolf Scherer scored against the run of play. Scherer was familiar to myself and my Rangers colleagues as he had scored twice at Ibrox back in 1959 when Rangers defeated Red Star Bratislava 4-3 in a European Cup tie. And he showed exactly why he would go on to score 22 goals in 36 internationals when he ran at our defence and shot low beyond Bill Brown in our goal.

But Scotland rallied. I had had a hooked shot cleared shortly after the Czechs went ahead but Denis got his first goal of the game after 62 minutes after some probing by Baxter. And he scored the winner with seven minutes to go to put us in the box seat for qualification.

I had always dreamed of playing at the World Cup and now I was on the cusp of realising the dream of playing on the biggest stage of them all. The Czechs now had to beat the Republic of Ireland twice to force a play-off against us in Brussels. My team-mates and I were therefore on tenterhooks ahead of the first match in Dublin but a goal from Scherer and a brace from Kvasnak gave Czechoslovakia a 3-1 win. And those two and the great Josef Masopust were among the goals when the Czechs emphatically booked their play-off place with a 7-1 win in Bratislava.

The stage was therefore set. On 29 November we faced the Czechs for a third time and Wilson was hoping to be on the wing again. But I missed the game through injury – in a European Cup tie for Rangers against ASK Vorwaerts six days earlier I aggravated a thigh muscle problem I had been suffering from – and despite a double from Ian St John, Scotland went down 4-2, conceding two goals in extra time after we were tied at 2-2 after 90 minutes.

There was no great shame in being bounced by the Czechs – they reached the 1962 World Cup Final where they lost 3-1 to Brazil – but that was my one and only shot at playing in a World Cup. By the time qualification for the next World Cup came about I was no longer part of the Scotland squad.

In between the two games with Czechoslovakia, Scotland faced Northern Ireland at Windsor Park, Belfast. And that occasion was a triumph for the Rangers boys in the team. If you look at the Scotland squad nowadays, there are not that many Rangers players in it. But back in the early 60s we dominated the starting XI and that day five of the team that started the game were plying their trade at Ibrox.

But that afternoon in Belfast we Rangers lads weren't just content in providing the lion's share of the playing personnel. Scotland won 6-1 and all the goalscorers were Rangers players; Alex Scott scored a hat-trick, I netted twice and Ralphie chipped in with a goal too.

The fixture that followed our painful play-off defeat was the 2-0 win over England at Hampden that I mentioned earlier. But there were only two more caps for me in 1962, one against Uruguay at Hampden and the other against Wales in Cardiff.

The Uruguay match was nothing short of barbaric. It was the first time Scotland had faced the South Americans since suffering a 7-0 hammering at the 1954 World Cup, but our visitors came and battered and bludgeoned their way to a 3-2 victory. But that barely told the story of a match that degenerated so badly that the police had to intervene at one point. I was victim to some of the treatment doled out, their full-back, Eduardo Gonzalez, earning a booking for taking me out the game in the 13th minute. But I got off lightly. Two of our players, goalkeeper Eddie Connachan and right-half Paddy Crerand, were so badly injured that they had to be replaced.

We didn't play well on the night and Gair Henderson of the *Evening Times* savaged our inside-forwards for their display. Myself and Alex Scott were absolved of any blame – Mr Henderson even said that I ventured infield eventually to 'show

St John how a centre-forward should play' – but it took us until late in the game to score our goals, my Rangers mates, Baxter and Brand, pulling it back to 3-2 after we had trailed 3-0.

It would be another five months before I donned a dark-blue jersey again. I was selected to face Wales at Ninian Park in our opening Home Championship match and I was up against some fine players. In the Welsh XI were Ivor Allchurch of Newcastle United, Cliff Jones, who had won the double with Spurs in 1960/61, and the Charles brothers, Mel and John.

John was a formidable player. He could play centre-half or centre-forward and had just returned to British shores to sign for Leeds United after five successful years in Italy with Juventus. Don Revie had paid £53,000 to get him back to Yorkshire – he had played for Leeds before leaving for Italy in 1957 – and I recall he had a fine match for Wales that day, capping his display off with Wales's second goal after 88 minutes.

In contrast, I had a rather lean night. My old pal Gair Henderson commented that I was 'tenacious and fast [but] should have had more opportunity to use [my] speed and shooting'. He was pretty scathing about the team's performance even though we won 3-2 and he hinted that the selectors, who were due to meet the week after the Wales match, would be ringing the changes for our next international against Northern Ireland at Hampden.

Changes were indeed made and one was enforced. The Saturday before the game I had played for Rangers and scored from the penalty spot in our 1-1 draw against Dunfermline at Ibrox but picked up an injury that meant I had to withdraw from the Scotland squad. Initially Willie Henderson was due to deputise, with Stevie Chalmers set to win his first cap at outside-right. But Stevie went down with flu so Willie patrolled his usual beat on the right while George Mulhall of Sunderland took my place on the left wing.

I wasn't absent from the Scotland squad for too long though. Our next match was against England at Wembley in April 1963 and this is the match I mentioned earlier that witnessed my good pal, Eric Caldow, breaking his leg.

The 2-1 win over the English, in what many view was the finest hour and a half of my career, saw Scotland retain the Home Championship and set us up for the visit of Austria to Hampden a month later. And what a match that turned out to be! In what was ostensibly a friendly, our visitors had two players ordered off and the match ended abruptly when the referee, Mr Finney, called for an abandonment as he feared someone was going to get seriously injured.

The first Austrian to see red was their centre-forward, Horst Nemec, who played for Austria Vienna. It was initially thought he had been sent off for dissent, but it later emerged that he had spat at Mr Finney which was, quite frankly, disgusting. The catalyst for the incident appeared to be the second of the two goals I scored that evening. I latched on to a pass from Jimmy Millar to score but our opponents were adamant I had received the ball in an offside position. In truth, Mr Finney wasn't convinced either but, after consulting with his linesman, he awarded the goal.

All hell then broke loose and it took almost two minutes for Herr Nemec to accept his punishment and leave the field. He was adamant he had done no wrong but the tone was set after that and he was joined for an early bath by fellow forward Eric Hof, who was dismissed for a robust tackle on Henderson.

Two further goals from Denis gave us a 4-1 win, but it was a bittersweet night for us.

Scotland had three more internationals to play before my team-mates and I got our summer holiday. They were played inside nine days in June and took us to Bergen, Dublin and Madrid. We lost the first two matches – going down 4-3 to Norway and 1-0 against the Republic of Ireland – but the third match against Spain must rank among the best ever played by a Scottish side.

In the Santiago Bernabeu we demolished Spain 6-2, with six different Scottish names on the scoresheet, one of which was mine. We trailed after just six minutes but then led when Denis and Leicester City's Davie Gibson scored. Davie's Leicester team-mate, Frank McLintock, fired us 3-1 ahead and that prompted the Spaniards to withdraw their centre-half, Jose Mingorence of Cordoba, and replace him with a chap called Zoco.

But the new boy couldn't plug the gaps quickly enough as I immediately picked up a pass from Baxter and slotted the ball home to make it 4-1. Fishing the ball out the net after I scored was one of the last things their goalkeeper did as he too was replaced as our opponents tried to sort themselves out at the back. The Spaniards did pull a goal back before half-time, but wee Willie got our fifth goal after 51 minutes and Ian St John, who was magnificent that night, rounded off the scoring seven minutes from time.

The natives were not best pleased with the result, though, and soon cushions were raining down on the pitch. This was commonplace in Spain at the time as a sign of displeasure but we were delighted although the performance against Spain summed up Scotland at that time. On our day we could be among the best teams in the world, but on others, like the night we lost against Norway, we could be abject.

Remarkably, my contribution against Spain would be the last I would make in a Scotland jersey for almost a year. The next fixture scheduled was the Home Championship match against Northern Ireland in Belfast on 12 October 1963. But ten days earlier I had broken my leg playing for Rangers against Berwick Rangers and that injury also cost me the chance of adding further to my cap collection as I also missed wins over Norway (6-1) and Wales (2-1).

After returning against England and creating the winner for Alan Gilzean, I was selected again when we travelled to Hannover to play West Germany. And the team selected showed just one change from the one that had defeated the Auld Enemy, Jim Cruickshank, who I would later sign when I was manager of Dumbarton, winning his first cap in goal at the expense of Campbell Forsyth.

It was a hot night in Hannover and we soon found ourselves 2-0 down, Uwe Seeler scoring twice inside a minute in the first half. I wasn't having the best of games on the wing, but I managed to cross for Gilzean to pull a goal back for us and, after Law had struck the post, big Alan was on hand to net the rebound to earn Scotland a 2-2 draw.

The match with West Germany was my 19th cap for Scotland. And I marked my 20th appearance in dark blue on 25 November 1964 with a double in a 3-2 win over Northern Ireland at Hampden. A knee injury had counted me out of matches against Wales and Finland, but I was back in position for our second British Championship tie of the season.

And I was joined in the forward line by a familiar face. Jimmy Baxter had made his name as a left-half but in a match for Rangers against Hearts at Tynecastle on 17 October, Scot Symon had redeployed him at inside-left. Rangers had won just two of their opening seven league matches, but moving Baxter forward had reinvigorated our season and helped secure the League Cup too. The Scottish selectors seemed to have recognised that the move could also be beneficial for the national team so Jimmy was in the number-ten jersey when we took to the field against the Northern Irish.

In opposition to us that evening was one George Best and he was instrumental in the two goals our visitors scored in the first half. Burnley's Willie Irvine was the beneficiary but his two goals were cancelled out by two from me, with Gair Henderson telling the readers of the *Evening Times* that I had 'turned the clock back to the days when I was the greatest matchwinner in Britain'. I was really pleased to score and was now starting to rediscover my best form after returning from breaking my leg.

Alan Gilzean, the subject of transfer speculation linking him with a move from Dundee to Tottenham Hotspur, scored the winner for Scotland after the interval, pouncing on the loose ball when Pat Jennings fumbled a header from Law.

The victory over Northern Ireland set us up for the final British Championship match against England at Wembley in April 1965. We arrived needing a win to have any chance of winning the tournament, but we ended up with a 2-2 draw against an English side that ended the match with, to all intents and purposes, nine men. Their left-back, Ray Wilson, was carried off with a suspected rib injury and, in the second half,

Johnny Byrne was injured following a challenge with Willie Henderson. He did return to the fold but was nothing more than a passenger on the left wing.

But my team-mates and I failed to capitalise on our numerical advantage. At one stage we trailed 2-0, Bobby Charlton and Jimmy Greaves scoring for England, but a Gordon Banks error gifted Denis a goal. And with just over half an hour left, Ian St John equalised when he beat Banks after George Cohen had only partially cleared my header.

And that would be the last time I would face the Auld Enemy. Just over a month later I was in the team that beat Finland 2-1 in a World Cup qualifier in Helsinki and that would be the last time I would play for my country. It would also be a first for me that night too as I played under Jock Stein for the first time, big Jock having succeeded Ian McColl when the latter took over the manager's job at Sunderland.

I had missed the last two matches for Scotland against Spain and Poland, but I was back at outside-left against the Finns. And I signed off from international duty with a goal, our equaliser on the night. Denis had missed a penalty after 17 minutes but he made amends by playing a pivotal role in my goal, for it was from his cross that I struck the ball past the Finnish goalkeeper from 12 yards. My clubmate, John Greig, scored the winner six minutes into the second half.

That match was on 27 May 1965. When Scotland played again on 2 October against Northern Ireland at Windsor Park I was barely getting a game for Rangers so it was no surprise that I wasn't involved. And given that my game time with the Rangers first team became more sporadic after that, my international career was over.

Although I had five good years at Dundee United the call from the SFA to play for Scotland again never came. Nonetheless, I am proud of each and every one of my 22 caps and the ten goals I netted for my country. And to crown it all, in 2014 I was inducted in to the Scottish Football Hall of Fame. I got a phone call in the September of that year to let me know but I had to keep it quiet which was quite a challenge for me as I was honoured to be inducted. It was humbling to be included in the list of luminaries and the award has pride of place in a display cabinet in my house.

CHAPTER 6

RUSSIAN RANGERS

PRE-SEASON TRAINING ahead of season 1961/62 was, as always, tough, but, similarly to the training in the Royal Engineers, the fact I was a fit lad meant I could handle what we were asked to do. We would run up and down the sloping terraces at Ibrox and would often go across to The Albion to do running too. That, however, presented an altogether different challenge. The pitch was surrounded by a greyhound track and as we ran around we had to dodge the dog dirt. I often felt sorry for the apprentices who had to clean the boots, though, as the players were not always successful in avoiding the faeces that littered our route round!

The training stood us in good stead and our preparations were completed on 7 August with the annual trial match at Ibrox. And the first-team lads got a bit of a fright when the young upstarts in the reserves beat us 1-0. I always viewed the match as a great chance for the lads in the second and third teams to go out and showcase their talents and that was certainly the case on this occasion. Willie Henderson was the standout performer and it was he who created the game's only goal for our new signing, Jim Christie.

The season kicked off in earnest five days after the Ibrox trial when we travelled to Cathkin Park to face Third Lanark in the League Cup. The wee ground was bursting at the seams and it was little old me who put the smiles on the Rangers supporters' faces, scoring both our goals in a comfortable 2-0 win. Thirds were managed by the great Ranger, George Young, but his side were a goal down after just ten minutes. Such was the extent of the crowd and their proximity to the pitch, I had struggled to find room to take a corner kick in the early exchanges. But I had plenty of space to exploit when I latched on to a perfect pass from Ian McMillan and ran forward ten yards before slotting the ball behind Jocky Robertson in the home goal.

Usually I would be joined in celebration by my team-mates, but on this occasion my back was also slapped on numerous occasions by the Rangers supporters as well. My goal sparked a pitch invasion but the police soon restored order and Rangers proceeded to entertain the crowd with a dominant display. My second goal after 31 minutes was the least our fine play deserved.

My goals that day were the first two of five I scored as we breezed through our section, dropping just a single point. We had struggled to get out the group for the past couple of seasons but there was no danger of that happening this time.

In our second game Dundee were beaten 4-2 at Ibrox and we were breath-taking in the opening quarter of an hour. Ralphie netted twice in that spell but should have had four, for he also struck the post and the crossbar. Yet after such a whirlwind start, we went in level at 2-2 at half-time – in fairness this was a very good Dundee side which included the likes of Andy Penman, Alan Gilzean and Alex Hamilton – but I fired us back on to the road to victory with just nine minutes left. Jimmy Millar was the creator, slipping a fine pass to me and I stepped away from the challenge of three defenders before shooting the ball beyond Pat Linney. I returned the favour to Jimmy a few minutes later when I crossed for him to head our fourth goal.

A late Harry Davis goal preserved our 100 per cent record when we defeated Airdrie 2-1 at Broomfield and I netted another double against Third Lanark when we hammered them 5-0 at Ibrox. I was particularly pleased with my second goal that afternoon as it was another header. I once again belied my lack of inches in height to head home a lobbed pass from McMillan, although my boots that day must have been spring-loaded as Jimmy Dunbar, writing in the *Evening Times*, was of the opinion that I had jumped 'at least three feet in the air' to reach the ball!

We lost our 100 per cent record the following midweek when we drew 1-1 with Dundee but, under the circumstances, it was a fine result. Early in the game Harry Davis picked up an injury which saw him move to outside-left and me move back to fill in for him at right-half. And it was from that position that I created our equalising goal for Ralphie.

We rounded off the section with a comfortable 4-1 win over Airdrie to progress to the quarter-final stage for the second successive season. We were joined there by Motherwell, Hearts, Hamilton Accies, Ayr United, Stirling Albion, St Johnstone and East Fife and it was the latter we were paired with when the draw was made.

The Fifers arrived at Ibrox for the first leg as one of only three unbeaten teams in Scotland – ourselves and Ayr United were the others – and fielding the country's top goalscorer, George Dewar. He added to his tally against us but by then we had cantered into a 3-0 lead. That made the second leg pretty much a formality and that was confirmed when I opened the scoring in Methil after 17 minutes. We registered another 3-1 win to secure a 6-2 aggregate but in the semi-final we found ourselves in a spot of bother when we trailed 2-0 against St Johnstone.

We were without Harry Davis for the match at Celtic Park – he had been injured in training – so Willie Stevenson came in at right-half. But we were really poor in the first half and St Johnstone – managed by the former Rangers goalkeeper, Bobby Brown – took full advantage.

Ian Gardiner headed them in front after 31 minutes and a minute shy of the interval it was 2-0 when John Bell fired the ball past Ritchie. It's fair to say we were on the ropes at this stage, but we managed to get back in the game almost immediately after the restart. Alex Scott was the architect, his cross finding the head of Jimmy Millar, and when Jimmy's header fell at my feet I touched the ball into the net via the far post. Scotty was involved in our equaliser too. He was impeded by the St Johnstone left-back, Jim Lachlan, and referee Phillips awarded a penalty which Eric Caldow despatched.

There were no further goals in the final 12 minutes which meant extra time was required to try and separate the sides. We dominated the extra half hour and two minutes before the end of the first period, wee Wilson used his head again to score the winning goal.

Victory over Hearts in a replayed final meant I had now doubled my medal tally in the League Cup. We drew 1-1 after extra time on 28 October but it would be 18 December before we managed to contest the replay. And that match started like a whirlwind. Alex Scott set up Jimmy Millar for our opening goal in the seventh minute, but a minute later Norrie Davidson equalised. We were soon back in front, though, my cross picking out the head of Ralphie after 15 minutes. And by the 20th minute the scoring was complete when Ian McMillan netted on the rebound after his initial shot hit the crossbar.

But while the League Cup was retained, we relinquished the league title to Bob Shankly's Dundee. They had come to Ibrox in November and battered us 5-1 – Alan Gilzean scored four times in a match played out in dense fog – and were seven points clear of us by Christmas time, although Rangers had a game in hand. But we came back off the ropes and by the time we beat Falkirk at Brockville on 17 March we were three points ahead at the top. That match was my most memorable in a Rangers jersey.

Our centre-half, Doug Baillie, was injured so Harry Davis deputised for him, meaning Jimmy Millar was moved back to cover for Harry at right-half. That meant I was picked to play at centre-forward, a position I'd filled throughout my school days, with wee Willie Henderson taking my number-11 jersey.

This was just my second game back in the team following a spell on the sidelines. A pulled muscle ruled me out of matches against Hearts, Motherwell and Third Lanark, but I was back now and raring to go. I was also intent on adding to my goal tally for the season. I was in the middle of a bit of a dry spell as I hadn't scored in a league game since 2 December. But the goals came flooding back at Brockville as I scored SIX, three with my right foot and three with my left.

I only scored once in the first half. That came in the 24th minute when I controlled a fine pass from McMillan and thumped the ball beyond Willie Whigham in the Falkirk goal with my left foot. There then followed a burst of four goals in 15 second-half minutes. After 47 minutes I scored another with my left foot after good work from Baxter and Henderson, and although Alex Duchart scored for the home side three minutes later I completed my hat-trick in the 52nd minute. It was another strike with my left foot too as I pounced on a rebound after Whigham had saved a shot from Ralphie.

Not content with scoring a hat-trick with my left foot, I proceeded to do the same with my right foot! My fourth goal in the 56th minute was a ferocious right-foot drive, my fifth six minutes later was a shot from 20 yards and I completed the scoring eight minutes from time with a chip following a Henderson pass. Alex Scott scored as well to give us a 7-1 win but then denied me a seventh goal when I scored again but it wasn't given on this occasion because of the linesman's flag, Alex having strayed into an offside position.

The day was made all the more special as it was my mum and dad's wedding anniversary and my dad was in the crowd to see me. The Falkirk chairman, Duncan Ogilvie, was a friend of the family and he presented me with the match ball after the game. That was a lovely gesture as in those days you didn't get to keep the match ball if you scored a hat-trick. My son, David, still has the ball and it is one of his most prized possessions.

Incidentally, I remain the only Rangers player to score six goals in one game for the club in the post-war era. Jimmy

Fleming netted nine times against Blairgowrie in 1934 and Jimmy Smith hit six against Ayr United six months earlier in a 9-1 mauling of Ayr United. But since 1945 only six players have come close to matching my tally. Don 'The Rhino' Kichenbrand scored five times in Rangers' 8-0 win over Queen of the South on 7 March 1956 and, in later years, Jim Forrest (twice), Derek Parlane, Marco Negri, Kenny Miller and Kris Boyd also racked up what is often referred to as a 'nap hand'. In fact, if you refer to the evening paper, *The Green Citizen*, for that day then you would have thought I had also gone 'nap'. The journalist covering the game, big Malky Munro, left prior to me scoring my sixth goal to ensure his match report was submitted in time to meet the copy deadline and therein he had me scoring just the five goals rather than six.

My glut of goals continued the following midweek when I was selected to play for the Scottish League against the English League at Villa Park, home of Aston Villa. Inter-league matches had been taking place since April 1892 when the Scottish and English Leagues drew 2-2 at Pike's Lane in Bolton. They usually drew huge crowds – in March 1947 84,000 were at Hampden Park to watch Stanley Matthews inspire the English League to a 3-1 victory – but the advent of European competition meant these games lost their popularity. Nevertheless, I am extremely proud of the seven league caps I won, the first of which was against the League of Ireland back on 5 October 1960.

That match was at Celtic Park and I was joined in the team by my clubmate Eric Caldow. The Scottish League won 5-1, with my corner kick creating the fourth goal for Clyde's George Herd. That completed his hat-trick and Alan Gilzean and future Ranger Andy Penman, then of Dundee, scored the others.

I made my debut against the English League later that same season – we won this one 3-2 at Ibrox thanks to a late Caldow penalty kick – and season 1961/62 brought further league caps against the Irish League (7-0 with seven Rangers players in the XI) and the Italian League (1-1).

There were familiar faces in the opposition side in the latter match. Denis Law, who was playing with Torino then, Gerry Hitchens (Inter Milan) and 'The Gentle Giant' John Charles, who was at Juventus, were selected for the Italian side, as were Fiorentina's Santi Albertosi and Kurt Hamrin who I had faced a few months earlier in the European Cup Winners' Cup Final. If I remember correctly it was a wretched night weather-wise, but we still attracted a crowd of about 70,000. And they witnessed a Scottish League side passing up a glut of scoring chances before a late goal from Ralphie earned us a 1-1 draw.

Given that the manager of the Scottish League side was also the manager of the national side – former Ranger, Ian McColl – getting selected for the inter-league matches was no mean feat and I was delighted when it was announced I was in the squad for the match at Villa Park.

In the match programme for what was my fifth Scottish League appearance, I was described as 'a tear-away winger' and the writer alluded to the fact that I was 'particularly dangerous when [he] cuts inside and has scored many goals'. That may have been true, but prior to the match against our English counterparts in March 1962 I had never scored for the Scottish League. But that would all change over the 90 minutes in Birmingham.

The squad gathered at Glasgow's Central Station on the Tuesday morning, the day before the game, to travel by train to England. That was the norm for fixtures south of the border back then and the chat amongst the players would almost exclusively be about football. Our travelling party was three players light when the train pulled away from the platform; the Edinburgh-based trio of Eddie Connachan, Jimmy Millar and Ralphie Brand would join us when we got to Carstairs.

We didn't train on arrival in Birmingham but Ian McColl took us to St Andrew's, home of Birmingham City, on the day of the game and we went through a tough 45-minute session before returning to the hotel at lunchtime. He had introduced a training session on the day of the game prior to our draw against the Italian League back in November, citing that getting us out into the fresh air stopped us lounging around the hotel and alleviated any boredom and stopped us stiffening up ahead of the game. Can you imagine that in today's game, training with intensity a matter of hours before a big game?

On completion, we travelled to Villa Park to inspect the playing surface so we could select the appropriate studs for our boots before retiring to the hotel. Both teams stayed at the same hotel – my room-mate was Alex Hamilton of Dundee – and I was joined in the squad by team-mates Caldow, Scott, Millar and Brand. Baxter missed the game through an injury he had picked up the previous weekend playing for Rangers. His place was taken by Stewart Fraser of Dundee United.

The English League side were formidable and many observers reckoned that the majority of the XI that faced us would be in the squad selected for the World Cup in Chile in the summer. Their number included Liverpool's Roger Hunt,

Bobby Charlton of Manchester United and the £100-a-week man, Johnny Haynes of Fulham. Indeed, such was the height and weight advantage of our opponents – Cyril Horne of the *Glasgow Herald* opined that the English League had more pace in their side too – many observers felt we were the underdogs.

But we proved everyone wrong when the referee, Mr R. J. Leafe from Nottingham, got proceedings underway. After myself (twice) and Celtic's Paddy Crerand had gone close to opening the scoring, Ralphie broke the deadlock when he fired the loose ball into the net after Ron Springett had parried a shot from Pat Quinn of Motherwell. And six minutes later we were 2-0 ahead. Dundee United's left-half, Stewart Fraser, bulldozed his way through a couple of challenges and fed the ball to me. Faced with my old adversary, Jimmy Armfield, I strode past him, and as Springett advanced I shot the ball past him with my left foot.

However, the game was turned on its head when the English League roared back and took a 3-2 lead courtesy of goals from Hunt (2) and Haynes. We were behind, however, for a mere two minutes. Billy McNeill fired in a high ball that Jimmy Millar got his head to and when the ball dropped in my vicinity I gleefully tucked it away into the net.

It really was an enthralling game and the Scots claimed victory in the final minute, becoming the first Scottish League XI to score four goals on English soil in the process. Millar and Quinn combined to create the opening and I was in the right place at the right time to complete my hat-trick. It was something of a landmark goal too as it gave the Scottish League their first win in England for almost 30 years. Somewhat ironically, our first win in England had also been at Villa Park back in 1898 but our 4-3 win this time around was the first time we had been victorious since a 3-0 win at Maine Road in 1933. Since then the Scots had lost nine of the ten inter-league matches played in England, with the only match that didn't end in defeat being a 1-1 draw at Newcastle in 1948.

The press waxed lyrical about my performance. In his match report in the *Evening Times*, Gair Henderson said I 'wrote my name across international football with speed, fluency and a three-goal flourish' and referred to me as the new wee blue devil. The magnificent Alan Morton had been dubbed with this nickname after his sumptuous performance against England in 1928, and Gair felt that this was the first time since then that a player had tormented the English defence. As you can imagine, it was very humbling to once again be compared to such a legendary figure but such comparisons made me a little uncomfortable given the stature of the gentleman I was being compared with.

I played twice more for the Scottish League. In September 1963 I was part of the side that defeated the Irish League 4-1 at Windsor Park and, six months later, I was at Roker Park in Sunderland to help preserve my unbeaten record in a Scottish League jersey. We trailed the English League by two goals to one going into the final minutes of the match, but Hibernian's Neil Martin scored an equaliser to make it 2-2.

Back at Ibrox, the league title was ours to lose and that's exactly what we did. At the turn of the year we trailed Dundee by eight points. But from 10 January until 3 March, we won ten straight league games, and, although that run was ended with a no-score draw against Dundee at Dens Park, we led our opponents by three points with just seven games to play.

However, defeat at home to Dundee's city rivals, United, the week after my six-goal show against Falkirk was costly, and when we drew 1-1 against Celtic at Parkhead, we were only ahead of Dundee on goal average.

I rescued a point for us against Celtic 12 minutes from the end of a match played on a Monday evening, this being the rearranged date for the New Year fixture which had been postponed due to heavy snow and thick fog. Playing league games at any time other than 3pm on a Saturday was a rarity back then, but in January alone we played a midweek league match every week bar one. And the only reason why we didn't do likewise in February was due to our European Cup commitments. These were the days before sports science and the concept of resting players, so, for our six fixtures in January, myself and six others played 90 minutes in all of them. The fixture pile-up and the tiredness that went hand in hand with that was no excuse for missing out on the league title, though. Others teams had fallen foul of the weather too and on the same day we drew at Parkhead, Dundee beat Dundee United 2-1 in a rearranged Dundee derby.

Despite the dropped point at Parkhead, we still had it in our own hands with two games to play. We had a trip to face a struggling Aberdeen at Pittodrie followed by a home fixture against Kilmarnock, while Dundee had St Mirren to face at home then St Johnstone away. Two wins would be enough to secure the championship.

But we lost 1-0 to the Dons – an uncharacteristic error from Eric Caldow proving costly – and with Dundee winning 2-0 against St Mirren, they now led by two points and needed only a point in their last league match to clinch the title. In the end we rendered their result meaningless as we drew our 'must-win' match against Kilmarnock, which meant we couldn't overhaul their lead. By the time I equalised in that match with seven minutes remaining there were huge gaps on the Ibrox terracing, our followers resigned to the fact that we would miss out on retaining the title.

Losing out on the league meant Rangers missed out on a domestic treble as a couple of weeks earlier we had beaten St Mirren 2-0 to lift the Scottish Cup. We survived a tough trip to Pittodrie in the third round, drawing 2-2 before I scored one of our five goals in the midweek replay. And I was among the goals again in the semi-final as we avenged our defeat the previous season at the hands of Motherwell.

Max Murray, in for the injured Jimmy Millar, scored twice in the first half of a match that saw young Ronnie McKinnon drafted in at left-half as Baxter was playing for the British Army against the Belgian Army. I created Maxie's first goal, but Roberts halved the deficit early in the second half. However, I ensured we would progress to the final when I dodged a couple of tackles and cut inside on to my right foot to send a shot past Alan Wylie in the Motherwell goal.

I grabbed a goal in the final too. Big Jim Clunie, the St Mirren centre-half, had an excellent game as we pummelled them from the start. He appeared unbeatable until, five minutes before half-time, I managed to fire the ball across the goal for Ralphie to tap in and put us in front. I sealed the deal later in the second half when I outwitted the St Mirren goalkeeper, Bobby Williamson. Harry Davis and Ian McMillan combined and the ball came to me on the left. I ran along the byline and as I reached Bobby I dropped my right shoulder, suggesting I was going to move to the right. Bobby moved in that direction, exposing his near post, so I squeezed the ball in the gap he left. Bobby got his hand to my shot but couldn't keep it out.

Despite the setback of losing the league it was another good, solid season for me. I missed only five first-team games and scored 29 goals. And one of those goals was scored in Liege in the quarter-final of the European Cup.

Home and away wins against Monaco – both 3-2 – took us through to a tie against East German champions ASK Vorwaerts. We beat them 2-1 away from home in the first leg but had to play the return leg in Malmo, Sweden, as our East German opponents had to face us in a country that was not affiliated to NATO. The first match was abandoned after 45 minutes due to thick fog, but we returned the next day to seal our progress. We won 4-1 but I aggravated a thigh muscle problem I had, which ruled me out of our next league game, a 3-2 win over Dundee United at Tannadice.

The win over Vorwaerts took us through to the quarter-final where we drew Belgian champions Standard Liege. A toe injury ruled out Eric before the game so Bobby King came in at left-back. That added a more youthful complexion to our side as we also had Henderson and Greig, both of whom were aged 18, in the starting line-up.

We fell behind after only six minutes, but I pulled us level 13 minutes later when I despatched a pass from Jimmy Millar into the net. Thereafter we were undone by the controversial lad Johnny Crossan, who had played against us a couple of years earlier for Sparta Rotterdam. He scored a goal either side of half-time – the first of them fairly screamed past Billy Ritchie – and a deflected free-kick in the 54th minute consigned us to a 4-1 defeat. Hopes of a third successive European semi-final were all but extinguished, but we nearly turned the tie around at Ibrox when Ralphie and Eric scored to give us a 2-0 win.

I loved playing in Europe and at the end of the season the lads and I were afforded the chance to continue our continental escapades when we embarked on a tour of Russia. We departed from Renfrew Airport just after 9am on Wednesday 30 May. From there we flew to Copenhagen, then on to Moscow on a Russian-built Tupolev Tu-34 jet. We had to survive a scare on landing too. At the airfield that had welcomed the astronauts Yuri Gagarin and Gherman Titov back to terra firma after their escapades in space, it took the pilot two attempts to get the wheels of our aircraft on the tarmac.

We eventually reached the sanctuary of the terminal building to collect our luggage and were met by the famous goalkeeper Alexei 'Tiger' Khomich. He was no stranger to Rangers as he had kept goal when the famous Moscow Dynamo side had played at Ibrox in 1945. Thereafter, we were bussed to our hotel, dubbed the Cathedral by the locals, and it was lucky I had a head for heights as our accommodation towered up 25 storeys into the Moscow skyline.

We travelled to Russia without Jimmy Baxter as he was away on National Service, so Mr Symon added a young John Greig to the squad. Greigy had broken in to the team earlier in the season and I remember him scoring a terrific goal up at Aberdeen. He smashed it in to the net from the edge of the box and he struck the ball so hard I thought the net was going to burst!

You could tell even in the early days that John was captain material. He always wanted to talk about the game and when

Symon made him skipper he was always invited to have his say after the manager had spoken to us. He deserves to be regarded as the greatest-ever Ranger.

John was an inside-right initially but the regular in the number eight at that time was Ian McMillan. Dubbed 'The Wee Prime Minister', Ian signed for Rangers in October 1958 and one of his first outings for the club was a reserve game at Ibrox. Scot Symon phoned me up and asked if I would play in the game at outside-right, and I scored a hat-trick, with all three goals created by through balls from McMillan. It would be Willie Henderson who profited more than most from service like that from Ian but, any time I was deployed on the right flank with McMillan inside, I could guarantee top quality service for the 90 minutes.

We also got our first taste of Russian cuisine on day one. On the flight from Copenhagen we were served caviar accompanied by red cabbage, cold meat and salad. And in the hotel we had soup, but it was a far cry from the homemade soup that my mother used to make. This potage featured some floating pieces of orange, apple and olive which led me and my team-mates to rename it 'fruit salad soup'. We would get chicken too but the portions were tiny.

We had our own tour guides and they would come to the hotel each day and take us to places like the Kremlin. However, everywhere we went we were followed by agents from the KGB which was a bit unnerving to say the least. They never engaged with us but you were aware they were there.

Our first tour match was against Locomotiv Moscow. The star man for our opponents was a chap called Valestin Bubikin. He had plundered over 40 goals in the season that had just finished so was expected to provide a stern test for our defence. We had expected to face searing temperatures too. After rain had lashed the stadium when we trained a couple of days before the game, the following day the Lenin stadium was like a furnace. However, dark clouds hung over us when the game started, and by half-time it was raining pretty heavily.

The team were welcomed by a message emblazoned on the electronic scoreboard which read 'Greetings to the Sportsmen of Great Britain' and although there were only 16,000 in attendance at a stadium capable of holding 100,000 people, they watched Ralphie do what he did best seven minutes before half-time. He picked up a pass from Jimmy Millar and despatched the ball into the net and he could have had another goal 60 seconds later but his effort rattled the crossbar. Although I wasn't involved in the goal, I had been prominent throughout the first half, running at the Russians when given the opportunity, and I came close to teeing up a goal for Eric Caldow just prior to Ralphie giving us the lead.

Locomotiv got themselves back on track after the restart, though. They deployed a successful offside trap that I was sucked into on a number of occasions and, after Gratchishanikoff had missed a harshly awarded penalty, our hosts were level. And it was a splendid goal from Bubikin, the inside-left thumping a shot beyond Billy Ritchie from all of 25 yards.

The goal stung us into action and with the descending dusk forcing a change to a white match ball, I picked it up and after beating the right-back had the goalkeeper at full stretch to prevent us regaining the lead.

With time running out Mr Symon sent on Willie Henderson for Alex Scott – it had been agreed before the game that both teams could use any number of substitutes – and wee Willie made an immediate impact. It was his pass that created Rangers' second goal, scored by Ian McMillan, and I secured our win when I scored with only five minutes remaining. My goal evidently impressed the locals because at the end of the game they came on to the park and carried me shoulder high towards the dressing room!

It was a fine start to the tour and I had enjoyed a fine 90 minutes. I got the measure of their right-back, Sorokin, fairly early in the game and beat him time after time. His frustration eventually got the better of him in the second half and I remember one tackle in particular that sent me spinning into orbit!

We travelled to Tbilisi in Georgia for our next game but we did so against a backdrop of player revolt. And I was one of the players involved. In those days you were offered the terms for your contract ahead of the new season, but myself, Jimmy Baxter, Harry Davis, Alex Scott, Eric Caldow, Ralphie Brand and Jimmy Millar were less than enamoured by the offer of £30 per week, £5 appearance money plus bonuses. We were looking for £45 per week and our rationale was that we were playing in front of huge crowds – for cup finals there was usually more than 100,000 at Hampden – and our counterparts in England were being paid far more handsomely than we were.

We won the match against Dynamo Tbilisi – Henderson scoring the only goal of the game – but, despite the issues some of us had with the club's hierarchy, it's fair to say it was still a happy camp that travelled to Kiev for our final match against the Russian champions, Dynamo Kiev. As testament to that, after a tough training session at the Krushev stadium in Kiev we all gathered in the centre circle and belted out 'Auld Lang Syne'!

The Kiev match was considered to be the toughest of the tour and that's exactly how it proved. We led 1-0 thanks to another Brand goal but Biba, Kiev's outstanding centre-forward, lashed in an equaliser from 25 yards to earn the home side a draw.

In truth we were also playing against the referee in that match. A number of his decisions were baffling, but none more so than when he denied Rangers a blatant penalty kick. I was involved in the incident and the refusal to award a spot kick meant I had to defend my good name afterwards.

I had been saddled with the nickname 'Polaris' after the famous nuclear-armed, submarine-launched ballistic missile as some folk reckoned I went down too easily in the penalty box. I was, in their opinion, a diver but I was no such thing. And it was that unwanted reputation that, in my opinion, cost us against Kiev. Ralphie played me in and I was bundled to the ground by a Kiev defender. As I was small and slight and played at pace, the slightest contact would send me spinning and that's exactly what happened that afternoon. But the referee waved play on and saw no infringement which was extremely infuriating.

Nevertheless, it was a fantastic achievement to come home undefeated and it was felt that our trip had enhanced the prestige of Scottish football in the European arena. We flew back to Renfrew Airport the next day, but as we were on the final approach the pilot suddenly pulled up and the aircraft started to climb again. It turned out he was unable to land as the runway was filled with thousands of Rangers fans who had come out to welcome us home!

It was estimated that 10,000 followers had flooded on to the tarmac and, sitting at a window seat, I had seen the masses gathering as we came in to land. The pilot of our Icelandair DC6 eventually got the aircraft down but we faced a long wait on board. The pilot announced over the intercom that he would be keeping the doors firmly closed until the crowd had been brought under control. That meant a bit of a wait for me and the 50-odd others in the stuffy cabin on the aircraft. In addition to the Rangers party and the nine members of the Scottish press who had accompanied us on the trip, we had been joined on our flight from Copenhagen by a touring hockey side.

When the doors eventually opened and the fresh air surged in, our ears were met with choruses of Rangers songs and the tunes of an accordion band. For me and the lads, to be welcomed home like that was just a fantastic way to end our trip. However, understandably the flood of fans caused consternation at the airport, prompting Mr H. G. Hendry, the airport manager, to meet with police chiefs to try and ensure this kind of thing didn't happen in the future.

Although Mr Hendry recognised that our fans had been in good spirits, he was correct in his assertion that it was extremely dangerous for them to encroach on an operational area of the airport. One solution put forward was to ensure that arrival times of flights carrying footballers should be kept out the public domain.

And that was that. Season 1961/62 ended on a high and we went our separate ways to enjoy some family time and recharge the batteries ahead of our return for pre-season training. The tour had placed Rangers Football Club at the forefront on the continent and we would be coming back intent not just on winning domestic honours but on making an impression in European competition too.

CHAPTER 7

A GLUT OF GOALS AND A TREMENDOUS TREBLE

I THOROUGHLY enjoyed the tour of Russia but had circumstances been different I may not have been part of the Rangers squad that travelled. Earlier in the season Harry Catterick, manager of Everton, had bid £100,000 for me and I have to admit I was tempted. Everton were building a very good team, with the likes of Alex Young, Billy Bingham and Bobby Collins in their ranks. They would eventually win the English First Division in season 1962/63, and if I had joined I would have made history. I would have been Britain's first £100,000 footballer – Jimmy Greaves was a pound shy of that magic number when he was transferred from AC Milan to Tottenham Hotspur in December 1961 – and I would have more than trebled my wages too.

The maximum wage of £20 per week had recently been abolished and I was on £30 a week at Rangers. But Johnny Haynes of Fulham had blazed a trail by becoming the first player to earn £100 a week, and that was what was on offer to me should I opt to move to Merseyside. I found that out when a Rolls Royce turned up at the pigeon loft one day. My uncle George, my dad's brother, went out to see who it was and was met by the driver of the car, Mr John Moores, the chairman of Everton.

Mr Moores proceeded to make an offer to sign me for Everton that included a car and a signing-on fee of £2,000. I spoke to Scot Symon and he made it clear he didn't want me to leave Rangers. I was integral to his plans going forward so that and my dad convinced me to turn down the lucrative offer and stay put. My dad was still working down the pit at the time and at the end of his shift he would head to watch me wherever I was playing. He wouldn't have been able to do that if I was in England so I politely declined Mr Moores's offer.

With the warm welcome home from Russia still fresh in our minds, we reported back for pre-season training on 17 July but with our pay dispute unresolved. That meant that since midnight on 30 June I and my other team-mates who had not re-signed for Rangers had gone without pay. But, along with Ralphie, I eventually relented and agreed to sign on for the new season two days after we got back.

That meant I was eligible for selection when we travelled to West Germany at the end of July to face Borussia Monchengladbach. The occasion was the opening of their redeveloped Stadion Bokelberg and, by then, only Jimmy Baxter hadn't put pen to paper for the forthcoming season. This was the same Monchengladbach side we had hammered 11-0 on aggregate a couple of years earlier in the European Cup Winners' Cup, but on this occasion the match ended with honours even. We created a vast array of chances to score but only had an early goal from Ralphie to show for our efforts.

The trip to West Germany came off the back of a tough training programme at home. Training was good as it varied, although Mr Symon didn't take training, it was Davie Kinnear and Joe Craven who fulfilled that role. In all my time at Ibrox I don't think I ever saw Mr Symon in a tracksuit. He always wore a suit and sometimes a trilby hat, but he would watch us train at The Albion across the road from Ibrox from his office as the window overlooked the pitch. If we weren't putting enough effort in, we would be pulled up. But Symon wasn't a hard man. He got our respect through how he went about his business and he was a very successful Rangers manager.

I got more minutes under my belt three days prior to the season starting when I was chosen as part of a Glasgow Select that faced Manchester United at Hampden. The prize was the Glasgow Merchants' Charity Cup I had won twice with Rangers, and, with the exception of George Niven of Partick Thistle, all the players were drawn from either Rangers or Celtic. A mammoth crowd of 82,000 watched United win 4-2. But with 16 minutes to go we were 2-1 ahead – Danny Divers of Celtic and my club mate, Ian McMillan, scoring the goals – and we looked set to seal the deal when Willie Henderson was felled in the penalty area by Maurice Setters. A spot kick was awarded but the normally reliable Eric Caldow missed after he was ordered to retake the kick. Having scored with his first attempt, he failed with his second, his effort striking the United goalkeeper David Gaskell.

This was the first year that the Charity Cup ceased to be a knockout tournament and for the next four seasons it was decided a Glasgow XI would take on a team from England for the trophy. In August 1963 Manchester United once again provided the opposition and I was at outside-left when the Glasgow select secured the silverware. Bobby Charlton gave United the lead after just three minutes but Celtic's Stevie Chalmers equalised before Maurice Setters had the misfortune of heading beyond his own goalkeeper to give Glasgow a 2-1 win. That would be my last involvement in the Glasgow XI. I wasn't selected when a Baxter-inspired Glasgow beat Tottenham Hotspur in 1964 nor was I chosen when Glasgow were comfortably beaten by Chelsea in 1965 or when the competition concluded with a meek 1-1 draw between Glasgow and Leeds United in 1966.

Part of the Glasgow XI on the night we lost 4-2 to Manchester United was Jimmy Baxter. Having completed his National Service with Black Watch in early August, he eventually signed on the dotted line at Ibrox and, with a full complement of players to choose from, we blasted out the blocks at the start of season 1962/63.

With a young Willie Henderson taking over the number-seven jersey from Alex Scott, Rangers had a frightening forward line that would go down in folklore. We became the fabled Henderson, McMillan, Millar, Brand and Wilson and that was a phenomenal season for us. Jimmy, Ralphie and myself scored a total of 118 goals in all competitions. I'm sure Steven Gerrard would have to pay a lot of money to get that kind of goals return in his Rangers team today! My own personal breakdown was 23 league goals – including all four of the goals in a 4-1 win over Partick Thistle in April 1963 and three from the penalty spot – five in the Scottish Cup, three in the League Cup and one in the European Cup. For good measure

I also scored against Celtic in a 2-2 draw in the opening round of the Glasgow Cup.

The penalty goals were an added bonus. Hubby, dubbed the Penalty King, had been the main man from the penalty spot when I initially joined, but since he left in 1959 the responsibility had predominantly fallen to Eric Caldow. He was calmness personified although he did miss a couple of notable spot kicks, one against Fiorentina in the European Cup Winners' Cup Final and another against Kilmarnock in the 1960 Scottish Cup Final.

It was against Dumbarton in the first leg of the League Cup quarter-final on 12 September 1962 that I netted my first penalty. And I scored from 12 yards again ten days later in a 5-1 win over Hibernian at Easter Road. I won the award myself when I was fouled by the Hibernian left-half, John Baxter, and I then took advantage of some dithering by Ronnie Simpson in the Hibernian goal to score. As I placed the ball I saw Ronnie checking his goals, looking at the posts. After he had looked at one I saw him motion to check the other and as he did I stroked the ball in to the net. Ronnie was raging and demanded the kick be retaken as he wasn't ready. But the referee awarded the goal which was our fifth of the afternoon.

I wasn't always successful from 12 yards as witnessed by the penalty I missed a few weeks later at Cathkin Park against Third Lanark. But I was a victim of uncertainty in that instance. I had scored directly from a corner kick earlier in the game and we were leading 3-1 when wee Willie was brought crashing to the turf. I stepped up and thundered the ball in to the net but the referee ordered a retake. There was a bit of debate as to whether it was for encroachment by Ralphie or because Thirds goalkeeper, Ian McKinlay, had moved before I struck the ball. Nonetheless after I re-spotted the ball I shot wide of the target. My miss mattered little in the grand scheme of things, though; barley a minute later Ralphie made it 4-1 and the two points gained allowed us to leapfrog Hearts at the top of the league.

The last penalty I can recall taking for Rangers was our goal against Dunfermline Athletic in a 1-1 draw on 3 November 1962. When we were awarded our next penalty Ralphie took it and scored the second goal of what would prove to be a hat-trick against Raith Rovers. Incidentally, the collective goalscoring return of myself, Ralphie and Jimmy that season was a European record for forward players until the terrific trio of Messi, Suarez and Neymar broke it in 2015 when they scored 122 goals between them for Barcelona.

The secret of our success was the extra training we did together in the afternoon. Ralphie, Jimmy and I all decided to stay back and work on developing our relationship and Rangers reaped the rewards of those additional sessions. Our understanding became almost telepathic and some years later, when Ralphie and I were playing in an old crocks game, we reproduced one of our signature moves. Ralphie would play the ball to me and I would stand still as he ran forward. He was lightning quick so I would chip a pass over the defence in to his path and he would time his run to perfection and run on and score.

Jimmy was magnificent too. When he signed from Dunfermline in 1955 he was a half-back, but Mr Symon converted him into a centre-forward. He scored goals but also ruffled feathers in the opposition rearguard with his all-action style of play. He made us all laugh one day too when he somewhat unconventionally trapped the ball. A long ball was played in his direction, but rather than control the ball with his head Jimmy allowed it to drop and, as it bounced off the turf, he tamed it by sticking out his arse! The ball struck him and landed perfectly at his feet and we enjoyed a long laugh about that after the game had finished.

It's sad to see Jimmy and Ralphie as they are now, both in a nursing home and bedevilled by dementia. There are a number of players from the era I played in that are suffering from this horrible illness and more and more tests are being carried out as awareness grows. I have been tested myself and was invited to Ibrox a few years ago to establish if there were any signs of the early onset of dementia. I spoke to the doctors for 45 minutes about my career and they were happy with my responses so I got the all-clear.

Ralphie and Jimmy would also join me before games for what became, for me, a pre-match ritual. At ten o'clock on the Saturday morning I would go and see a chap called Mr Chester at his house in Shettleston. He was a masseur and was fantastic. After he had finished with you, you felt as if you could jump over the moon! His wife would make fish for us too, and my wife, Avril, still makes fish for me today the way Mrs Chester did back in my playing days. Jimmy and Ralphie would travel through together from Edinburgh to see Mr Chester too and we valued him so much that when we went to Pittodrie to face Aberdeen we paid his train fare to ensure we still got our matchday massage.

Not surprisingly, producing the stats we did meant Rangers won the league again that season. We dropped points in just nine of the 34 league fixtures – seven draws and two defeats –

and enjoyed a swashbuckling 18-match unbeaten run between 8 December 1962 and 13 May 1963. The sequence included a 6-1 thrashing of Kilmarnock at Ibrox – yours truly opened the scoring against a team who would finish runners-up, nine points adrift of us – and that was the first of ten straight wins.

Celtic were hammered 4-0 on New Year's Day and 52 goals were scored with only 12 conceded. In the Old Firm game there was a mass exodus of Celtic supporters well before the end of the game, so the majority of them missed me scoring our fourth goal. The win was inspired by Jimmy Millar who had been bed-ridden with flu. He dragged himself through from his home in Edinburgh and, after getting some pills from Dave Kinnear to relieve the congestion, he proceeded to rampage through the Celtic defence. Harry Davis had us ahead after 12 minutes, his deflected shot deceiving Haffey, and two goals in two minutes from Ralphie and John Greig signalled the start of the Celtic fans heading for the exits. I completed the rout when Bobby Shearer and Davis combined and I rifled Harry's cutback into the net.

Although I didn't quite manage to notch up another six-goal haul in one game, I did find the net with breathtaking regularity in the league. After missing the opening league match against St Mirren with a leg injury, I chalked up my first goals of the season when I scored twice in a 5-1 win over Hibernian at Easter Road on 22 September. I then scored in four successive league games between 13 October and 3 November. Amongst those fixtures was a tight contest against Aberdeen at Pittodrie.

Travel arrangements for an away fixture were different when we faced the Dons. This was the only away fixture where we would stay in a hotel the night before the game; for all other away games we would travel through on the bus on matchday. Clearly on this occasion our overnight stay had left us all refreshed, for we got off to a flying start when Jimmy Millar and I scored to put us 2-0 ahead after just four minutes. But a double from Bobby Cummings – who a couple of years earlier had become the first Englishman to score a hat-trick against Rangers – restored parity and it took a goal from John Greig nine minutes from time to secure the two points.

Such was the form of myself, Jimmy and Ralphie that season, it was inevitable there would be casualties in the first-team squad, and on 21 November Max Murray was sold to West Bromwich Albion for £15,000. Maxie was a real character and a great goalscorer. He came from Queen's Park in 1955 and in his first season scored nine goals in 13 appearances. In season 1956/57 his 29 league goals in just 30 games went a long way to securing the title for Rangers and he had the distinction of scoring the club's first goal in European competition when he netted against OGC Nice in October 1956. Almost as regular as his goals was his puffing on a cigarette, and when we came in at half-time he would make for the toilets and have a fag before we went out again for the second half.

When Mr Symon moved Jimmy Millar to centre-forward, Maxie's time was up and if he ever needed convincing he made the right choice to leave then he had to look no further than our match against Dundee United at Ibrox on 16 March. United had beaten us 2-1 at Tannadice in November but we avenged that defeat in spectacular fashion, winning 5-0, with Jimmy helping himself to four of the goals.

That match was only our second in the league since we had beaten Celtic on New Year's Day. The whole of the UK went into deep freeze and we endured the coldest winter for more than 200 years. In Glasgow we had our first white Christmas since 1938 and, although our game with Celtic went ahead on 1 January, the Edinburgh derby was postponed as there was eight inches of snow covering the pitch at Tynecastle.

We eventually returned to action against Dunfermline Athletic at East End Park on 9 March and trailed 1-0 until I scored with 17 minutes remaining. I scored from a tight angle after I latched on to Jimmy Millar's flick and, remarkably, that was our first goal at East End Park for THREE years which showed how good a side the Pars were back then.

They were always a doughty opponent and as the game entered its dying moments we looked set to drop a precious point and bring to an end our four-match winning run. But in a heart-stopping final 60 seconds we grabbed both points and left our vanquished opponents enraged.

The frenetic conclusion started when George McLean, making his first-team debut at inside-right, forced a corner kick. Willie Henderson took it and I leapt high in the air to meet the cross coming in. Also intent on fielding the ball was the Dunfermline goalkeeper, Jim Herriot. We collided, accidentally, and Jim was knocked out cold. With Jim lying prone, the ball broke to Jimmy Millar who, from around 20 yards, promptly dispatched the ball into the net. Despite the protestations from the Dunfermline players the referee, Mr Crossman from Edinburgh, allowed the goal to stand. In fairness it had been a busy day for Mr Crossman for we had no fewer than FIVE claims for a penalty waved aside!

The chilly spell had certainly not frozen my hot streak of goalscoring, and over the course of four weeks, between

20 March and 17 April, I scored 11 goals in just four games. I kicked the run off with a hat-trick against Airdrie at Broomfield in the second round of the Scottish Cup and then grabbed a late double in our 5-0 league win against Hearts at Tynecastle. This was followed with another brace when we beat Hibernian 3-1 at Ibrox. And to cap it all off I scored all four of Rangers' goals in a 4-1 midweek win over Partick Thistle at Firhill.

Willie Thornton, the man I had rebuffed as a youngster, was now manager at Thistle and he had recruited my old team-mate, George Niven, in February 1962. George was a splendid goalkeeper and, at 32, still had a good few years left in him. He had lost his place at Rangers to Billy Ritchie and had not played a first-team game at Ibrox since 25 March 1961.

It was good to make his acquaintance again when we beat Thistle 2-1 at Ibrox back in September, and both he and Thistle were in fine form when we met on 17 April. Thistle were third in the league, just three points behind us, although we had four games in hand. And George had been a big part of taking Thistle to that lofty perch, but try as he might he could not keep us at bay that evening.

By the 48th minute, I had netted four times. I got my first after just ten minutes when Jimmy Millar played me through on goal with a fine pass inside the Thistle right-back, George Muir. I powered a shot past George and had completed my hat-trick before the referee, Mr Syme, had blown his whistle for half-time. Neil Duffy had got Thistle on the scoreboard after 35 minutes but I finished the scoring three minutes after the restart when I pounced to net on the rebound after George McLean's shot had struck the post.

I still talk about that game any time I meet up with Martin Ferguson, Sir Alex's brother. Martin had signed for Thistle the previous summer having been with Kirkintilloch Rob Roy but missed the match against us. He was a right-half and he keeps telling me that there was no way I'd have scored four goals that night if he had been playing! 'Nonsense' is usually my reply, as I was riding the crest of a wave of confidence and it would have taken some performance from him to stop me in my tracks in that game.

My final two league goals came on the last day of the season against Aberdeen at Ibrox. The fixture backlog due to the big freeze meant this was our third game in five days and my goals preserved our proud unbeaten home record that season. George Kinnell had the visitors ahead after seven minutes, but I equalised ten minutes later. Aberdeen centre-forward Billy Little had them 2-1 ahead at half-time, but I beat their goalkeeper, John Ogston, again in the 69th minute to earn a 2-2 draw.

We finished on 57 points and only Motherwell (twice), Dundee (twice), Kilmarnock, Raith Rovers, Dunfermline, Dundee United and Aberdeen had taken points off us in the title race. Of the 94 league goals we scored, myself, Ralphie and Jimmy Millar were responsible for 69 of them.

Kilmarnock gained a modicum of revenge when they eliminated us from the League Cup in the semi-final, but we did add the Scottish Cup to the trophy cabinet. I was among the goals there too. In the second round we drew Airdrie at Broomfield and it turned out to be a day their centre-half, Adam Thomson, would rather forget.

There were only seven minutes on the clock when we broke forward but our attacking endeavours looked set to be curtailed when the linesman raised his flag for offside. But the referee, Mr Stewart, waved play on and I headed a cross from Willie Henderson against the crossbar. When the ball broke to Thomson he, still thinking that the offside decision stood, picked the ball up and placed it down for a free-kick. The referee immediately pointed to the penalty spot and Ralphie made no mistake to put us 1-0 up. You had to feel for Thomson but the old adage of 'play to the whistle' never rung as true as it did here.

Two minutes later we were 2-0 ahead when Ian McMillan's long pass picked me out and I beat the Airdrie goalkeeper, Jim Samson, with a shot from 20 yards. It was one-way traffic after that and Samson had to be at his best to keep us at bay. But our relentless pressure eventually paid off when I scored from a free kick after 22 minutes, my shot striking the post on its way into the net. We coasted through the second half, adding three more goals to our tally. Willie Henderson made it 4-0 after 49 minutes and I completed my hat-trick 19 minutes from time, latching on to a flick from Ralphie and shooting low past Samson. The hapless Thomson then completed the scoring at 6-0 when he scored an own goal in the 88th minute.

I scored again in round three, our second goal in a 7-2 thrashing of East Stirling that saw Ralphie net four times. And to cap it all off, I grabbed Rangers' third goal in the 3-0 win over Celtic in the final. That was in a replay after the first match on the Saturday ended 1-1. However, we could consider ourselves fortunate to have made it that far. In the fourth round we drew 1-1 with Dundee at Dens Park but with only 16 minutes of the replay remaining, we were trailing 2-1 and facing the exit.

It was a terrific match, with 81,190 in attendance and a reported 5,000 more outside. My direct opponent and often my room-mate when on international duty, Alex Hamilton, inadvertently put us in front after 15 minutes, heading my pass beyond his own goalkeeper, but a double from Alan Gilzean looked like sending our opponents through to the last four. But the luckless Hamilton gave us a helping hand once again when he impeded me in the penalty area as I looked set to equalise. Ralphie did the business from the penalty spot and scored again with only two minutes remaining to send us through to face Dundee's city rivals, Dundee United.

We beat United 5-2 – Jimmy Millar grabbed a hat-trick – and should have beaten Celtic when we faced them at Hampden on 4 May in the final. But we were defied by Frank Haffey in the Celtic goal. I mentioned Frank earlier when discussing my Scotland career, but that afternoon in the wind and rain he appeared to be unbeatable. We got past him once when Ralphie put us ahead after 43 minutes, but Bobby Murdoch equalised on the half-time whistle. In truth I was guilty of spurning our best chance to win the match when, in the closing minutes, eight yards from goal, I fired the ball tamely at Haffey when it seemed easier to score.

Baxter was simply majestic in the replay. He toyed with Celtic and, with Ian McMillan coming in for the injured George McLean, we cantered to a convincing victory. Ralphie put us ahead after just six minutes and a minute before half-time I atoned for my miss on the Saturday when I pounced to score after Haffey parried a shot from Ralphie. The shine was put on matters after 73 minutes when Ralphie hit a speculative shot from 18 yards that caught Haffey napping.

This was the first cup success of the John Lawrence era. Mr Lawrence had become chairman of the club in February 1963 following the death of John Wilson. Mr Wilson, a bailie or magistrate, had taken over from Roger Simpson in 1950 and he passed away after a short illness. His son, also John, became vice-chairman and he used to wear a bowler hat. In the celebrations that followed winning the Scottish Cup in 1964 I am pictured wearing that hat. I took it off him at the side of the pitch and I believe Jimmy Millar still has the hat in his house somewhere.

Back in the dressing room at Hampden, Davie Kinnear opened the hamper and brought out magnums of champagne to toast our success. The cup was duly filled and passed around my team-mates to take a swig in celebration. As a teetotaller I didn't take a drink, but Davie had my celebration tipple covered. Alongside the champers in the hamper were bottles of Irn Bru and that's what I used to mark adding another success to the Rangers Roll of Honour.

As was the tradition at the time after we showered and changed, we boarded the team bus with the trophy and were joined by our wives before we headed to the St Enoch Hotel. That was a popular haunt for us and we would go there for a meal prior to every home game. However, on this occasion, as we set off for the city centre from Hampden, the bus was pelted with bottles thrown by disgruntled Celtic fans. It was scary at the time but we came through unscathed and enjoyed our night at the hotel.

With champions Dundee taking Scotland's place in the European Cup, it was a return to the European Cup Winners' Cup for Rangers in season 1962/63. But any notion we had of repeating our run to the final two years earlier was halted abruptly by Bill Nicholson's tremendous Tottenham Hotspur team, a wonderful side including the likes of Jimmy Greaves, Danny Blanchflower, Cliff Jones and my Scotland team-mates Dave Mackay and John White.

They called big John 'The Ghost' as his runs in to the opposition box were such that he seemed to appear as if from nowhere. Tragically he was killed in July 1964 when he was struck by lightning while sheltering from the rain on a golf course in Enfield. He was only 27. A few months later I was part of a Scotland XI that travelled to White Hart Lane to take part in a benefit match for John. It was fitting that the scoring that night was opened by John's brother, Tommy, who played for Hearts. I equalised a couple of minutes later with a left-foot shot and the Scots eventually ran out 6-2 winners. But it wasn't about the result that night; it was about paying tribute to one of the finest Scottish footballers of his generation.

Before we met Spurs we had to resist some barbaric behaviour in Spain in the opening round. After winning 4-0 against Seville at Ibrox – Jimmy Millar scored a hat-trick – our 2-0 defeat in the place famous for its orange crop ended with our players being battered from pillar to post. Bobby Shearer ended up with broken ribs and scratches on his throat, Ronnie McKinnon was bitten on the ear, Baxter was subjected to a challenge that was so robust that it knocked him off the field and left him with a bloodied mouth and loose teeth, John Greig was butted and kicked and little old me was in the thick of it too, sustaining a badly bruised thigh and being subjected to a head-butt.

My room-mate on that trip was big Davie Provan. For my early European trips I would share with Bobby Shearer but eventually Davie took over the role and we were great pals. He stayed near Falkirk back then so rather than travel back through there after a game on the Saturday, he would come back and stay with me at my mother and father's house in Halfway. My mother would come in on the Sunday morning and Davie's feet would be sticking out of the bottom of the single bed in my room and what with me being a tad smaller than Provan, she would know instantly that that was the 'other' Davie!

We would go out to the dancing at The Barrowlands and one night, after we had beaten Celtic in the cup, Ronnie McKinnon came with us. As we went in someone deliberately bumped into big Ronnie, and when Ronnie found out the chap had done it deliberately the red mist descended. Ronnie went after the guy and I tried to get myself in between the two of them to stop things kicking off. Next thing I knew the guy has pulled out a bayonet and all of a sudden I realised that we were in a bit of bother. But before the fear could sink in, I saw the blur of a fist above my head and Ronnie had caught the guy square on the jaw. His jaw was skewed and he hit the floor, whereupon Ronnie picked him up and threw him down the stairs! You didn't mess with big Ronnie, and the following weekend we met the guy again and this time there were no issues.

We had now emerged as one of the greatest-ever Rangers teams. And in season 1963/64 we achieved something that, until then, only one team in Scotland had done – we won the domestic treble. The only other team to do it had been Rangers back in season 1948/49 and I am proud to have been part of the second Rangers team to do the triple crown.

There was talk ahead of the season about me getting a run at centre-forward. Jimmy Millar was struggling with a groin injury and the media were suggesting I had all the necessary attributes to fill the number-nine jersey in his absence. But in the end I stayed on the wing, with young Jim Forrest replacing the injured Millar as the spearhead of our attack. And young Jim made his mark as we topped a tough League Cup section that included Kilmarnock, Queen of the South and Celtic.

Jim scored in both Old Firm games – twice at Parkhead and once at Ibrox – with both fixtures ending in 3-0 wins for Rangers. I scored the first goal in our win at Ibrox with another header and was also on the mark in our two ties with Queen of the South, scoring twice in a 5-2 win at Ibrox and striking again when we repeated the scoreline in Dumfries. Forrest was on fire in that one, for he helped himself to four goals to take his tally to eight in just five games.

He added a ninth of the season when he and I scored again as we completed our group with a 2-2 draw at home to Kilmarnock, and before September was finished we had another Old Firm scalp, winning 2-1 at Ibrox in the league. It seemed no one was going to stop us and when we faced Division Two Berwick Rangers at Hampden in the semis of the League Cup, another final beckoned. But that night, despite scoring our first goal in a 3-1 win, my season came to a shuddering halt.

As the game was drawing to a close, I passed the ball to Jimmy Millar and just as Jimmy received it, their right-back, a chap called Hogg, whacked me and immediately I felt pain coursing through my body. In fairness to the chap he did come in to the dressing room afterwards to ask how I was doing but, at that time, everyone thought it was just a muscle problem. As I hadn't heard any bones cracking that was the immediate thought and for the next ten days when I reported to Ibrox I would get a rub to try and help with the healing process.

But I couldn't shift the pain so I ended up being referred to a specialist. I had to go in a wheelchair and our trainer, Davie Kinnear, called me a coward, but I was adamant that there was something more serious wrong with my leg. Archie McDougall was the Rangers doctor at the time and he was angry that he hadn't been made aware of my injury. He took one look at me and delivered the shattering blow that my leg had been broken. X-rays taken later showed a four-inch long break running vertically down my shin bone, and it would be another five months before I would see action for the Rangers first team again.

The road to recovery began when the plaster cast came off. Davie Kinnear was responsible for my rehabilitation and he pummelled me relentlessly until the day came that I was allowed to return to full training. Davie, perhaps feeling a touch guilty over misdiagnosing my injury initially, was brilliant with me and so was the manager, Mr Symon. Once I was back training he arranged several practice matches to help rebuild my confidence. They were huge for me as, initially, I was reluctant to enter into any 50-50 tackles for fear I'd get injured again.

But gradually I got myself back to my old self, although there were a couple of false starts during my comeback. I played for the reserves against Celtic at Ibrox on Hogmanay but I soon realised that I wasn't sharp enough. It was February before I decided to give it another go and this time, in a reserve match against Falkirk, I felt much better. Mr Symon must have agreed, for a week later I had my number-11 jersey back when I turned out for the first team on 8 February against St Mirren at Ibrox.

It was a day of mixed emotions. I set up Ralphie for our first goal and scored our second, but we lost at Ibrox for the third time that season when the Saints won 3-2. The other defeats had come against Hearts (0-3) and St Johnstone (2-3), with a certain Alex Ferguson scoring a hat-trick in the latter game. But although we lost it was a happy day for me. In some quarters I had been written off as being finished, so I was determined to prove the doubters wrong. Given that I didn't miss a game for the rest of the season after that, I think I achieved what I set out to do.

It was a tough run-in. We were neck-and-neck with Kilmarnock and we found ourselves effectively down to nine men at Pittodrie in March when we lost Henderson and Forrest to injury. Willie went off after 22 minutes with ankle ligament damage and Jim spent the last 20 minutes hobbling on the left wing. But after Ian McMillan was tripped by Jimmy Hogg, Jimmy Baxter scored a penalty and we drew 1-1. And the following week, with Ralphie deputising for Willie at outside-right, George McLean, who came in at number ten, and I scored when we beat Kilmarnock 2-0 to all but clinch the title. We eventually finished six points clear to seal the treble.

I had missed the League Cup Final – cousins Jim Forrest (4) and Alex Willoughby scored the goals in a 5-0 win over Morton – and the emphatic wins over Stenhousemuir (5-1) and Duns (9-0) in the opening rounds of the Scottish Cup due to my broken leg. But I was back on the wing when we faced Partick Thistle in the third round, scoring twice in our 3-0 win.

This tie was played just a week after my comeback against St Mirren and the football correspondent in the *Glasgow Herald* commented favourably on the return of my 'exuberance and positional sense' and how I struck up a good partnership with Baxter. My old pal, Gair Henderson, was praising me again too, saying in his *Evening Times* match report that my performance was 'masterly' and that my speed and courage were still evident. He also felt that my natural instinct to be in the right place had not been curtailed by my injury absence.

I opened the scoring after 26 minutes when I followed up after George Niven had saved from both Henderson and Brand. A Forrest goal three minutes into the second half effectively killed the tie before I scored my second goal with a right-foot shot 18 minutes from time. I could have had a hat-trick too but for the intervention of the legendary referee Tom 'Tiny' Wharton, who ruled out another goal from me for an infringement.

Celtic were beaten 2-0 in the last eight at Ibrox and my goal a minute before half-time was the only one of the game in the semi-final against Jock Stein's Dunfermline. That took us through to face Dundee at Hampden and what a day that was! Their goalkeeper, Bert Slater, repelled almost everything we threw at him, but a good old dose of 'M & B' secured the trophy.

We eventually breached Slater's goal in the 71st minute thanks to Jimmy Millar, only to concede an equaliser within a minute when Kenny Cameron scored for Dundee. As the game entered its final minute, we were still all square but a bit of magic from wee Willie Henderson ensured the Scottish Cup was Ibrox-bound. Taking up position on the left wing, he slung in a cross that Millar headed home, and barely a minute later he teed me up to score our third. Big Bert was defiant again, but he could only parry my shot into the path of Ralphie, who slotted the ball home via the post to make it 3-1.

In the celebrations that followed I donned vice-chairman John Wilson's bowler hat and Ralphie found a bucket of water that he doused us all with as skipper Bobby Shearer was hoisted up on the shoulders of Ronnie MacKinnon.

It is fair to say that life was good as the season ended in May 1964. My injury hell was over and I was back doing what I did best, scoring and creating goals for Rangers and Scotland. The injection of youth into our forward line in the shape of McLean, Forrest and Henderson appeared to bode well for the future of the club. But rather than help nurture that talent as the experienced man in the front five, season 1964/65 would prove to be the beginning of the end of my Rangers career.

CHAPTER 8

THE END OF THE ROAD
AT RANGERS

SEASON 1964/65 started as every other one did in that era, with the sectional ties in the League Cup and, drawn alongside Aberdeen, St Johnstone and St Mirren, Rangers went goal-crazy. We faced the Dons first and I notched the last of our four goals in a 4-0 win at Ibrox and scored again when we beat St Mirren 6-2 in what was our penultimate fixture. We had drawn a blank against the Saints at Love Street in a 0-0 draw, but that was the only point we dropped. In between those fixtures, Jim Forrest scored four times in a 9-1 thrashing of St Johnstone and notched a hat-trick in an epic 4-3 win over Aberdeen. Another Forrest hat-trick against St Johnstone at Ibrox made it 26 goals in six games for Rangers and booked us a quarter-final tie against Dunfermline Athletic. Remarkably, Jim had helped himself to 18 of those 26 goals and would end the season with 57 goals across all competitions.

That match at Ibrox against St Johnstone saw me move from outside-left, where I had played in the previous five ties and also the opening league fixture, to outside-right. I was filling in for Willie Henderson, who had flu, and as the early part of the season progressed, I did that more often than not as Willie was sidelined from November to late January with bunion trouble.

I had my own injury issues prior to that, missing seven league games between 7 October and 21 November after I broke a bone in my ankle in the League Cup semi-final against Dundee United. Another talented youngster, Willie Johnston, who had made his debut in the 3-1 win over St Johnstone in the League Cup, came in at number 11 to replace me, and such was the impact he made, he would eventually claim my coveted jersey and regular berth in the team.

It was me that turned young Willie into an outside-left. He was a centre-forward initially, but he came to me one day after training and asked me to show him how to play as a winger. I recognised immediately he had the pace required to be a success on the flank and he was a goalscorer too. I worked with him a lot in training and we talked at length in the dressing room. I guess this was an early indication that I had a talent for spotting a player and coaching them.

I was reinstated at outside-left for the League Cup quarter-final ties – we beat Dunfermline 5-2 on aggregate – and again in the semi-final at Hampden Park against Dundee United. We needed extra time to see off Jerry Kerr's side. We trailed 1-0 with only four minutes to go before the prolific Forrest scored to force an additional half hour. And it was Forrest who netted again after 106 minutes to book us a rendezvous with Celtic at Hampden. That was on 24 October, but despite playing in every match up to the final, my injured ankle deprived me of the opportunity to add to my medal collection. I played in a practice match a couple of days before the final but wasn't deemed fit enough for selection at Hampden.

Although I was not enjoying the best of fortunes on the field, I had more joy off the pitch. I attended my cousin's wedding late in 1964 and one of the bridesmaids caught my eye. Her name was Avril Finlay and folk at the wedding said we would be the next ones up the aisle. They were right! We were engaged within six months and a further six months later, 30 November 1965 to be exact, we were married. The ceremony was in Paisley Abbey and my best man was a chap called Billy Gordon, who used to sing at the Pavilion Theatre with the great Scottish comedian and legendary Rangers supporter Lex McLean.

My marriage to Avril meant it was time to cut the apron strings. Even though I had been a professional footballer for almost ten years, I still stayed at home with my mother and father. I had become something of a local celebrity and folk used to swarm round my car looking for an autograph every morning when I left for training at Ibrox. But now it was time to fly the nest and build my own family home, which Avril and I did in the village of Kilbarchan, which is about 16 miles outside of Glasgow.

Back at Rangers before I lost my place in the team, we had had an inconsistent start to the league season. We drew two and lost two of our opening four league games – I scored a late consolation goal in our 3-1 defeat against Celtic at Parkhead – and although our first win was emphatic, 9-2 at home against Airdrie, we lost 4-2 at home to Hibernian and drew 1-1 with Hearts at Tynecastle. After eight games we were in tenth place, eight points adrift of the early pace-setters, Kilmarnock.

After a couple of games for the reserves against Aberdeen and Kilmarnock, I made my first team comeback on 18 November against Rapid Vienna in the European Cup. And I was at outside-right again three days later when I made my first league appearance since 26 September in a 1-0 win over Motherwell at Ibrox. I replaced Ralphie on the wing, with my buddy unfit after injuring his thigh late on in our 1-1 draw with Kilmarnock at Rugby Park. Ralphie had been one of three players to don the number-seven shirt since Willie Henderson had last played for the first team in late September – Jim Forrest and Craig Watson were the others – but I was back on the left wing the following week when we travelled to Falkirk.

Bud was left out of the team which placed me alongside Jimmy Baxter, who was now strutting his stuff at inside-left, with Wilson Wood at left-half. And it was Jimmy who created my third league goal of the season after 75 minutes, returning the favour after I had crossed for him to net Rangers' third goal of the game four minutes from half-time. He was brilliant that day, but it would be the last time he would play in the league for the first team until 10 March.

As for me, after the Falkirk game I missed just two more league matches. Over the festive period I was among the goals too, scoring two goals in our 5-0 win over Third Lanark at Ibrox. I flitted across the forward line in that spell but I was at outside-right when we beat Celtic at home on 1 January. It was a typically rugged Old Firm battle – there was a tousy end to the game with Jimmy Johnstone ordered off minutes after Bobby Murdoch had missed a penalty for Celtic – but we edged it 1-0 thanks to a Jim Forrest goal.

Although I kept my place in the league, I didn't play at all in our three Scottish Cup ties, which culminated with us relinquishing the trophy when Hibernian won 2-1 at Easter Road in the quarter-final. And three days prior to that our run in the European Cup had been ended by Inter Milan.

In my opinion we should have won the European Cup that year, and, in so doing, become the first British club to win the trophy. The fact we did not was, I believe, down to an incident that happened in the dying seconds of our match against Rapid Vienna in the Prater Stadium. It was there that, after turning in arguably his finest hour and a half in a Rangers jersey, Jimmy Baxter broke his leg.

We had qualified to face Rapid by edging out Red Star Belgrade in a thrilling opening-round tie. We beat them 3-1 at Ibrox in the first leg but we should have been out of sight by half-time. Baxter and I combined to set up Ralphie to put us ahead after ten minutes, and before half-time John Greig had rattled the crossbar twice and I had also struck a shot against the inside of the post. But a minute after the restart we doubled our lead when I cut the ball back for Forrest to score from close in.

Back came the visitors, though, and they halved our lead ten minutes into the second half. They then enjoyed a sustained spell of pressure and also struck the woodwork, but a last-minute goal from Ralphie completed our victory.

We went to Belgrade for the return match a week later and got a pummelling. Although it was 1-1 at half-time, our hosts scored three times inside ten second-half minutes to put themselves 5-4 ahead on aggregate. We were shell-shocked, but in the last minute I scuttled down the wing and forced a corner kick. My delivery landed perfectly on the head of Jim Forrest, and although his header struck the bar the rebound fell to Ronnie McKinnon, who dived to head into the net and force a play-off at Highbury. What a time to score your first goal for the Rangers!

I missed the play-off – Willie Johnston was handed his European debut at my expense – but we won 3-1 and faced old foes Rapid Vienna with a place in the quarter-final at stake. In the first leg at Ibrox they defended stoically. We had plenty of possession but struggled to pierce their solid defensive armour. When we did get behind them we would invariably be caught in their offside trap, which was incredibly frustrating for us and the Rangers fans.

We eventually found a way through in the 55th minute. Jimmy Millar, playing at inside-right, beat two players in midfield and fed the ball to me on the right flank. I transferred it quickly to Jimmy Baxter, who took a touch and then played a sumptuous defence-splitting pass that I, having continued my run after releasing my pass, latched on to before firing the ball beyond their goalkeeper, Andrija Veres.

We were rarely troubled in an attacking sense that night, but we were conscious that a 1-0 lead was a precarious one to take with us to Austria for the return leg. We arrived in Vienna two days ahead of the game to heavy snowfall and the pitch at the Prater Stadium was three inches deep with the white stuff. The forecast suggested that the temperature was set to rise over the next 48 hours, so we expected the snow would turn to slush and we would be facing the Austrians on a very wet and muddy playing surface.

Mr Symon named the same XI that had won at Ibrox but made a tactical switch, with myself and Willie Johnston switching wings such that I would now be playing on the left up against the Rapid right-back Wilhelm Zaglitsch.

Although the surface was indeed slippery and sticky, Baxter thrived. Just over a year after Rangers had rejected a bid of £70,000 for Jimmy from Stoke City, he toyed with the Austrians and delivered what is regarded as his finest 90 minutes in a Rangers jersey. Inevitably, he was involved when we opened the scoring after 19 minutes, his perfectly timed pass releasing Jim Forrest to advance unchallenged to score his fifth goal in the competition.

The tie was sealed six minutes after half-time thanks to yours truly. Willie Johnston made it for me, running through the heart of the pitch, before finding me in the inside-right position. I despatched the ball clinically into the net and our place in the last eight was secure.

But the night ended on a sour note. Baxter received the ball on the touchline and, not for the first time, turned adroitly away from his marker, Walter Skocik. The Rapid right-half had clearly had enough and launched in to a challenge that caught Jimmy just above the Achilles tendon on his right leg. Those in close proximity heard the snap, Jimmy had broken his leg and it would be 11 weeks before we would see him back in first-team action.

Our European odyssey would have to continue without Jimmy. The other teams in the hat for the quarter-finals were world and European champions Inter Milan, Bill Shankly's Liverpool, Benfica, Real Madrid, DWS Amsterdam and the season's surprise package, Hungarian champions Vasas ETO Gyor. We drew Inter Milan who were managed by the legendary Helenio Herrera.

It was Herrera who had introduced the infamous *catenaccio* – or 'door bolt' – tactics where the onus was on defence. He utilised four defenders and a sweeper, with the remit of the defenders being to mark the opposing forwards. Should one of the forwards slip their marker, the sweeper was to be on hand to mop up the danger. Purists felt it was 'anti-football' – this coming some 40 years before Lionel Messi badged Walter Smith's Rangers with the same tag – but Herrera pushed his full-backs forward to supplement the attack, thus creating a devastating balance between effective defence and punishing attack.

In those days the dates for the ties were agreed between the two clubs, and Mr Symon was outfoxed by the wily Herrera. The Argentinian selected dates that would mean we would be without Jimmy Baxter and Mr Symon succumbed. We would play Inter in Milan on 17 February, with the second leg scheduled for Ibrox on 3 March.

In the league match that preceded our trip to Italy, I played inside-right in a 1-1 draw with Hearts at Ibrox. Jimmy Millar had had possession of the number-eight jersey for the previous 13 league games but was now set to start a 21-day suspension. Remarkably, his 'crime' was to have accrued three cautions that season and, despite the club appealing, the decision of the referee committee was upheld.

The suspension could also have ruled Jimmy out of the Milan game. Unlike today when suspensions picked up domestically only apply to league and cup games in Scotland, back in 1965 the SFA held the view that suspensions also applied to European competition too. For this to happen they were obligated to report Jimmy's alleged misdemeanours to the European Football Union but, on this occasion, feeling that Jimmy's absence may hamper our chances of winning the European Cup, they elected not to.

Thus, with Jimmy eligible to return at inside-right I was back patrolling the left flank in Europe's fashion capital as Willie Johnston was ruled out, having suffered cuts above his eyebrows against Hearts. And my big pal Jimmy was outstanding on a night when we were unfortunate to lose 3-1.

Luis Suarez, who had arrived at the San Siro in a £142,000 deal from Barcelona, was the principal reason we returned to Glasgow trailing by two goals. We frustrated our hosts in the first half with our disciplined defending, but Suarez opened the scoring after 48 minutes with a sumptuous half-volley. And within 60 seconds we were 2-0 behind when their Spanish centre-forward, Joaquín Peiró, deflected a long-range shot from Mario Corso beyond Billy Ritchie. When the same player made it 3-0 in the 50th minute with a dipping shot from 16 yards it looked like we were in for a mauling.

But we were a plucky lot, and rather than cave in we regrouped and, after 64 minutes, who else but Jim Forrest scored to get us right back into the tie. We survived the remaining 26 minutes unscathed to give us a fighting chance of turning the tie around at Ibrox.

The second leg coincided with the return to action of Baxter. While Wilson Wood's goal was giving the first team a 1-0 win over St Mirren at Ibrox, Jimmy was playing alongside me for the reserve team at Love Street. I opened the scoring in that one – we eventually won 7-1 – but although Baxter emerged unscathed, in the end Mr Symon elected not to gamble on throwing him into action against Inter. I missed out too when Willie Johnston was brought back in at outside-left. Young George McLean, scorer of over 40 goals for the reserves that season, also came in at inside-right. And big George came within an inch of forcing a play-off on a dramatic night under the lights at Ibrox.

There was concern about the match going ahead, though. On the Monday prior there was four inches of snow on the Ibrox pitch, but a team of 30 men worked from first light to remove the snow and by early afternoon the West German referee Herr Tschenscher was able to declare the pitch was playable. That meant I was able to watch along with 77,206 others as Jim Forrest fired us ahead after six minutes when he snapped up the loose ball after their goalkeeper, Giuliano Sarti, spilled a shot from Roger Hynd. It was now game on, but try as we might we could not find a way through the black and blue line that was superbly marshalled by Armando Picchi and Aristide Guarneri.

We did, however, get one chance when, after 69 minutes, a poor clearance fell to George McLean. Big Dandy had been in red-hot form for the reserves, with 46 goals to his name, and he looked like adding a European Cup goal to his tally when he unloaded a searing shot that rose majestically towards the top corner. However, it was just a fraction too high and the ball thudded against the underside of the crossbar. We were that close to forcing a play-off in Stuttgart. Instead it was a tale of what might have been and all that was left for us was to try and win the league.

After our uneven start we had settled down and embarked on a 13-match unbeaten run. In that sequence I added to goals against Falkirk and Third Lanark when I scored the opening goal against Airdrie at Broomfield on 16 January. But we could not sustain that run of form and defeats against Hibernian, Aberdeen, Morton, Dunfermline and Dundee United left us with an insurmountable mountain to climb. We eventually finished fifth, six points behind champions Kilmarnock. It was Rangers' lowest league finish for almost 40 years. It was the first time we had finished outside the top three since season 1953/54.

Personally the season had been stop-start. I eventually made 40 appearances, scoring 14 goals, but the old guard was on its way out. At the end of the season Jimmy Baxter went to Sunderland and 'Captain Cutlass', Bobby Shearer, joined Queen of the South. Within a few months Ralphie would also be off to pastures new, signing for Manchester City for a fee of £30,000.

I remained, but I had precious few opportunities in the first team in season 1965/66. The campaign opened with a trip to Tynecastle to face Hearts in the League Cup. I thought I had a good chance of playing as Willie Henderson had been injured in the annual 'trial' match five days earlier, but Mr Symon picked Craig Watson instead. I wasn't often overlooked for selection during my time at Rangers when fully fit, so I guess the writing was on the wall.

But a 4-2 defeat in Edinburgh clearly irked our manager for he ordered all first- and second-team players to report to Ibrox ahead of our next match against Clyde the following midweek. And I profited when Mr Symon made three changes to the XI that lost to Hearts as I was selected at inside-left at the expense of Tottie Beck.

With Eric among the players left out by Mr Symon, he chose me as captain, and what an honour that was for me. But despite the personnel changes we still didn't play that well – the *Glasgow*

Herald said we 'lacked a personality with a brain to think up goal-scoring moves' – but Alex Willoughby scored twice and laid on another for Jim Forrest in a comfortable 3-0 win.

I lost my unbeaten record as captain three days later when we lost 2-0 against Aberdeen at Pittodrie. This was the match I talked about earlier when I took over in goal from Norrie Martin. Remarkably, at the halfway stage we were third in the four-team Section Two, three points behind Aberdeen and facing an uphill battle to qualify for the quarter-final. Indeed, had we lost at home to Hearts in our fourth outing, we would have been out of the tournament. We scraped a 1-0 win to keep hopes of progression alive – an early goal from Bud did the damage – and we completed a remarkable recovery with wins over Clyde (3-1) and Aberdeen (4-0) to top the group and advance to the next round.

Leading the team out didn't make me immune to being left out, though, and by the time we faced Aberdeen I was no longer part of the starting XI. And it was the same story when the league action got underway as I had to wait until early October for my first league appearance. I came in on the right wing, replacing Willie Henderson who was playing for Scotland against Northern Ireland. Can you imagine that today? A full international taking place on the SAME day as eight top division matches? In any case I tried to make the most of my chance and marked my return by scoring twice in a 6-0 win over Stirling Albion. But that would be the first of just six appearances in the opening 28 league games. In all, I made just 12 appearances in the league, with that figure swelled by the fact I played outside-left in each of the final six fixtures.

It was evident that Mr Symon was looking to inject a bit of youth into the team, and while I was spending most of my time in the reserves, the forward line in the first team comprised the likes of Henderson, Willoughby, Forrest, McLean and Johnston. In fairness, I could have no complaints as the young lads were terrific, particularly Forrest and McLean who between them scored 49 goals in the league.

While being out of the first team reckoning was frustrating, I was never one for chapping on the manager's door demanding to be reinstated or else I'd be looking for a transfer. Instead I simply kept plugging away in the second team waiting for an opportunity, but the form and fitness of our front men meant that those chances were rare.

I was joined in the reserve team that season by some emerging youngsters like Colin Jackson and Sandy Jardine. I like to think playing alongside me and my experience in the game helped their development, particularly Sandy, who was an inside-forward back then. You could see that he had the potential to be a Rangers great, and so it proved, although he cemented his place in the hall of fame as a full-back. He was a colossal figure off the park too, especially when the club entered the abyss in February 2012. Sandy was instrumental alongside Ally McCoist as a figurehead during those toughest of times, and it's so sad that cancer caught up with him and he passed away before he saw Rangers return to the summit of the Scottish game.

Eric was part of the reserve team too and it was his goal from the penalty spot that gave us the lead in one of our opening Reserve League games against Partick Thistle at Ibrox. I was the one fouled to earn us the spot kick, but Thistle came back to win 2-1 and that defeat was one of many the second team suffered in the early weeks of the campaign.

Just six days later we lost 1-0 to Celtic Reserves at Parkhead and on 9 October, while the first team were thrashing St Mirren 6-1 at Love Street, I was part of the reserve side that suffered a harrowing 5-1 defeat at home by St Mirren Reserves. I was at outside-right for that one and we were 5-0 down at the interval. Definitely a day to forget!

I obviously didn't play too badly that day, though, as a couple of weeks later I was playing for the first team at Hampden against Celtic in the League Cup Final. We had won the first Old Firm league encounter 2-1 at Ibrox, but we lost out to them on this occasion. Although I hadn't played in the quarter-final or semi-final, I was chosen at inside-left to replace George McLean, who wasn't risked due to the badly swollen tendons in his ankle. But we were 2-0 behind at half-time after John 'Yogi' Hughes had successfully converted two penalties, and, although I was switched to outside-left after the break, all we could muster in response was an own goal from Ian Young six minutes from the end.

I played for the first team again the week after the League Cup Final, replacing wee Bud for our visit to Douglas Park to face Hamilton as he was nursing a toe injury. This was another triumphant day for Jim Forrest as he scored our first five goals in a 7-1 win. I got myself on the scoresheet too, netting with five minutes to go. The Accies took a real pounding from Rangers that day as the reserves also dished out a drubbing, winning 10-1 at Ibrox.

My top-team return was a brief one, though, and I was back in the reserves in November, opening the scoring in a 5-2 win against Hearts Reserves and playing at outside-right in a 5-3 win over Kilmarnock Reserves that featured a first-half double for Dennis Setterington and a goal from my old pal Jimmy Millar. The scintillating form of Jim Forrest meant Jimmy was now second fiddle at centre-forward but, irrespective of the level, he could always be relied upon to score goals.

The two of us still had that old chemistry and that was demonstrated when Jimmy created a goal for me when Rangers Reserves beat Falkirk Reserves 5-2 in the Second XI Cup. But just a few weeks later I was back in the first team. In our 4-0 New Year's Day win over Partick Thistle, Willie Henderson had picked up a muscle injury which ruled him out of our visit to Parkhead to face Celtic two days later. Symon opted to play me at outside-right and on my inside was young Setterington as Alex Willoughby was also on the casualty list.

The match was played out on an ice rink of a pitch. I had us ahead after barely a minute, firing a left-foot shot beyond Ronnie Simpson after a shot from John Greig had broken off a defender, but we capitulated in the second half. The reason for that was simply down to footwear. At the behest of their manager, Jock Stein, the Celtic players took their boots off at the interval and donned training shoes, which were more adept at helping maintain balance on the sanded, frosty surface than our conventional boots were. They scored five times without reply in the second half, with Stevie Chalmers grabbing a hat-trick.

That defeat did not derail our title challenge, though, as five straight wins took us back to the top of the table by the end of February. I kept my place at outside-right for the first of those victories – a George McLean hat-trick securing a 3-0 away win against St Johnstone – and even the late postponement of our match with Dundee at Ibrox the following week failed to disrupt our momentum.

The break wasn't beneficial for me, though. It gave Willie another week to recover and when we faced Stirling Albion in our next fixture, the wee man was back in the number-seven shirt. I didn't even have the fallback of a reserve fixture that day either as our Second XI Cup tie against Aberdeen at Pittodrie was postponed.

But I was back among a much-changed forward line when St Mirren came to Ibrox at the end of January. Willie had picked up another injury, a pulled muscle this time, so I deputised and there was also a place for Derek Traill on the other wing as Bud Johnston had flu. Alex Willoughby and Jim Forrest were also absent, their replacements being our big Icelander Therolf Beck and George McLean. Jimmy Millar was all set to take over from Forrest but his chances were scuppered when we were doing sprints at The Albion the day before the game. He pulled up and indicated he was having trouble with his back. Jimmy had had back trouble before and now it had returned, he was out of contention.

The impact of the changes on the team was minimal. I was involved in our first two goals, releasing Beck with a fine pass to allow him to create an opening for McLean to score and then firing in a cross that their goalkeeper, Liney, could only parry into the path of Beck. Big George scored again before half-time and a further goal in the second half from John Greig gave us a 4-1 win. And when news filtered through that Celtic had lost 3-2 against Hearts at Tynecastle, Rangers were back at the summit of the league table.

It was nip-and-tuck at the top, and Celtic overtook us after the next round of league fixtures. I was floored with flu so missed Rangers' 2-0 win over Hibernian, but Celtic took top spot on goal average after winning 4-0 against Falkirk. Remarkably, both games were home fixtures. Nowadays, there is no way Police Scotland would allow this to happen but it was a common occurrence during my playing days.

But daylight emerged between the teams at the end of February. With Bud and Willie fit again, I was with the reserves at Hamilton – I scored our second goal in a 5-0 win – but in the corresponding first-team fixture, Rangers won 4-0. And that, coupled with Celtic's shock 1-0 loss away at Stirling Albion, took us two points clear and into pole position to regain the First Division title.

The month of March would prove pivotal and it was a nightmare for us, the league fixtures therein ultimately costing us the title. We lost twice – to Falkirk and Dundee United – and drew twice, and although we won our last seven games Celtic topped the table, two points better off than ourselves. I played in six of those last seven games, scoring against Morton at Cappielow and Clyde at Ibrox.

We secured a crumb of comfort a couple of weeks before the end of the season when we beat Celtic to lift the Scottish Cup. Again I featured intermittently, scoring in the 5-1 win over Airdrie in the opening round, then securing a starting berth again at outside-right when we beat Ross County 2-0 in the second round. That match was memorable for the state of the pitch. The match was originally scheduled for 19 February, but blizzard conditions and snowdrifts resulted in a postponement. When the white stuff eventually disappeared and the tie went ahead nine days later, the pitch was a mud heap. It was so bad that Willie Waddell, who was being touted as the next Scotland manager and was attending the match as a journalist, lost his wellington boot! We scored twice inside a minute through Johnston and McLean and thereafter simply kept the ball as best we could until the 90 minutes was up.

I missed the quarter-final win over St Johnstone and both the semi-final and semi-final replay against Aberdeen, but I was named in the 14-man squad for the final. I felt I was in with a good chance of playing as I had played on the left wing in each of the previous four league games. George McLean had been dropped for the first of those matches – a 1-0 win over Aberdeen at Ibrox – with Willie Johnston replacing him at inside-left, allowing me to reclaim the number-11 jersey. Big Dandy bounced back from his omission, though, and in the week leading up to the final he netted an astonishing eight goals in two reserve matches.

The squad had a weather-disrupted session 24 hours prior to the match – the heavens opened and torrential rain lashed Glasgow, forcing us to train in the Ibrox gymnasium rather than at The Albion – but Mr Symon kept us all waiting to the day of the game to announce his starting XI. When he did, Messrs McLean, Willoughby and Sorensen were the ones to miss out and I was given the opportunity to collect another Scottish Cup medal.

When the teams took to the Hampden turf on 23 April, both defences were on top. Although I was listed at outside-left, we made a tactical switch early in the match that saw me and wee Willie switch wings. I was deployed on the right to try and stop the marauding Tommy Gemmell causing our defence trouble with his attacking surges. That had the effect of curbing my attacking instinct, though. In the end it was Celtic captain Billy McNeill who came closest to breaking the deadlock when he headed against the crossbar.

Four days later we met in the replay and it was a day we hailed the coronation of a new king, King Kai! Kai Johansen had arrived at Ibrox from Morton and was a very good full-back. And 20 minutes from the end he carved his name into Rangers folklore when he scored the winning goal. Willie Johnston created the chance with a slaloming run to the byline, and after George McLean – who had replaced Jim Forrest at centre-forward – fluffed his chance a few yards out and Willie Henderson's shot was blocked on the line, Kai, stationed 25 yards from goal, struck a venomous shot beyond Ronnie Simpson.

I was delighted to end what had been a disappointing season on a personal level with a medal, my fifth in the Scottish Cup. But little did I know as I bounded up the Hampden stairs to collect my gong that it would be the last time I climbed those stairs as a winner with Rangers.

CHAPTER 9

TERRIFIC TIMES ON TAYSIDE

I MADE history in the early weeks of season 1966/67. On 3 September Rangers faced Kilmarnock at Rugby Park in the quarter-final of the League Cup and won 1-0 thanks to a Jim Forrest goal after 74 minutes. I was not part of the starting XI, but I was named as our solitary substitute, and when I replaced Willie Henderson I became the first-ever sub to play in a competitive match for Rangers!

The media felt I was tailor-made for the recently introduced role. Writing in the *Evening Times*, Gair Henderson opined that the substitute's role was best suited to players that were versatile and could play in numerous positions. Gair reckoned that emerging youngsters should look to learn how to play in two or three different positions and also that, when signing players, managers would now be looking to establish not only the position a player played but also the positions they could fill if required. Although I wasn't quite a youngster anymore, I had played in a variety of positions for Rangers and Scotland so it looked as if the advent of this role would be a good thing for me.

My impact in the Kilmarnock match was immediate, with Allan Herron of the *Daily Record* calling me a 'human terrier' and opining that I 'fought for every ball like a sparrow fights for its daily bread'. Allan thought that my performance merited an extended run in the starting XI, but I remained a peripheral figure. The two Willies – Henderson and Johnston – were the main men on the wing, and I only appeared in six of the first 20 league games.

I did start the season in the team, playing at outside-left in our opening League Cup sectional tie against Hibernian at Ibrox. Bud was in the midst of an SFA-imposed suspension at the time so I took his place in the team. I hit the post with a header in the first half and John Greig thumped the upright in the second half too, before, with five minutes remaining, I looped in a cross that Alec Smith headed down to George McLean to net the only goal of the game.

I started again the following midweek when we visited Annfield to face Stirling Albion. My direct opponent that night was none other than Eric Caldow. Since his leg break Eric had only featured intermittently for the first team. Davie Provan had established himself in Eric's position so my old pal left Ibrox in the summer of 1966. However, our reunion was an unhappy one for him. We romped to an 8-0 win, with Jim Forrest scoring five times. I scored after 19 minutes and that opened the floodgates, with four goals scored in each half.

Eric may have been at right-back that night but, for me, his best position was left-back. He was a great guy and an immaculate footballer, never once being booked, and some years later the great Paco Gento of Real Madrid hailed him as his toughest opponent. With Eric at left-back, Baxter at left-half, Ralphie at inside-left and me outside him, our team had a formidable left-hand side, which was complemented superbly by the likes of Shearer, Greig, McMillan and Henderson on the right. I talked about the match in which Eric broke his leg earlier in the book but, suffice to say, he was never the same player after he came back from that injury. We stayed in regular contact after we both finished playing, but, alas, Eric is another who is no longer with us. He passed away in March 2019 and I was among the mourners at his funeral.

Our eight-goal feast was followed by famine, though, as the following Saturday we drew a blank against Kilmarnock at home. Bud was back from suspension so I warmed the substitute's bench. And that's where I remained for our 3-2 defeat against Hibernian at Easter Road and the rather humiliating 1-1 draw at home to Stirling Albion before I was eventually called into action in Ayrshire.

It was good to be part of the top-12 for every first-team game, but I was becoming increasingly aware that my role was going to be, more often than not, the 12th man. It was only when either of the two Willies were absent through injury or suspension that I got a place in the starting XI, with my longest run in the team coming after Bud broke his leg against Berwick Rangers in January. I started 13 of the last 14 league games, but my days as a regular fixture in the first team appeared to be all but over.

It was me who replaced Bud when he broke his leg at Berwick, thus earning an unwanted place in the history books. I was part of the team that lost that day, Sammy Reid's goal giving the home side a 1-0 win. Try as we might we couldn't score. I hit the outside of the post and Jock Wallace, in goal for Berwick, was heroic. That meant we exited the Scottish Cup at the first hurdle to lower league opposition and the hullaballoo that followed saw our strikers, Forrest and McLean, jettisoned. They never played for the club again.

The Berwick loss was a big blot on our copybook, but, that aside, we were in with a shout of honours right to the end of the season. Despite struggling in our League Cup section, the win over Kilmarnock was enough to take us through to the knockout stages. And we made it all the way to the final where, unfortunately, we lost out to Celtic. However, we went toe-to-toe with them in the league and also had a fantastic run to the final of the European Cup Winners' Cup.

As I said, I appeared in all but one of our last 14 league games but, crucially, the one I missed was our last fixture against Celtic at Ibrox. We went into the game knowing anything but a win would hand the title to our Old Firm rivals. They led the title race by a point but this was our last league game while they still had a game in hand.

Wee Bud had now returned to fitness, making his comeback three days earlier when we beat Slavia Sofia 1-0 at Ibrox to seal our place in the Cup Winners' Cup Final. And he was on the left wing again when we faced Celtic while I was relegated to the bench.

Celtic hadn't won on their last eight visits to Ibrox, but they didn't need to on this occasion. Young Sandy Jardine put us ahead five minutes before half-time and had we held on to the interval it may have been a different outcome. But no sooner had I and my fellow Rangers supporters acclaimed Sandy's goal, we contrived to lose a poor goal less than a minute later. Norrie

Martin, our goalkeeper, parried a shot from Willie Wallace but hesitation from our defence allowed Bobby Lennox to shoot against the post before Jimmy Johnstone netted the rebound. Wee Jinky scored again 16 minutes from the end to all but seal our fate, although Roger Hynd set up a grandstand finish when he made it 2-2 six minutes later.

The Celtic match was played on 6 May so there was now a gap of some three weeks until we faced Bayern Munich in the European Cup Winners' Cup Final. To ensure we maintained our match sharpness, we played three matches in that spell, the first of which was in Toronto against Sparta Prague. This was an exhibition match arranged to launch football as a major sport in the USA and Canada. We took 13 players with us on the flight from Prestwick, the 11 who had started against Celtic plus myself and Billy Ritchie.

In truth, the match, played on front of a crowd of 21,940, was anything but friendly as our opponents doled out some rough treatment. They went ahead inside the first four minutes then resorted to kicking lumps out of us for the rest of the game. Willie Henderson, who had a great game, bore the brunt of the heavy challenges. Try as we might, we couldn't restore parity and we flew back home on the back of a 1-0 defeat.

I was back in the starting XI for our next friendly against newly promoted Morton at Cappielow. Willie Henderson had suffered a cut leg against Sparta, so I played at outside-right and created our opening goal when my corner kick on the stroke of half-time found Bobby Watson and he headed the ball into the net. Ian Anderson equalised for a plucky Morton side after 65 minutes, but Roger Hynd sealed a 2-1 win for us when he scored with four minutes to go.

It was good to get some minutes under my belt, but I still felt sure I wouldn't be considered for Nuremberg. And when we faced Motherwell in Charlie Aitken's testimonial seven days before travelling to West Germany, that uneasy feeling was made worse when I wasn't selected. Willie was fit again and back in the number-seven jersey, and he was joined on the pitch by Dave Mackay, Ian St John and my former team-mate Billy Stevenson, who guested for the home side. Roger Hynd put us ahead after 25 minutes, but a Mackay penalty 11 minutes from time meant it ended with honours even.

As Rangers were drawing at Fir Park, Celtic were in Lisbon preparing to face Inter Milan in the European Cup Final. And they heaped more pressure on our team by defeating the Italians 2-1 to become the first Scottish side to lift a European trophy. Incidentally, to illustrate how strong Scottish football was at that time, while we were battling it out at Fir Park, down in Ayrshire Kilmarnock were attempting to reach the final of the Inter-Cities Fairs Cup. This was the predecessor of the UEFA Cup – now, of course, the Europa League – and the Rugby Park side faced Leeds United in the semi-final. They had lost the first leg at Elland Road by four goals to two and they were unable to overturn the two-goal deficit, drawing 0-0 against Don Revie's side.

Although uncertain if I would play in the final, I was included in the 16-man squad that left Glasgow on 29 May bound for our date with destiny. I had only played in three of our eight matches prior to the final, home and away in the quarter-final against Real Zaragoza and in the first leg of the semi-final against Slavia Sofia. It was my goal after 31 minutes of that match that gave us a 1-0 win, but the man that created the chance for me, Alex Willoughby, was not on the aircraft bound for West Germany.

Alex had come into the side in the wake of the defeat at Berwick, ironically taking his place in the team just as his cousin, Jim Forrest, was being cruelly jettisoned. Alex was a good player and he hit a rich vein of goalscoring form. He joined me on the scoresheet the week after our Scottish Cup loss, netting a hat-trick in our 5-1 win over Hearts at Tynecastle. Willie Henderson scored the other goal and remarkably, four days later, it was the same scorers and the same scoreline as we defeated Clyde 5-1 at Ibrox.

Alex and I made it three successive scoring games when we got one goal each in a 2-1 win over Kilmarnock, and by the end of April Alex had netted 16 goals in just 11 games. I was in good form in that spell too, scoring twice in an enthralling 4-3 win over St Johnstone at Ibrox and the opening goal in what proved a costly 1-1 draw at home against Clyde.

A week later we dropped another point at Dens Park – remarkably we had now gone eight years without a win there – and it was Alex who netted our goal. But that would be the last goal he would score for Rangers that season. The following midweek he was dropped for the return leg against Slavia Sofia, with Roger Hynd coming in at centre-forward and Alex Smith taking Willoughby's place at inside-right. Alex was quite rightly annoyed at his omission as big Roger hadn't played for the first team for over a year and wasn't even a forward! However, he had scored four goals when deployed up front against Dundee Reserves and Mr Symon reckoned that form could be replicated in the first team. It was harsh on Alex, a fine player and a real Rangers man, and in the wake of that match he submitted a transfer request. He ended up at Aberdeen with his cousin, Jim Forrest, and won the Scottish Cup there in 1970.

Back to our trip to Nuremberg and we were 90 minutes late leaving due to some issues with air traffic control. During the delay we had lunch and tried to relax in the airport lounge before we took to the air at 1.30pm. We were accompanied by Clyde manager Davie White and Morton impresario Hal Stewart, and we touched down safe and well. When we emerged from the aircraft we were greeted by mist and a chill in the air, but we were soon warmed up by the sight of around two dozen of our supporters who had come to meet us at the airport.

In all, around 6,000 followed us, and among them were two young lads from East Kilbride, Malcolm Graham and Bobby Sorbie. These chaps took 37.5 hours to travel from Hamilton Cross to Nuremberg as they hitch-hiked all the way! En route they stopped at Beattock, London, Dover, Ostend and Cologne before a wee wander along the side of the autobahn secured a lift to Nuremberg. That for me epitomised the Rangers supporters, they are second to none and I am fortunate to have had, and still have, an excellent relationship with them.

Mr Symon had decided to stay outside the centre of Nuremberg, clearly feeling we could focus on the task in hand without the distractions that staying in the hub of a busy city can bring. We stayed in a wee village about 24 miles away, and after checking in we were soon back on the bus and heading for an evening training session at the Nuremberg Stadium.

We trained hard for around an hour, but it was after that 60-minute workout I received confirmation that I would not be in the team to face Bayern. Naturally I was disappointed – although I did suspect I wouldn't be picked – but I was a

Rangers man so I was still supportive of my team-mates and willing them to win.

The weather was typically Scottish in the days before the final – it was 'bucketing' down – and that should have been to our advantage. But on the night we simply couldn't find a decisive goal. We huffed and puffed but lacked that finishing touch that a forward like Jim Forrest, George McLean, Alex Willoughby, or even myself, could provide. The match went to extra time wherein Franz Roth, the Bayern right-half, scored the winning goal.

And that would be my last involvement with a Rangers squad. It was time up for me and Mr Symon told me as much. It was hard to accept that, at 28, it was felt I could no longer hold down a regular first-team place. From my return from National Service until I broke my ankle I had been a first pick, but now I was a peripheral figure. With most of my contemporaries leaving – for example, Jimmy Millar was handed a free transfer in July 1967 – it made sense for me to seek pastures new. I ended up joining Dundee United as part of a deal that brought the Swedish winger, Orjan Persson, to Ibrox. If you include Glasgow Cup, Glasgow Merchants Charity Cup, friendlies and testimonials I made a total of 408 appearances in a Rangers jersey and scored 163 goals. That puts me in a very select group of wingers in the club's history as only two others, Alec Smith and Sandy Archibald, have scored more goals for the club than me.

The whole deal to take me to Tannadice was a bit of a saga due to issues between Persson and United which left myself and Wilson Wood, who was also part of the swap deal, in limbo. We reported to Ibrox for pre-season training at the end of July knowing that we were surplus to requirements, yet unsure where our respective futures lay. In the interim, Rangers signed Alex Ferguson for a record fee of £65,000 but I never got the chance to play alongside him. Eventually all the technicalities were sorted out and I was off to Tannadice.

One of those technicalities involved a pay-off for yours truly. I had expected I would have received some sort of payment as part of the deal, but Mr Symon steadfastly refused to give me one. I informed him that I would be taking this up with the chairman, John Lawrence. I went up to Mr Lawrence's office and he couldn't believe Mr Symon hadn't offered me anything. He alluded to the fact I had been at the club since I was 14 and asked me to pretty much name my price. I said I was looking for £3,000 and a cheque was promptly written to cover that amount. But I could have got myself a bit more if I had wanted. Mr Lawrence had been so impressed with my loyalty and service to the football club that he said he would have given me £5,000 had I asked for it.

The United manager, Jerry Kerr, was a good man and I developed an excellent relationship with him. In fact, our relationship was that good that I went fishing for him one day. We were in the dressing room when he came in and asked me to help him recover his false teeth. It turned out he had been sick in the toilet and, in the process, his teeth had come out and went down the pan. None of the other lads were prepared to retrieve the gnashers so it was left to me to stick my hand in to the toilet water to get them!

I joined a decent Dundee United team on 3 August 1967. As recently as 1959 they had been languishing in the lower reaches of the Second Division, but following Jerry's appointment they had regained their First Division status. In his first season in charge – 1959/60 – Kerr, who insisted upon his appointment that United went full-time, led United to second place in the league, securing promotion to the top flight on the final day of the season. They had been mainstays in the First Division since then.

Jerry was a bit of a visionary. Along with Hal Stewart, who was manager of Morton, he tapped into the Scandinavian market, recruiting excellent players like Lennart Wing (Sweden), Finn Dossing and Mogens Berg (both Denmark). The man who had been part of my transfer from Rangers, Orjan Persson, was also from Scandinavia.

United were not just a threat domestically. In the Inter-Cities Fairs Cup in 1966/67 Kerr's team beat Barcelona 4-1 on aggregate, winning 2-1 in the Camp Nou. This was United's first-ever European tie and they met another stellar European club in the next round, the Old Lady herself, Juventus. After losing 3-0 in Turin, United could not rescue the tie at Tannadice, Dossing's goal ten minutes from time merely being a consolation.

Notable guys in the dressing room were our inside-forward Dennis Gillespie, who would score over 100 goals in more than 300 appearances for United, and left-back Jimmy Briggs, who would make almost 400 first-team appearances between 1955 and 1970. Tommy Millar, younger brother of Jimmy, was the right-back I would usually be up against when Rangers faced United and he was a solid, dependable player. Speaking of Jimmy, he was on the books at Tannadice too, having moved to United just a few weeks before I joined.

Just two days after I signed for United I was making my debut. We faced Sheffield United at Tannadice in a friendly, and the man I had scored past on my debut for Rangers against the British Army, Alan Hodgkinson, was between the sticks for the visitors. We lost 1-0 – Mick Jones, who would join Leeds United a month later for £100,000, scored the goal – but it was good to get to know my team-mates before we faced Celtic at Parkhead in the opening League Cup sectional tie.

This would be the first competitive match the Lisbon Lions would play after lifting the European Cup a few months earlier, and their manager, Jock Stein, selected the same XI to face us. Although the admission prices had been raised to five shillings (25p), there was a good crowd of 51,101 in attendance.

The arrival of Jock Stein had brought the fans flooding back to Parkhead. As recently as season 1964/65, Celtic's average attendance at home games was a paltry 18,284 and it was only really for Old Firm games that Parkhead would be full. To be honest it was a similar story when I was at Rangers, with the terraces at Ibrox only densely populated on European nights or when Celtic visited. Indeed, by the time I went to United average attendances were dwindling across the country. United's average gate at that time was around 7,500 but that had dropped markedly from an average of 11,382 at the start of the 1960s. The decline in attendances eventually prompted league reconstruction although it would be the summer of 1975 before that came to pass.

In the tie against Celtic I was up against Jim Craig but we set ourselves up to play defensively so I didn't get many chances to take him on. But although Celtic had a lot of possession and carved out a few chances it looked like United would take a point until, in the last minute, a Bertie Auld cross from the byline was met by the head of wee Jimmy Johnstone. Our goalkeeper, Don McKay, who had had an excellent match, saved Jinky's header but the rebound fell back to the feet of the Celtic outside-left and he fired in the winning goal.

Joining ourselves and Celtic in our section were Aberdeen and Rangers and my home debut for United would be against the Dons on 16 August 1967. It would be a goalscoring debut too as I managed to net the second goal of the evening. It was 0-0 at half-time but Billy Hainey put us in front and I doubled our lead with a solo effort. I beat several players then dummied the goalkeeper, Bobby Clark, before walking the ball into the net. Our Norwegian outside-right, Finn Seemann, then helped himself to a double before Dennis Gillespie rounded off the scoring to set us up for a trip to my old stomping ground, Ibrox.

Similarly to our earlier visit to Glasgow to face Celtic, we were not overawed by Rangers and once again defended stoically. Although they had a certain Alexander Chapman Ferguson rumbling up our defence all they had to show for their efforts at the end of the match was a 72nd-minute penalty converted by Kai Johansen. It was a soft award – Doug Smith was adjudged to have fouled Orjan Persson but many observers felt his challenge was a fair one – and I could have nicked a point for us in the dying minutes when I fired in a shot that beat Eric Sorenson in the Rangers goal but rose too high and cleared the crossbar.

That 1-0 reverse, coupled with a similar scoreline when Celtic visited Tannadice, meant we were all but out of the competition, something that was confirmed when we drew 2-2 at Pittodrie and went down 3-0 to Rangers at home. Ferguson scored his first goals in a Rangers jersey that afternoon at Tannadice.

In the league we didn't start too well, winning just two of our first eight games. In that sequence Aberdeen exacted revenge for our League Cup win by hammering us 6-0 at Pittodrie before I got my first league goal for United the following weekend in a 2-2 draw at home to Partick Thistle. Tommy Rae had the visitors ahead after just four minutes but I equalised six minutes before half-time. Ian Mitchell, who would have a fine season for us, put us in front after 66 minutes before Frank Coulson earned the Jags a point with an equaliser after 71 minutes.

Our league form continued to be erratic and inconsistent up to the end of 1967. In December we were heavily defeated by Clyde at Shawfield, losing 5-0 just a fortnight after drawing 1-1 against Celtic at Parkhead. I played particularly well in the latter game. Although the onus was again on defence, when we did spring forward I was at the heart of our attacking forays, none more so than when I gave United the lead. Twice in the first half I had tested the reflexes of the Celtic goalkeeper, Ronnie Simpson, but the big man could do little to stop my 20-yard shot with my left foot 17 minutes from full time. Celtic equalised less than a minute later through Stevie Chalmers but the match ended in controversy when Willie Wallace of Celtic was sent off by the referee, Mr R. C. Greenlees. Mr Greenlees had dismissed Alex Ferguson and Colin Stein in the Rangers v Hibernian match nine days earlier and he sent off Willie on the say so of his linesman. Willie, usually a centre-forward, had been redeployed at right-back and we had a bit of a battle in the closing stages, culminating in an off-the-ball incident when Willie struck me. The referee didn't see what happened but the linesman did and Willie went for an early bath.

A fresh-faced six-year old me circa 1943

Captain of the school football team. That's me in the centre of the front row, holding the ball

With some of my fellow members of the 194th Glasgow Boys' Brigade company on our annual camp in Arbroath

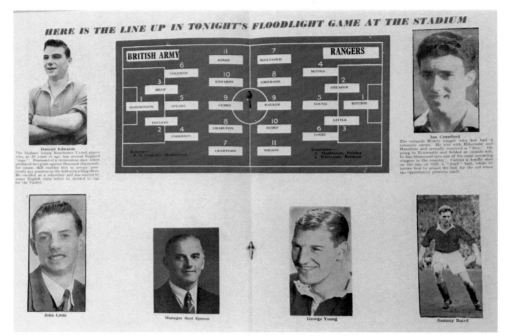

The centre pages of the match programme listing me at outside-left for my Rangers debut against the British Army in December 1956

Scot Symon hands me my train ticket as I prepare to depart for National Service in January 1958

Arriving back from Holland after beating Sparta Rotterdam 3-2 in the European Cup in March 1960. I am flanked by fellow goalscorers, Max Murray (left) and Sammy Baird

With the Main Stand looming in the background, Billy Ritchie and I make our way to the Albion training ground across the road from Ibrox

Thwarted by the England goalkeeper, Ron Springett, at Wembley in April 1961. I scored twice that day but Scotland lost 9–3

Netting with a flying header during a 4-0 win over Falkirk at Ibrox in 1961. Four months later I scored six times against the same opponents

Peering in through the window on the day of my sister Grace's wedding, 17 November 1961

Recording Rangers songs at a studio in Glasgow in 1963. I also recorded a World Cup song with my Dumbarton players in 1978

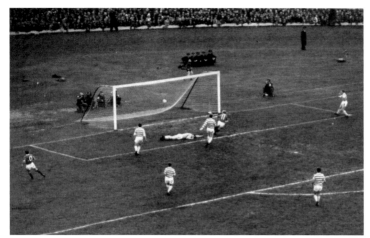

Scoring Rangers' third goal in the 1963 Scottish Cup Final replay against Celtic. I won five Scottish Cup medals and had an excellent record against Celtic too

Taking a walk with the irrepressible Jim Baxter in December 1963. He was one of the best players I played with

Celebrating Burns Night with (L–R) John Greig, Davie Provan, George McLean, Bobby Shearer, Jimmy Millar and Ralph Brand

The squad celebrate winning the Scottish Cup and completing the domestic treble in 1964. I am crouched on the right wearing a bowler hat

Avril and I not long after we met at a family wedding. It was love at first sight and we were married within a year

Training with Ralph Brand at Ibrox. We struck up an almost telepathic understanding and, along with Jimmy Millar, netted a glut of goals for Rangers

The Scotland forward line in training at Hendon ahead of the match with England in 1965. I am joined by (L–R): Willie Henderson, Bobby Collins, Denis Law and Ian St John

Dressed in our training gear, here I am with Eric Caldow, Jim Baxter and Ralphie Brand

30 November 1965, the day I married my Avril. One of the best days of my life!

In action for Dundee United against Motherwell. I had five great years at Tannadice and was inducted into their Hall of Fame

Pictured during my second spell as manager at Dumbarton. I remain the only manager in the club's history to lead them to the Premier League

Breaking open the bubbly to celebrate Dumbarton's promotion to Division One in 1972. The man with the glass is one of the Dumbarton directors.

I trained, bred and raced pigeons for over 60 years. This is me at the pigeon loft in Newton

With the greyhound we call ROL, Rangers Outside Left. She won over ten races for me before a broken hock ended her career

Out and about with the dogs and my grandkids, Harry, David and Anna. I'm the doting grandad and love spending time with them

With my daughter, Sheena, son, David, and granddaughter, Carly, at Ibrox in 2016

We ended the year in style with a 9-0 thumping of Stirling Albion and sitting mid-table. However, we were not afforded the opportunity to have a long run in the Scottish Cup. We beat St Mirren 3-1 at Tannadice in the opening round but were then eliminated at the next hurdle following a titanic match against Hearts.

We found ourselves two goals down inside the opening 15 minutes in that match, Donald Ford and Rene Moeller scoring for the Jambos. But I pulled one back in the 20th minute, pouncing on a poor backpass from Eddie Thomson to score with my left foot. And we were level five minutes later when my cross from the right-hand side of the box was headed into the path of Andy Rowland, who rattled the ball into the net.

I was involved again when we took the lead in the 30th minute. I took a quick free kick to Tommy Millar and scampered towards the penalty area. When Tommy flighted the ball forward I managed to stoop and get my head to it and direct it into the path of Ian Mitchell who fired one home. Remarkably, Mitchell scored again after 37 minutes and suddenly from 2-0 down we were 4-2 ahead.

Eddie Thomson atoned for his earlier error when he headed a third goal for Hearts just before half-time and it was all-square again when Moeller scored his second of the game after 50 minutes. The tie see-sawed back in our favour with 20 minutes to go when Billy Hainey drove a left-foot shot into the net from 20 yards. But we couldn't hold on, and, after George Miller made it 5-5 from the penalty spot, Jim Irvine scored the winner for Hearts four minutes from time.

The attendance at our match was 9,021. Remarkably, a couple of hundred yards away Rangers took on Dundee at Dens

Park on the same day at the same time. Such events wouldn't be allowed to happen nowadays but approximately 33,000 watched that one – it ended in a 1-1 draw – so you can imagine what the congestion was like afterwards.

United bounced back from the cup exit with a five-match unbeaten run in the league. I opened the scoring in the first of those matches, a 3-1 win over Motherwell at Fir Park, and was on the mark again when we drew 3-3 at home to Raith Rovers. The run also allowed us to exact some revenge on Hearts when we beat them 2-1 at Tannadice. We were behind inside the first minute but Ian Mitchell scored 16 minutes into the second half and I got our winning goal eight minutes from time when I capitalised on a mistake from George Miller.

Heavy defeats were dished out by Celtic (0-5), Rangers (1-4), Kilmarnock (0-4) and Dunfermline (1-4) before the season ended, but Dundee United were never in any danger of being drawn into a relegation dogfight. We eventually finished 11th, 12 points clear of Motherwell, who were relegated along with Stirling Albion.

I had a productive first season as a United player. I made 37 appearances and my goal in a 2-1 defeat against St Johnstone at Muirton Park on 24 April was my tenth of the campaign. And my debut season at Tannadice also saw me pick up another winners' medal. In November we beat St Johnstone 5-1 in the final of the Dewar Shield – I scored one of United's goals – but I missed out on a second medal when we lost out to Dundee in the final of the Forfarshire Cup. We were beaten 4-3 at Tannadice, but I eventually got my hands on this piece of silverware in March 1970, scoring one of our goals in a 2-0 win over Arbroath.

The season was concluded with a three-match tour of Norway and, after a short break, I got a good pre-season under my belt in the summer of 1968. I was on the sub's bench for the first two pre-season friendlies against Preston North End but was back in the starting XI when we drew 4-4 with Hartlepool United. Kenny Cameron continued his fine start to the season in the latter match, his hat-trick making it five goals in just three games.

The competitive action got underway four days after our trip to Hartlepool but I was absent from the squad that travelled to face Dunfermline Athletic in the League Cup. I had some concerns over my future with Dundee United as I was finding the travelling to and from Glasgow difficult. As a result, I lettered the manager to inform him that, with reluctance, I wished to leave the club. But Jerry Kerr didn't want me to go and, after my letter was passed to the board of directors for their consideration, my transfer request was rejected. Jerry spoke to me soon after that and told me I didn't need to come to Dundee every day to train. Instead he arranged for me to train with Partick Thistle. They were managed by my old boss, Scot Symon, who had succeeded Willie Thornton after Mr Thornton had left to return to Rangers as assistant manager. The arrangement was that I would train with the first team during the day and work with their youngsters and reserves in the evening.

I returned to the fold for United in our 4-0 win over Arbroath in the semi-final of the Forfarshire Cup – Kenny Cameron scored all four goals – and was back at outside-left for our fourth League Cup tie against Dunfermline at Tannadice. We were all but out of the tournament by then – we lost each of our first three ties, with my old pal Jim Forrest scoring twice for Aberdeen when the Dons beat United 4-1 – but we came from behind to beat the Pars 2-1. It was nice to be back patrolling my usual beat on the left wing and I was there again when we completed our Section Three fixtures with wins over Clyde (4-0) and Aberdeen (1-0). The run of three successive victories wasn't enough to progress to the next round, though; Clyde's 3-0 win over Dunfermline saw them top the section, two points ahead of ourselves and Aberdeen.

If we had started the League Cup campaign poorly then our form in Division One was a complete contrast as we won each of our first four matches. This included a 3-1 win in the Dundee derby and a first league goal of the season for yours truly in a 4-2 win over Arbroath at Tannadice. Our home ground was a bit of a fortress – we won each of our first nine games there – and we were top of the table for a spell. A couple of defeats against Celtic and Kilmarnock knocked us off our lofty perch but, in early December, Dundee United were second in the table, two points behind leaders Celtic. And when Celtic lost 1-0 at Ibrox on 2 January, the same day we beat Dundee 2-1 at Dens Park, United were back on top of the pile, joint top of the league with reigning champions, Celtic.

I had come on as sub in both our New Year games – we completed a Tayside double, beating St Johnstone 4-2 on 1 January – and I was on the bench again when we welcomed Aberdeen to Tannadice to complete our third game in just four days. Confidence was sky high in the dressing room but it was rocked that day as Jim Forrest once again got on the scoresheet as the Dons, who were lying near the foot of the table, inflicted upon us our first home defeat of the season, winning 4-1.

That was the first of three straight league defeats. Restored to the starting line-up, I scored the equaliser after 65 minutes against Arbroath at Gayfield, but the league's bottom side recorded just their second win of the season when they beat us 3-1. And seven days later we lost at home again, this time to Celtic, although it took two goals in the last five minutes to give the league leaders a 3-1 win.

We enjoyed a temporary distraction from league business when we defeated Queen's Park and Ayr United in the Scottish Cup. In the latter tie we burst out the blocks, and when I scored our fifth goal with a left-foot shot only 28 minutes had elapsed. That was my fifth goal of the season and we eventually won 6-2, but we exited the cup in the next round, losing 3-2 at home to Morton.

February 1969 also saw a dear friend off to pastures new. At the ripe old age of 33, Jimmy Millar accepted an offer to become manager of Raith Rovers. Ironically, in his last match for United Jimmy scored an equaliser for the reserves against Raith Rovers in a Second XI Cup tie.

Our blip of three successive league losses had seen us tumble to sixth place, but we got back to winning ways when our reunion with Jimmy Millar ended in a 3-1 victory for United. I wasn't slow in rubbing that one in when I saw Jimmy after the match!

That was our first league match for over a month as bad weather had wreaked havoc during February. Kenny Cameron was the main man again, scoring twice, and after that United lost only two of their remaining ten league matches. Included in that run was a 2-1 win over Rangers at Tannadice – I was an unused sub for that match – and those two points helped us finish the season in fifth place which secured European football for the following season in the Inter-Cities Fairs Cup.

We ended the season with a trip to the USA. Two years earlier United had gone stateside and represented Dallas Tornado in the NASL – the fledging United States Soccer Association invited foreign clubs to represent North American franchises initially – and we were asked to do so again in May 1969. United played eight matches under that guise against Wolves, Kilmarnock, Aston Villa and West Ham.

United started with a 4-2 defeat against Wolves – I came on for Ian Scott after 60 minutes – and followed that with back-to-back matches with Villa. We drew the first match 2-2 but the Villa Park side, who were representing Atlanta, beat us 2-0 in the second tie which was staged in Dallas.

Match four was against a Kilmarnock side that were representing St Louis. We trailed 1-0 at half-time in this one, and with 13 minutes to go we were 3-1 down. But I crossed for Alan Gordon to pull one back and then scored our equaliser with only two minutes to go.

Against West Ham two days later we took a bit of a battering. On the same day that Colin Stein scored four goals for Scotland in an 8-0 win over Cyprus at Hampden, Trevor Brooking, Geoff Hurst and Bobby Moore were among the scorers for the Hammers in their 6-1 win. We lost to them again on 21 May, it was 3-1 this time, before ending the tournament with a 1-0 win over Kilmarnock – I notched the only goal of the game – and a 3-2 win over Wolves in the Cotton Bowl in Texas. Wolves won the tournament but Ian Mitchell scored twice for us to ensure United finished third out of the five teams that competed.

Sandwiched between the Kilmarnock and Wolves games was a friendly – we were Dundee United in this one – against West Ham at the Civic Stadium in Portland, Oregon. The match was played on astroturf, and at the conclusion a number of players reported burns to their legs sustained as a result of slide tackling. I have to confess I wasn't a fan of the surface. Although the ball moved well, I thought there would be a significant rise in cartilage injuries as it was hard to turn quickly.

Aside from the surface issues, we were comprehensively beaten again – a certain Harry Redknapp was among the goals as we lost 8-2 – and the tour was wrapped up with wins over Dallas Tornado and Juventus. I scored our opening goal in Dallas but I have to admit by this time I was absolutely knackered and ready for a wee summer break.

The trip stateside also had an impact on our attire for season 1969/70. We kicked off with a friendly against an Everton team that would win the English First Division championship that season. We lost 4-1 at Goodison Park but the match was more significant for the orange kit we were wearing. When I joined United we wore white shirts with black collar and cuffs. United today are, of course, synonymous with tangerine jerseys and that match on Merseyside was the first time that colour of jersey was sported. The change came about at the request of the wife of the manager, Barbara Kerr. Dallas Tornado wore a burnt orange home kit and Mrs Kerr felt the vibrancy of this colour would be beneficial to us so we adopted it from then on.

We followed our defeat on Merseyside with another two losses. We were defeated 2-1 by Millwall at The Den – I was pulled back to earn us a penalty in that one, which was duly despatched by Dennis Gillespie – and went down 3-0 to Bobby

Robson's Ipswich Town at Portman Road. But these matches were about getting match sharpness and I felt we were in good shape for the new campaign. Although many felt United had punched above their weight in season 1968/69, the players and the manager were intent on ensuring we remained in the upper reaches of the league table in season 1969/70 too.

However, as seemed to be our wont at that time, we started poorly in the League Cup. We lost 3-2 at home to Hearts, despite leading 2-0 at half-time, and we then went to Cappielow and went down 4-1 to Morton. We were 4-0 down in that one when I crossed for Ian Scott to net a consolation goal, and although we bounced back to beat St Mirren home and away we lost again to Hearts and Morton to exit the competition.

I played at outside-left in four of the six fixtures and was handed the number-11 jersey again for our first league match of the campaign against Rangers at Tannadice. Rangers, who had just re-signed Jim Baxter, should have beaten us, but Donald MacKay had a fine match in goal and we earned a point from the goalless draw.

We drew our next match too, 2-2 against Clyde, before we were hit for six against Morton at Cappielow. I was on the bench for that game, but by the time I replaced Davie Hogg at outside-right with seven minutes to go, we were 4-0 down. Two late goals from Joe Mason, which completed his hat-trick, capped a miserable day for us.

This kind of result was worrying, particularly as we were due to play Newcastle United in the opening round of the Inter-Cities Fairs Cup. But we got back on track before the first leg against Newcastle with a 5-2 win over Airdrie. That match featured my first goal of the season and I was involved in United's fifth goal, scored by Ian Scott. Remarkably, all five United goals were scored inside 38 first-half minutes.

We faced Newcastle two days after our win over Airdrie and the match was watched by a crowd of over 15,000, an estimated 5,000 of whom had travelled up from England. It was a fantastic match and we were very unlucky to lose 2-1. I had a chance to score in the first half when I beat their goalkeeper, Willie McFaul, with a header, but Alwyn Burton cleared the ball off the line. As it was, we fell behind 11 minutes after half-time when the big Welshman, Wyn Davies, who had hit the woodwork three times in the first half, scored. And he doubled his tally six minutes later with another header. We looked to have been weakened further when, with 17 minutes to go, MacKay had to be replaced in goal by 16-year-old Ged Reilly when he sustained a head wound. But Newcastle didn't manage to score again and a late goal from Ian Scott gave us some hope of retrieving the tie when we travelled to St James' Park a fortnight later.

We warmed up for that match with back-to-back wins in the league over Dundee and St Johnstone. I missed those matches and the return leg in Newcastle – which we lost 1-0 – but was back at outside-right for United's 2-0 win over Motherwell. And following successive doubles from Alan Gordon in 3-1 wins over Ayr United and St Mirren, United were second in the table, a point adrift of leaders Hibernian.

I really enjoyed playing in that United team and Alan was one that I struck up a particularly fruitful partnership with. He had come to the club from Hearts in March 1969 for £8,000 and he was great in the air. He would tell me to cross the ball to the back post as he would always get a header on the ball as no one would beat him in the jump. And that was the source of so many goals for United in my time on Tayside. In season 1970/71 Alan, who sadly passed away in 2010, netted 20 goals in 44 appearances and he would later credit me with creating around 80 per cent of them.

United were still there or thereabouts at the top of the league when we travelled to Ibrox to face Rangers on 13 December. A couple of weeks earlier I had returned to haunt my old team-mates, Jimmy Millar and Ralphie Brand, when I scored the only goal of the game against Raith Rovers at Starks Park. Ralphie had joined up with Jimmy earlier in the season, signing from Sunderland, but I pounced on a loose ball in the 20th minute to slam a shot into the net via the underside of the crossbar.

The match against Rangers was significant as it was Willie Waddell's first match in charge of my old side. Celtic had won two successive titles in my final two seasons at the club, which increased the pressure on Scot Symon. And he eventually lost his job early in season 1967/68 despite having led Rangers to the top of the league table. Davie White replaced him but he too could not derail Jock Stein's Celtic juggernaut and was dismissed in the wake of a dismal defeat against Polish side Gornik in the European Cup Winners' Cup.

Waddell – who was manager at Kilmarnock when they won the league in season 1964/65 – gave up his job as a journalist to take the Ibrox reins and his tenure got off to a winning start against United as Rangers won the match 2-1. Jerry Kerr sent us out to contain the home side but we held out for just 13 minutes, Willie Henderson scoring after good work from Colin Stein. But we were level just two minutes later when I fired in a low cross that was turned beyond the Rangers goalkeeper, Gerry Neef, by Alan Gordon. We defended stoically thereafter but our rearguard was eventually breached with five minutes remaining when Colin Stein scored the winner.

Despite the defeat, United were still well-positioned in the table. Ahead of a midweek visit to Glasgow to face Celtic, we were fourth, four points behind Hibernian and three adrift of Celtic and Rangers. But we took a dreadful hiding at Parkhead that December evening, losing 7-2. Celtic were in irresistible form and we had no answer save our two goals, a penalty from Ian Mitchell that brought us back to 2-1 and a header from Alan Gordon from my cross that made the score 6-2.

We ended the year with a 2-2 draw against Hearts at Tynecastle but, after losing 1-0 to St Johnstone on New Year's Day, we scored perhaps our best win of the season on 3 January when we defeated Dundee 4-1 at Tannadice. We mastered an icy surface to lead 3-0 at half-time. Kenny Cameron put us 1-0 up in the tenth minute before the unfortunate Jim Easton scored an own goal on the half-hour. Two minutes later it was 3-0 and this time I was the goalscorer, rising to meet a Kenny Cameron cross and thumping a header beyond Ally Donaldson from eight yards. Kenny scored his second of the game after 69 minutes, 20 minutes after Gordon Wallace had pulled one back for Dundee.

We followed our derby win with two successive losses. We went down 3-2 at home to Hearts and then 6-3 away at Airdrie. In the latter match Ian Mitchell scored a hat-trick, yet remarkably ended up on the losing side. And Ian was on target again in another nine-goal thriller at the end of January, scoring twice in a 5-4 win over Morton at Tannadice.

Ian's first goal came about when he snaffled the rebound after Walter Sweeney blocked my shot at goal. That equalised an earlier goal from John Murray and, just nine minutes later, United were ahead. I was released in on goal by Mitchell's pass and, although my initial effort hit Morton's Billy Gray, I regained possession and found the net to put us 2-1 ahead.

Mitchell scored again to give us a 3-1 lead at half-time, but Morton fought back to 3-3 within six minutes of the restart. And they came back to level the game again at 4-4 when Billy Gray scored with five minutes remaining after Doug Smith's goal had given us a 4-3 lead. It was a shame that someone had to lose such an absorbing match, and even more unfortunate that it was an own goal that gave us victory, Morton's John Murray diverting the ball beyond his own goalkeeper.

Hopes of a title tilt had by now all but evaporated. Celtic topped the table ahead of Rangers by two points at the start of February, but both sides of the Old Firm were well ahead of United who lay fourth, nine points behind my old club. And hopes of a Scottish Cup run were dashed when we were beaten 4-0 by Celtic in the second round.

Nevertheless, it was another good season for United – we eventually finished fifth with 38 points, 19 behind champions Celtic – and I made a solid contribution to our efforts. I missed only two league games and made a total of 40 appearances, scoring six goals.

There was also a bit of personal satisfaction for me towards the end of that season. Scot Symon had left Rangers in 1967, not long after I signed for United, and was now manager of Partick Thistle. United faced Thistle on 21 March at Firhill and Mr Symon's side were struggling to stay in the First Division.

United hadn't won in Maryhill for 30 years, but we laid that bogey to rest that afternoon. I scored both our goals in a 2-1 win, the winner coming just two minutes from full time. I always knew Mr Symon had made a mistake selling me when he did – he later admitted that to me himself – and that day I was able to prove it to him. The defeat effectively relegated Thistle and they eventually finished bottom of the league.

When the season ended I was off on my travels again, this time to South America. United agreed to take on a Mexico XI and a Toluca XI and, although we were comprehensively beaten in both games, it was a fantastic experience.

The World Cup was due to take place in Mexico a few weeks after our visit and all our expenses were covered by the Mexican FA. In addition to the two matches scheduled, Jerry Kerr offered to play a full-scale practice match in Mexico City against the world champions, England, but this didn't materialise.

My abiding memories of the trip were the searing heat and humidity and the hostility from the local fans. The English team had borne the brunt of the latter but we avoided a similar barracking, largely because the Mexican side battered us 6-0 in our first match! In fairness we had barely enough time to acclimatise to the heat and high altitude, but to sum up how impotent we were in attack their goalkeeper, Ignacio Calderon, only touched the ball four times during the 90 minutes! We improved when we played a similar XI a few days later, a double from Javier Fragoso who played for Club America giving our hosts a 2-0 win.

I was now part of a Dundee United side that were regarded as a mainstay in the higher echelons of the First Division. We were now expected to challenge for domestic honours and as the 1970/71 season dawned, we set out on a quest for silverware that started with the sectional ties in the League Cup.

Alongside United in Section One were Clyde, Celtic and Hearts. We started off against Clyde at Shawfield and it took a late equaliser from yours truly to earn United a point. Clyde, managed by Archie Robertson, went ahead 13 minutes from time when Millar Hay blasted a free kick beyond Donald MacKay. But five minutes from time we were level. Tommy Traynor, who we had signed from Hearts in April 1970, got to the byline and whipped in a fine cross that I met with my head at the left-hand post and the ball flew beyond the Clyde goalkeeper, Tommy McCulloch.

Four days later we beat Hearts 2-1 at Tannadice and I was in scoring action again. Ian Reid, who had made his first-team debut in the draw with Clyde, put us in front after only 45 seconds and I scored to double our advantage five minutes before half-time. My former team-mate Wilson Wood, who joined Hearts as part of the deal that brought Tommy Traynor to Tannadice, halved our lead after 68 minutes but we held on for the win.

Next up was a trip to Parkhead to face Celtic, one of seven sides in the competition who boasted a 100 per cent record after the opening two games. But at the end of the 90 minutes that record was ended as we played superbly to earn a 2-2 draw. In fairness we took a bit of a pounding early in the match – Davie Hay striking the woodwork before Tommy Callaghan put Celtic ahead in the 11th minute – but we found an equaliser in the 69th minute when Ian Reid made it two goals in as many games. We were level for just 60 seconds, though – Bobby

Lennox putting Celtic ahead again – but although Lennox struck the post late on, we nicked a point when my corner from the left picked out Alan Gordon who made it 2-2.

At 31 I was now one of the oldest players in the team – only Doug Smith at 33 was older – and I was enjoying being one of the elder statesmen. We had a number of young players playing for the first team then – Ian Reid (19), Jim Henry (21) and Stuart Markland (22) – and it was good for me to be able to use my experience to help them through those early season games.

However, after back-to-back draws against Hearts (0-0) and Clyde (1-1), we were out of the League Cup – Celtic won the group to go through – but when we faced Celtic at home in our last sectional tie we came within four minutes of winning the match. Celtic played well initially and struck the woodwork, but it was United who drew first blood when I got myself in between two defenders to fire a shot high into the net from around 20 yards after 31 minutes.

It was still 1-0 going into the final ten minutes, and even though Davie Hay equalised in the 82nd minute, Alan Gordon put us ahead again with only four minutes left. But we couldn't hang on and Lou Macari scored with almost the last kick of the ball to eliminate United from the competition.

With three goals in six appearances, I was enjoying a good start to the season. But United couldn't shake off the habit of drawing games and we opened up our league campaign with successive 1-1 draws against Hibernian and St Johnstone. However, we got back to winning ways in our third outing, edging a five-goal thriller at home to Dundee.

That gave us confidence ahead of our Inter-Cities Fairs Cup match against Grasshopper Zurich. I still loved European nights under the lights and this was a special one. I was at outside-right, but after 50 minutes of the home leg we were 2-0 behind. But we mounted a stirring comeback and goals from Ian Reid, Stuart Markland and Alec Reid gave United a 3-2 win.

I knew Alec well as we had been team-mates at Rangers. Indeed, he had been part of the squad that travelled to Nuremberg for the European Cup Winners' Cup Final in 1967. He had started well at Ibrox, scoring twice on his league debut against St Mirren, but soon drifted out the first-team picture. Jerry Kerr picked him up upon his release from Rangers and he became a good servant for United, making almost 150 appearances and scoring 20 goals.

We completed the job 15 days later, drawing 0-0 in Zurich to progress to the next round and a tie against Sparta Prague. But when we travelled to Prague for United's first-ever match behind the Iron Curtain, we did so on the back of a poor run of form in the league. We had won just one of our previous five league matches, our 2-1 victory over Clyde at Shawfield witnessing my first league goal of the season.

United should have won the match in Prague. We were dominant but only had a Tommy Traynor goal to show for our efforts. And when we lost our goalkeeper, Donald MacKay, and Alan Gordon through injury and had Andy Rolland ordered off, we couldn't hold out. Two late goals from Josef Jurkanin gave our opponents a 3-1 lead to take to Tannadice.

With a young Hamish McAlpine deputising for the injured MacKay, we almost overturned Sparta's lead in the second leg. The pitch was a bit of a quagmire but we found our feet quickly and Alan Gordon put us in front on the night after 17 minutes.

He did ever so well to beat three players and feed the ball to me on the wing, and when I crossed the ball in to the box he was on hand to head the ball in to the net. But although we pummelled the Sparta back-line we couldn't breach their defence and they went through to the next round. There they faced Don Revie's Leeds United and were hammered 9-2 on aggregate.

The European exit at least afforded us the opportunity to focus on the league campaign. We had not enjoyed the best of starts, and rather than occupy our customary position at the top end of the division we ended 1970 in 11th place, 14 points behind leaders Aberdeen.

Our last league game of 1970 was a 1-0 win over Hibernian at Easter Road on Boxing Day. In the starting XI that day for the first time since 28 February was one Walter Ferguson Smith. Walter had been signed by Jerry Kerr in November 1966 and had made his first-team debut in a 4-0 defeat against Kilmarnock at Rugby Park on 20 March 1967. He had appeared fleetingly after that, but after being selected at Easter Road he was rarely out of the team for the remainder of the season.

I knew his dad, who was a crane driver with Redpath and Brown, and he was keen to ensure his son, who was also completing his apprenticeship as an electrician, was kept in line. He told me to boot his arse if required and I admit I did so on a couple of occasions! But Walter was a great lad, a much under-rated defender, and I developed a good relationship with him. In fact, when I went to Dumbarton and we needed an experienced defender I recommended Walter to the manager, Alex Wright, and we got two good seasons out of him.

1971 started with back-to-back defeats against St Johnstone and Morton before we travelled to Ibrox to face Rangers on 16

January. It was a harrowing return to my old stomping ground. Two weeks earlier 66 people had lost their lives when a crush barrier gave way on Stairway 13 following the Old Firm match. This was Rangers' first match since the disaster.

I had actually been at the game. United's derby match away to Dundee was postponed so I travelled through by car to Ibrox to watch my old club. I left oblivious to what had happened and drove home to tell Avril the match had ended 1-1. I was shocked when she told me that nearly 70 people had been killed.

It was horrible and there was, understandably, a very eerie atmosphere when we played Rangers two weeks after the disaster. For the record, the match ended 1-1. Rangers were excellent in the opening half hour and led through a John Greig goal. But United came in to the game in the closing stages and I crossed for Alec Reid to equalise in the 72nd minute.

January ended with a Scottish Cup replay win over Clydebank. After a no-score draw at Kilbowie, United took the lead at Tannadice when my corner kick found the head of Alan Gordon and he nodded the ball beyond Mike McDonald. But we couldn't build on our lead and just two minutes into the second half our Second Division opponents were level when Alan Munro scored. Alec Reid restored our lead three minutes later but our doughty opponents were still very much in the tie until I scored United's third goal in the 62nd minute. A late double from Jim Henry sealed our place in the next round.

We faced Aberdeen at that stage of the competition and I was involved in a wee bit of controversy in the match at Tannadice. I had been causing bother for the Aberdeen defence for much of the first half – their goalkeeper, Bobby Clark, doing well to deal with one of my swerving crosses – but Bobby had no chance when I fired a shot past him and into the top corner just after the half-hour mark. I turned to celebrate but my joy was short-lived as the referee had already blown his whistle to award a free-kick … to UNITED! Clearly the man in the middle wasn't keen on playing advantage.

A Doug Smith penalty got United in 1-0 up at the break but my old team-mate, Jim Forrest, forced a replay when he equalised in the 75th minute. Four days later we were outclassed in the replay, second-half goals from Henning Boel and Davie Robb earning the Dons a comfortable 2-0 win and a quarter-final tie against Rangers at Ibrox.

All that was left for United now was to try and climb the league table. Our league form had been erratic and we lost three on the bounce between the end of February and the middle of March. After the last of those losses – a 1-0 defeat against Ayr United at Somerset Park – we sat in 13th place, just six points ahead of St Mirren who occupied the last of the relegation places.

But from there on in there was an upsurge as we won six of our last eight matches to finish sixth. One of those victories was a 2-1 win over Motherwell at Fir Park on 27 March and it was in that match that I scored my last goal for Dundee United. Kenny Cameron had scored after 22 minutes to equalise a goal from the home side's John Goldthorp and it was down to me to score the winner six minutes before half-time. I found Alec Reid with a long pass and continued my run. Alec picked me out and I managed to fire a low shot beyond Keith McRae in the Motherwell goal.

Unfortunately our late season form was not enough to secure European football for season 1971/72. We faced St Mirren at

Love Street on the last day of the campaign needing a win to keep alive our hopes of playing in the Fairs Cup. My appearance against St Mirren was my 48th of the season. I missed just two competitive matches and all but one of my appearances had been as part of the starting XI. However, despite taking the lead through Alan Gordon, we lost 2-1. Our opponents were striving to avoid relegation, but despite their valiant display the Saints joined Cowdenbeath in dropping down to Division Two.

Pre-season in 1971 started off with an oriental flavour as the club embarked on a three-match tour of South Korea. The club had originally agreed to tour East Africa towards the end of May but that fell through so we went to Asia instead.

I played the full 90 minutes in Seoul on 22 July as we beat Paikho 1-0 – Alec Reid scored our goal just short of the hour mark – and came off the bench to replace Jim Henry when we played the same opponents four days later. We won a thrilling match 4-3 to complete the tour unbeaten. We had drawn our other match 3-3 against Chung Yong two days earlier.

Playing three games in that short period of time was tough going, as was the travelling, but getting the opportunity to sample new countries and cultures was one of the benefits of being a professional footballer.

The tour had a controversial conclusion as we arrived home to an SFA inquiry. It was alleged United had breached the rule that stated no Scottish club side could play in a match against a national team. The club had faced a similar sanction on our return from Mexico the previous year. To ensure this wouldn't happen again, Jerry Kerr had informed the Koreans ahead of our visit that we would not take part in a match against the national side. However, the Paikho side we played were, to all intents and purposes, the South Korean team and were even referred to as the junior national team in the small report on the match in the *Glasgow Herald*.

In the end the club escaped without sanction thanks to Jerry's pre-emptive strike. He reasoned that United couldn't be blamed for breaching rules if they had informed the Koreans in advance and the governing body concurred.

Back in the UK and back on the pitch we completed our preparations with matches against Blackpool and the German side MSV Duisburg. I was an unused sub at Bloomfield Road in a match we lost 3-1 and we were thumped by the Germans too, losing 6-0 and having Alec Reid ordered off after 20 minutes.

All this fine-tuning was the precursor for the start of the domestic season in the League Cup. This time around we avoided either side of the Old Firm and were bracketed with Kilmarnock, Hibernian and Motherwell in Section One.

An Alec Reid goal handed us victory in our opening fixture against Kilmarnock at Tannadice, but that was as good as it got for us. Four days later we lost 2-0 against Hibernian at Easter Road – I was an unused sub for that one – and then drew 2-2 against Motherwell. I came on for Alan Gordon just before Tommy Traynor put us 2-1 up, but Brian Heron, who had joined Motherwell from Rangers, equalised 12 minutes from time.

With three points on the board at the halfway stage, we trailed Hibernian by three points, which meant we had to beat them at Tannadice to stand any chance of making the next round. I was on the bench again but United took the lead after only nine minutes through Alan Gordon. Joe Baker levelled the match after half an hour but as the game entered the final ten minutes – by which time I was on the field having replaced Jim Henry –

the sides were still tied at 1-1. But our left-back, Jim Cameron, was ordered off and we couldn't hold out, Eddie Turnbull's side scoring three times to win 4-1. Our League Cup journey had thus ended once again at the sectional stage. We finished third behind Hibernian and Kilmarnock, completing our fixtures with a 4-2 defeat at Rugby Park and 3-1 away win over Motherwell.

I was restored to the starting line-up at Fir Park. After playing so many games the previous season it was frustrating not to be involved as much, but Jerry Kerr had decided to play younger lads like Joe Watson on the wing. Although nowadays players extend their careers into their late 30s, in 1972 aged 32, I was considered a veteran and it was becoming apparent that my time at Tannadice was coming to an end.

I kept my place for our opening two league games and they were both high-scoring affairs. We opened with a 3-3 draw at home to St Johnstone, which was followed by a 6-4 defeat across the road against Dundee at Dens Park. Gordon Wallace and Jocky Scott both scored twice for Dundee and, although we had a late rally after trailing 6-2, the bragging rights went to our rivals.

Two weeks later I was part of the side that lost 2-0 against Kilmarnock at Rugby Park, our third successive league defeat. That was on 25 September, but it would be 4 December before I got any action in a tangerine jersey for the first team again. I went in to the reserve team and, although I would have far rather been with the first XI, I just loved playing football so playing for the second string was never an issue.

I was recalled to the team for our visit to Tynecastle to face Hearts. I came back into a squad that was struggling badly. We were shipping a lot of goals – conceding five on three separate occasions against Rangers, Celtic and Falkirk – and had lost seven of our opening 13 league fixtures. And defeat number eight was registered on my return in Edinburgh.

The Hearts match was watched by the former Dundee coach Jim McLean. After 12 years at the helm Jerry Kerr had decided to take up the role of general manager and wee Jim was appointed as his replacement.

Jim wasn't much older than me and, aged 33, he was the youngest manager in the league. But it became very apparent very early that Jim and I wouldn't get on. One of the first things he said to me was that I had given him a torrid time when he was playing for Clyde and that had hastened the end of his playing career.

I also liked to talk a lot about the game and one day I was chatting to some of the guys when Jim came in and told me to shut up. Maybe he was just trying to flex his muscles and exert his authority, but I knew at that moment that my time on Tayside was up.

After missing Jim's first two matches, he picked me to start the home match against Dunfermline on Christmas Day. We led 2-0 at one point but needed a penalty from Kenny Cameron five minutes from the end to secure Jim the first win of his tenure.

I was on the bench again for our first match of 1972 – a 2-0 defeat against St Johnstone at Muirton Park – and I came on for Walter Smith in a bid to rescue something from the game. It was to no avail but my endeavours must have impressed Jim as he restored me to the starting XI for the derby against Dundee. We drew that match 1-1 but just five days later I played my last match for Dundee United.

The date was 8 January 1972 and the venue was Easter Road in Edinburgh. I was named as substitute and came on to replace Stuart Markland ten minutes into the second half. By then we trailed 1-0 – Pat Stanton scoring for the home side – and late goals from John Brownlie and Arthur Duncan earned Hibernian a resounding 3-0 win. Incidentally, future Rangers assistant manager Archie Knox made his Dundee United debut that afternoon. However, just as Archie's Dundee United career was starting, mine was coming to an end. A matter of days after the defeat at Easter Road I was off to Dumbarton.

I found out about that move from the long arm of the law. I was driving my car through Perth when I was stopped by the police. My immediate thought was that I had been putting my foot down and had been speeding but the officer told me I had to go to the police station and phone Dumbarton to speak to their manager and sort out the deal.

Since signing in August 1967 I had made 169 appearances for Dundee United and scored 27 goals. I thoroughly enjoyed my time there and I like to think I built up a good relationship with the supporters. And I was honoured to be inducted into the club's Hall of Fame in 2017. I am in there alongside luminaries like Doug Smith, Dennis Gillespie, Dave Narey, Paul Hegarty and Paul Sturrock and the club will always have a special place in my heart.

CHAPTER 10

THE SONS OF THE ROCK

ALTHOUGH I dropped down a division to play for Dumbarton, my new club were in the mix for promotion from Scotland's second tier when I signed on 10 February 1972. Cowdenbeath were top of the table, four points ahead of St Mirren and eight clear of fifth-placed Dumbarton, although the Sons had three games in hand.

Alongside me in the Dumbarton forward line would be Peter Coleman, former Celtic man Charlie Gallagher, Roy McCormack and Kenny Wilson.

Kenny was the main man at Boghead at that time. He had signed for the club in July 1970 from St Johnstone and scored 40 goals in 45 appearances in his debut season. He was on course to hit the 40-mark again when I joined and I was looking forward to supplying the ammunition for him to shoot us towards the First Division. Also in the first team squad were the McAdam brothers, Tom and Colin. Both would later play for the Old Firm, with Tom going to Celtic and Colin ending up at Rangers.

There's a great story about the McAdams and their appearance in a reserve game against Rangers. I was overseeing the reserves at the time and we hammered the Rangers second team 5-0 at Boghead, with Colin scoring a hat-trick and Tom helping himself to the other two. I phoned up Ibrox to inform them of the result and Willie Waddell answered. After telling me Rangers had won the first-team fixture he asked how the reserves had got on. When I said it had been 5-0 he assumed Rangers had won and put the phone down. I later found out from Alex Wright that Waddell had told everyone that Rangers had won the game. I took great delight, therefore, in phoning Willie back and telling him that it was in fact Dumbarton that went nap!

I made my debut for Dumbarton on 12 February 1972 against Stenhousemuir at Ochilview. It was a winning start as a McCormack double and a penalty from Gallagher gave us a 3-0 win. The penalty Charlie scored came about when my goal-bound shot was punched off the line by the Stenhousemuir right-back, Rooney, and I had a hand in our third goal too when I combined with my namesake Kenny to create Roy's second goal in the 50th minute.

We comfortably won my home debut the following week – a Kenny Wilson double helping us to a 4-0 win over East Stirling – and although we exited the Scottish Cup at home to Raith Rovers and lost 3-2 at Arbroath, we secured a crucial 2-1 home win over leaders Cowdenbeath on 11 March.

That was the first of nine straight wins in the league, including a 5-0 win over Raith Rovers that avenged our Scottish Cup loss. Kenny Wilson scored all five goals in that match, just three days after his double had helped us beat Queen's Park

3-0. Kenny's nap hand took us into second place with four games to go. We sat three points behind leaders Arbroath with two games in hand. And when we beat Brechin City at Glebe Park eight days later, we needed just a point from our last two fixtures to secure promotion to the First Division for the first time in 50 years.

Our penultimate game saw third-placed St Mirren visit Boghead. They were two points behind us, but by the end of the 90 minutes they had leapfrogged us as we dropped to fourth. Although we dominated the match the Paisley Saints scored five minutes from time to secure a 2-1 win.

Leaders Arbroath, St Mirren and Stirling Albion, the three teams above us, had now completed their fixtures, which left us with one match, against Berwick Rangers at Boghead, to claim the point we needed. But we actually went one better than that, picking up two points courtesy of a 4-2 win.

On the night, Charlie Gallagher was superb and it was from his cross that wee Peter Coleman headed us in front after just three minutes. Berwick equalised after 19 minutes but Charlie put us back in front again 12 minutes later. Our visitors were reduced to ten men early in the second half when Eric Tait was dismissed for a foul on me and we took full advantage; Charlie scoring our third before Roy McCormack made it 4-1. A late counter from Berwick failed to take the shine off our win.

And the two points didn't only secure promotion, they were enough to supplant Arbroath and give us the Second Division title. I had won numerous honours with Rangers, but I am extremely proud to have added a Second Division title medal to the four First Division titles I won at Ibrox.

At the age of 35 I was back in the big time, and in the summer of 1972 I was relishing the chance to ply my trade again at places like Ibrox, Parkhead and Tannadice. It was also fitting that in what would be their centenary year, Dumbarton were back playing at the top level in Scotland.

I would be joined in the Boghead dressing room by a familiar face ahead of season 1972/73. Jackie Stewart decided to sign Willie Whigham from Middlesbrough. If you recall, Willie was the unfortunate goalkeeper on the day I scored six goals for Rangers against Falkirk so I wasn't slow to remind him of that on his first day at the club!

After losing to Celtic in the opening round of the Drybrough Cup, the season started in earnest with the sectional ties in the League Cup. Dumbarton were grouped with Hearts, Berwick Rangers and Airdrie. We won two, drew two and lost two of the ties, and that was enough to take us through to face Dundee in the second round. And it was against the Dens Park side that I scored the first of only three goals I would net in Dumbarton colours.

That was on 20 September and Ron Trevorrow, writing in the *Evening Times*, talked about me being an 'evergreen veteran' and said that my 'experience and boundless energy was infectious' and inspired Dumbarton to a comprehensive 3-0 win. Johnny Graham fired us in front after 28 minutes and five minutes later I got myself on the end of a pass from Roy McCormack to make it 2-0. The irrepressible Kenny Wilson completed the scoring 12 minutes from time.

That was Kenny's 87th goal in just his 100th Dumbarton appearance. Three days later he made his 101st and last appearance for us in a 2-1 defeat against Aberdeen. I opened the scoring that day, but second-half goals from Drew Jarvie and Joe Harper took the points back to the North East. But after the match Kenny departed for Carlisle United for £40,000 and we now had the task of filling a huge void in our forward line.

Jackie Stewart attempted to do that by bringing in the former Lisbon Lion Willie Wallace from Crystal Palace. Willie made a scoring debut against Dundee on 14 October, the 2-2 draw that day at Boghead going some way to avenge the 4-0 drubbing we suffered at Dens Park in the second leg of the League Cup second-round tie.

Although we didn't make the best of starts in the First Division – we only won three of our opening 18 league games to end 1972 fourth from bottom – I was enjoying being back in the top flight. But just a week into 1973 it was all change at the club.

Jackie Stewart was approached by St Johnstone to take over the manager's role from Willie Ormond, who was leaving to become manager of Scotland. Although Partick Thistle boss Dave McParland was hotly tipped by the media to take the job in Perth, Jackie got it and it was his assistant manager at Boghead, Alex Wright, that was appointed as his successor. Alex had played with Partick Thistle and had previously managed St Mirren and Dunfermline. He was now charged with the responsibility of ensuring we maintained our First Division status.

We lost Alex's first match in charge – 2-1 at Arbroath – and it would be 17 March before he chalked up his first win in a 4-2 home win over Kilmarnock. In that run of games we lost heavily to Aberdeen (0-6) and Hibernian (0-5) and another drubbing at the hands of Celtic in April looked to have sealed our fate.

That defeat left us second from bottom with two games to play. But just when all seemed lost we found form, winning our last two games. First up we went to Fir Park and beat Motherwell 2-0. That put us level on points with 16th-placed Kilmarnock. I missed that match and the Parkhead pummelling, but I was back in the team that welcomed Dundee United to Boghead for a final-day showdown.

It was a day where nerves were shredded. We essentially had to better Kilmarnock's result to stay up – the Ayrshire side were facing Falkirk – and we started well but found ourselves a goal down when George Fleming scored after just ten minutes. But we fought back to level through Willie Wallace and, although the same man missed a penalty soon afterwards, we were 2-1 ahead at the break thanks to a header from Ross Mathie.

News filtered through that Kilmarnock were 2-0 ahead but that didn't stop us pushing on after the interval. Eighteen-year-old Tom McAdam, who came off the bench to replace Billy Wilkinson at half-time, headed in a brace of second-half goals to give Dumbarton a 4-1 win. And that completed a whirlwind few days for young Tom as just five days earlier he had scored four goals as Dumbarton thumped East Stirling 6-0 to win the Stirlingshire Cup.

We now faced an anxious wait to hear the final result of the Kilmarnock match. When it emerged they had been pegged back to draw 2-2 the celebrations started as we ensured First Division football would grace the turf at Boghead again in season 1973/74.

I more than played my part, with Ian Walker writing in the *Evening Times* that it was the guile of myself and fellow 'old campaigner' Willie Wallace and the hard work of Roy McCormack that had been big contributory factors in our success. And I was delighted for everyone associated with the club, but particularly the manager. Had we been relegated it would have given him an unwanted treble as in the previous two seasons teams he had managed, namely St Mirren and Dunfermline, had been relegated.

At 36 years and 117 days, I was the oldest player in the Dumbarton team that afternoon. It was time to call it a day and hang up my boots so I decided to bring to an end a playing career that had seen me play over 600 games and score just over 200 goals.

The dilemma I now had was what to do next? Other than my job with Redpath and Brown, I had known nothing other than football for the best part of 20 years so, naturally, I wanted to stay in the game. I had laid the foundations for future involvement by attending coaching schools at Largs and at the Butlin's holiday camp on the outskirts of Ayr, so I was delighted when, on 15 May, I was offered my first coaching role when the Dumbarton board ratified my appointment to the role of assistant manager at Boghead. I had, to all intents and purposes, been player-assistant manager since I had arrived at Dumbarton, and, in addition to assisting Alex with the first team, I would also be responsible for the reserve team and the development of the young players at the club.

The role was tailor-made for me. In addition to the courses in Largs and Ayr, I had helped the young lads out in the latter days of my time at Rangers when I was mostly playing for the reserves, and I had also done some coaching when I was training with Partick Thistle during my stint at Dundee United.

I worked with players like Alan Rough, who would go on to play for Scotland, and John Hansen, the older brother of Alan who also played for Thistle before moving on to great success at home and abroad with Liverpool. In fact, eight of the players I worked with formed part of the team that thrashed Celtic 4-1 in the League Cup Final in 1971 and, since I enjoyed working with them so much, I made up my mind that I would take up a coaching role at some point after my playing days were over. It therefore worked in nicely that the opportunity came up at Dumbarton.

Over the course of the next two seasons, Alex and I worked hard to consolidate Dumbarton's position in the First Division. Ahead of season 1973/74, we took the squad to Spain for a five-day training camp and returned with a trophy after beating a Lloret de Mar select side 5-1. That set us up nicely for the season, and although we started poorly we eventually finished in tenth place, which represented Dumbarton's best league season since 1918. The reserve team that I was looking after did well too, reaching the third round of the Second XI Cup and the last four of the Reserve League Cup, at which stage we lost to Partick Thistle.

Season 1974/75 was to be the last season before league reconstruction in Scotland. In 1975/76 the teams who had finished in the top ten in the First Division would form the Premier Division, with the rest joining the top teams in the Second Division to form the new First Division. Thus, if we placed the same or higher than we had done in 1973/74 part-time Dumbarton would have been part of the elite.

Alas, after scoring freely on a two-match tour of Spain and making an excellent start that saw us lose just one of our first five league games, we struggled for consistency and eventually finished 14th, nine points adrift of Motherwell who occupied the last of the coveted top-ten places. However, we had a bit of a run in the Scottish Cup, Alex and I guiding the club to the quarter-final where we lost narrowly to Celtic at Boghead. And we won the Stirlingshire Cup courtesy of a 4-1 win over Stenhousemuir.

Although disappointed to be in the second tier of the new league structure, season 1975/76 would be a memorable campaign for Dumbarton. We kicked off with a 2-1 win over Hearts in the League Cup, but we didn't manage to get out of the group. The Tynecastle side exacted revenge a few weeks later, winning 6-2, and Celtic also thumped us 8-0 at Boghead. Our league season started badly too, with four defeats in the first five matches. We drew the other game, 5-5 against East Fife at home.

In truth, it was a really topsy-turvy season in the league and we were never really in contention for promotion. Our squad was weakened by the departures of the McAdam brothers – Colin went to Motherwell and Tom joined Dundee United – and we eventually finished fourth, seven points behind runners-up Kilmarnock who were promoted alongside champions Partick Thistle.

But it was in the Scottish Cup that we almost pulled off an unlikely success. Victories over Keith, Partick Thistle (after a replay) and Kilmarnock put Dumbarton in the hat for the semi-final draw. In with us were Hearts, Rangers and Motherwell, and we drew the men from Tynecastle. The match was held at

Hampden on 3 April and we should have won what was a pretty scrappy match. In the end we drew 0-0 and, as is often the case, we didn't get a second chance as Hearts comprehensively won the replay 3-0.

That match is famous for the opening goal, which was scored by none other than Walter Smith. Trouble is, Walter was playing for Dumbarton and it was an own goal, a spectacular diving header! I had managed to broker a deal to bring Walter to Boghead from Dundee United in October 1975. We paid £8,000 for him and he made 33 appearances for us. He played 31 times in season 1976/77 too before I did a nice wee bit of business to sell him back to Dundee United. Jim McLean called to say he wanted Walter back, so I agreed, but only if wee Jim stumped up £14,000 for him. He duly did and I had managed to make Dumbarton a tidy wee profit.

The star turn in our cup run was our young centre-forward, Ian Wallace. I went to watch him play for Yoker Athletic and was mightily impressed, so much so that I asked his manager to substitute him as I was going to recommend he signed for Dumbarton. I guaranteed the chap we would pay Yoker £500 for Ian and that was pretty much how the deal was done.

It was actually Ian's goal that edged out Partick Thistle in the Scottish Cup. After a drab 0-0 draw at Firhill, we faced each other in the replay 11 days later. Thistle had lost star turns Alan Hansen and Alan Rough to injury and illness respectively, but I reckon we would have still won the replay had they been on the field. We were excellent that night and young Wallace was a cut above, scoring the only goal of the game after 53 minutes. That was one of the 19 goals he scored in 45 appearances that season.

Our journey to the last four of the cup stimulated interest in our 'wee' club and soon scouts were flocking to our games. Ian was one who stood out and pretty soon we were getting bids for his services. And when he played a starring role in a 3-3 draw against Celtic in August 1976 we simply couldn't hold on to him. Coventry City offered £70,000 and, in a heartbeat, Ian was off to Highfield Road.

I knew Ian was set for big things, so I advised the chairman at Dumbarton to insert a sell-on clause as part of the negotiations. I suggested we push for ten per cent of his next transfer fee but, for whatever reason, they didn't listen to me. And, ultimately, that was costly as I was proved correct. Ian played superbly at Coventry and, in July 1980, the then European champions, Nottingham Forest, bought him for £1.25 million. My maths suggests that that would have netted Dumbarton £125,000, which would have gone a long way to helping strengthen not just the club but the playing squad too.

Not long after Walter and Ian were sold I was no longer assistant manager at Boghead. Alex Wright had tendered his resignation in February 1977 but had been encouraged to stay on until the end of the season by the chairman, Mr Robertson. He moved 'upstairs' in the close season to become an executive director and I was asked to take over the managerial reins. I was only too happy to accept and a new chapter in my career was now opened.

CHAPTER 11

GAFFER

I INITIALLY took the manager's job at Dumbarton on a part-time basis – it would be March 1979 before I went full-time – and I set about putting my stamp on the playing squad. Money was tight but I felt I could use my first-hand knowledge of the younger players at the club, having worked so closely with the reserves, and construct a team that had a balance of youth and experience.

In the previous season Dumbarton had been among the top scorers in the First Division. Only four other teams scored more than the 62 we managed, but we also conceded 56 so, while I was looking for my strikers to maintain their scoring form, I was also looking to ensure we were much tighter at the back.

I wanted to make the squad much fitter too. Although we were only part-time and trained just two nights a week – usually Monday and Thursday – I introduced a rigorous programme comprising hill running, cross-country and weight-training circuits. I'd also have the players doing runs and sprints around the track that encircled the pitch at Boghead. There were plenty of moans and groans at the time, but I believe it was beneficial to everyone in the squad.

After completing a two-match tour in the north of Scotland – we drew 1-1 with Lossiemouth and defeated Nairn County 3-0 – my first competitive game in charge was the opening league match of the season against Hearts at Boghead. The first team I selected as a manager was:

Jim Cruikshank, Don McNeil, Don Watt, Jim Muir, Pat McCluskey, Alistair Brown, Derek Whiteford, John Whiteford, Murdo MacLeod, John Bourke and Brian Gallacher.

Jim Cruikshank and Brian Gallacher both made their Dumbarton debuts that afternoon. Jim was on the back nine of his career at that time, but I managed to get him to sign for us from Hearts. He was a hugely experienced goalkeeper and had earned six caps for Scotland. I was hoping his experience would help with the porosity of our defence, but it didn't really work out for Jim and he only made six appearances before being replaced by Lawrie Williams.

In contrast to Jim, Brian Gallacher was just starting out. Alex Wright and I had spotted him on a scouting mission and I was impressed with his pace and all-round ability. I had high hopes he would work well with big John Bourke and score the goals we needed to push for promotion. I was proved right with regards to his goalscoring as Brian netted a total of 31 goals in 117 appearances during my tenure. However, it was big John who made his mark against Hearts. He scored twice, but goals from Iain Smith and Willie Gibson ensured that it was honours even and the points were shared.

We drew 2-2 again the following week away to Arbroath before finishing the month of August with our first league win

– 2-0 at home to Queen of the South – and defeating Hamilton 4-1 in the first leg of our second-round League Cup tie. But just three days later I was sampling the bitter taste of defeat as a manager for the first time, and it was a real sore one.

I took my players to Douglas Park for the return leg against Hamilton, intent on maintaining the advantage we had after the first leg. And that's exactly what we should have done, yet we ended up somehow losing 6-0! With goals needed, Accies started well and Jim Cruickshank saved well from Jamie Fairlie in the early stages. We should have been ahead, though, moments later when Brian Gallacher was sent clean through on goal, but his shot was saved by the Hamilton goalkeeper. We were then hit by a double blow as Accies scored twice inside six minutes to reduce our aggregate lead to 4-3.

When the players came in at half-time I had no reason to fear for our place in the competition. Although we trailed we had had opportunities to score and perhaps Bourke should have put the tie to bed when he missed a chance with the goal gaping. But we collapsed in the second half, Accies scoring four times, and we even contrived to miss a penalty. The drubbing remains the heaviest defeat I suffered in my time as a manager.

My job now was to pick the players up and I managed that as we lost only three of our next 11 league matches. By the time we beat Arbroath 1-0 at Boghead on 29 October, we were second in the table, although we were tied on 18 points with Hearts, Dundee and Stirling Albion.

But then inconsistency crept in and we won just two of our next 12 league fixtures. It was proving difficult to get the right blend between seasoned pros, new signings and youngsters, but it all started to click into place around February. We lost just one of our last 13 games and also managed to reach the quarter-final of the Scottish Cup where we went down 2-1 to Partick Thistle at Firhill.

Unfortunately we left ourselves with too big a mountain to climb to achieve promotion. We did manage to beat the then league leaders Dundee at Boghead towards the end of the season – goals from Murdo MacLeod and Brian Gallacher giving us a thoroughly deserved 2-1 win – but we had too many draws – 17 in total – and that, coupled with our poor run towards the end of 1977, accounted for the fact we finished fourth, nine points adrift of the two promoted sides, Morton and Hearts.

I had, however, learned a lot from my debut season in the dugout, and I was intent on putting that to good use as I tried to plot a path towards promotion in season 1978/79. But before we got back down to business there was the small matter of the World Cup in Argentina. Ally MacLeod had us all convinced Scotland were going to conquer the world and the country were swept along with the hysteria.

The soundtrack was Andy Cameron's 'We're on the March with Ally's Army' but the Dumbarton players and myself also recorded a World Cup song. We teamed up with EMI America and Midge Ure at a recording studio in Glasgow to record 'Hey Argentina' and when we were there Billy Connolly popped in to say hello. It's fair to say that we weren't going to be giving up the day jobs any time soon, but it was still good fun to meet up with Midge and lay down the track.

But this wasn't the first time I had been cutting discs in a recording studio. Back in 1963 members of the Rangers squad joined the vocalist John Dunbar to record two songs entitled 'The Glasgow Rangers' and 'That's the Team'. Once again it was great fun and I believe the record sold in the region of 30,000 copies. We also performed the tracks at a charity concert in Glasgow a couple of weeks later.

Ahead of my second season in charge at Boghead, I wanted to get the players fitter than they had been before, and it's fair to say I was a hard taskmaster at times. I expected a high standard from my players and, initially at least, I was a bit of a bawler when things weren't going our way. Indeed, there were a number of games early in my tenure where our physio, Bobby McCallum, had to calm me down as I had gotten myself into such a frenzied state.

My shouting from the sidelines didn't abate much in the opening exchanges of my second season, though, as my team were once again bedevilled by inconsistency. Pre-season had gone well – our annual trip to the Highlands had witnessed us claim three victories and score 13 goals – but we just couldn't put together an unbeaten run of any sort when the competitive action started. While we scored emphatic wins like our 5-2 victory over Ayr United at Somerset Park and the 6-3 success against Airdrie at Broomfield, there were heavy defeats at the hands of Hamilton (0-5) and Kilmarnock (0-3). Dumbarton eventually finished seventh, 15 points behind runners-up Kilmarnock who would join Dundee in the Premier Division in season 1979/80.

My squad had, however, been weakened early in the season when we sold Murdo MacLeod to Celtic. Murdo, whose brother Alastair was also part of my squad, had made his debut in October 1975 aged just 17. He made 99 appearances for Dumbarton, had been capped by the Scottish League and was part of the Scotland Under-21 squad. But when Billy McNeill offered £100,000 to take him to Parkhead, it was an offer that a part-time club like Dumbarton couldn't refuse.

Murdo was an excellent young prospect but, unsurprisingly, I wanted him to go to Rangers. He had trained with my old club prior to signing for Dumbarton and I knew that they had been sending scouts to watch him. But when I went to Ibrox to speak to Jock Wallace, Willie Waddell, by then general manager at Ibrox, refused me permission to speak to him. I was disappointed I didn't get the opportunity to see Jock – I felt Murdo had all the attributes to be a success at Rangers – but in the end Murdo was enraptured by Celtic and I was there with him when he put pen to paper. He went on to have a stellar career at Celtic before moving on to play for Borussia Dortmund, and I'd like to think I played a small part in helping to develop him into the excellent midfield player he became.

The 1979/80 campaign was to be the third and last of my first tenure in charge at Dumbarton. Our chairman, Mr Robertson, again spoke of his desire to see Dumbarton in the top flight and I felt to do that we had to start turning draws into victories. And we managed that, with only three draws registered in our first 20 league games.

I had taken the players to Ireland this time to prepare for the season and wins over Coleraine, Finn Harps and Sligo Rovers were a great boost for the players' confidence. In the games I had placed more of an emphasis on youth and I stuck with that policy when the league campaign got underway. And it worked as the enthusiasm of the youngsters, allied to the experience of the likes of Pat McCluskey, helped us to a share of the lead at the top of the table at the start of December. A 1-1 draw at home to Motherwell took us to 25 points, the same total as Airdrie, who topped the table on goal difference, and Hearts.

Although we didn't start 1980 too well – from 5 January to 1 March we won only once, away to Berwick Rangers – my team were top of the table in the middle of February. But then came a disastrous run of three straight defeats against St Johnstone (0-1), Raith Rovers (0-4) and Ayr United (0-3). We arrested the decline with successive wins over Clyde and Dunfermline, but another three defeats on the spin at the end of March effectively ruled us out of the race for promotion.

Our cause wasn't helped by the fact we received an offer we couldn't refuse for our top scorer, Graeme Sharp. I had signed Graeme from Eastercraigs and given him his debut in December 1978. He fractured his cheekbone soon after that but still managed three goals in nine appearances in 1978/79.

I felt that Graeme had the makings of a great centre-forward. He was quick and a good finisher and, although just 19, looked like he would develop into a player who would play at the highest level. And when he started season 1979/80 in fine form it was no surprise when it came to my attention that more and more scouts were coming to our games to watch him.

Rangers were reportedly interested and, with Graeme being a Rangers fan, that must have been appealing. But I think his older brother, Richard, had had a bit of a chastening experience as a player at Ibrox so Graeme looked set to move south of the border.

At one point it looked as if he was moving to the Midlands to join Aston Villa. Myself and Sean Fallon, who had arrived from Celtic to become my assistant manager, travelled down to Birmingham with Graeme, and Villa manager, Ron Saunders, was suitably impressed so made an offer. However, after that the trail went dead and we didn't hear anything from Ron for about three weeks.

There then came a call from Gordon Lee, the manager of Everton. He was also interested in signing Graeme and called me the day after Graeme scored what would be his last goal for Dumbarton in a 3-2 home defeat against Arbroath. Gordon asked to speak to Graeme and it was arranged for myself, Sean and Graeme to go to Goodison Park and the training ground at Bellfield. As Graeme was shown round the ground, Sean and I negotiated a deal with the Everton secretary, Jim Greenwood, and after Graeme agreed personal terms, the deal was done. The price was £125,000.

The deal got Ron Saunders's dander up, though, as he thought HE had signed Graeme. He felt we had reneged on our agreement and had been unprofessional. But we simply got a better offer from Everton so concluded the deal with them.

As much as the £125,000 for Sharp was welcome for the coffers, losing Graeme hindered our promotion push. The Arbroath defeat was one of four we suffered in six league games in March. And when we started April with a 2-2 draw against Clydebank and a 4-1 defeat away at Arbroath, it was all over as a few days later I was out of a job.

I met with the board and we decided it was best that we part company. The parting was an amicable one, although I did feel that the lack of depth in the first-team pool and the sale of Sharp had contributed to our recent poor run of results. I was disappointed as I felt we had been on the cusp of achieving what I had set out to do when I took on the role, namely take Dumbarton in to the Premier Division for the first time in their history. But as the old saying goes, if at first you don't succeed, try, try again and I would be afforded that opportunity when I returned to Boghead four years later.

CHAPTER 12

BACK AT BOGHEAD

AFTER I left Dumbarton I initially found it very difficult to get back into football, although there were numerous openings, including an opportunity to go to Aberdeen to become assistant manager to Alex Ferguson and chances to manage Dundee and St Johnstone.

The Aberdeen role enticed me. The Dons were emerging as challengers to the traditional Old Firm hegemony – their title win in season 1979/80 would be the first by a club other than Rangers or Celtic since Kilmarnock had won the league back in 1964/65 when I was still playing – and Ferguson was regarded as one of the most talented young managers in the country. I felt I had the credentials that Alex was looking for but in the end the job went to my former Dundee United team-mate Archie Knox.

I also felt I was in with a good shout of replacing Tommy Gemmell at Dens Park. Dundee were heading for relegation from the Premier Division when Tommy resigned in April 1980. He did so in the wake of a remarkable 5-1 win over Celtic, but again I was overlooked for another ex-team-mate, Donald MacKay being the successful applicant this time around.

The best chance I seemed to have, though, was at Muirton Park, with the *Glasgow Herald* tipping me as the front runner to replace Alex Stuart who had recently been dismissed. But the former team-mate connection continued when Alex Rennie, who had been on the books at Ibrox when I was there although never played for the first team, was appointed after a spell as assistant manager at Hearts.

I was a bit perplexed to say the least. I thought my playing career and subsequent career as assistant manager and manager at Dumbarton gave me an impressive CV. Although I wasn't the most experienced manager in the country, I had more than both Don and Alex so I couldn't fathom why I wasn't being offered any of the roles. In the end I found out that it had been down to Alex Wright.

It transpired that Alex was the man providing the reference for me and he was being less than complimentary. Unfortunately, in football mud has a habit of sticking. Of course what Alex had been saying was untrue and I later found out it was borne out of jealousy. I was understandably livid. I had a family to feed and was being overlooked for jobs in football because a person I considered a friend was stabbing me in the back.

I eventually got a chance to get back in to the game when I became assistant manager to Jim Clunie at Kilmarnock. Jim had been a centre-half with Raith Rovers, Aberdeen and St Mirren and had also had a short spell in England with Bury. Once he retired he went into management and he had been on the coaching staff at Southampton when they beat Manchester United 1-0 to win the FA Cup in 1976.

Jim had taken over the reins at Rugby Park from Davie Sneddon towards the end of January 1981. By the time Jim came in, Kilmarnock were all but doomed and they were eventually relegated from the Premier Division in May. And that's when the call came in to me to ask if I'd come in on a part-time basis to help with the reserves and also assist him with first-team matters. Although Alex was still involved at Dumbarton, once the club found out about what had happened with previous references I was assured that next time the reference would be provided by another of the directors. Evidently this one was more favourable as it helped me secure the job in Ayrshire.

I enjoyed working with Jim and in season 1981/82 we were able to guide Kilmarnock back to the Premier Division at the first time of asking when we finished as runners-up to Motherwell in the First Division. We had to wait until the last day of the season to seal the deal; our 6-0 thrashing of Queen of the South coupled with Hearts' 1-0 defeat to Motherwell earning promotion at the first time of asking.

I worked with some familiar faces that season as John Bourke and Brian Gallacher, who had been part of the Dumbarton team I managed, were on the books. Jim also spent £44,000 to bring Alastair MacLeod, brother of Murdo and another former Dumbarton player, to Rugby Park. Our squad was also filled with local talent – around 14 were from in and around Kilmarnock – and one of them was a promising youngster called Sammy McGivern. Sammy was a good player and although he was only 17 or 18 at the time, he deserved his place in the first team. He scored a notable goal on our return to the Premier Division in season 1982/83 too, the opener in a 1-1 draw against Rangers at Ibrox in January.

There were some great games in my time at Kilmarnock. We ran Alex Ferguson's Aberdeen team close in the Scottish Cup quarter-final in March 1982 and the following season we had an epic tussle with Partick Thistle in the cup too. In the days before extra time and penalties, we eventually went to a THIRD replay before Maurice Johnston's goal took Thistle through.

But we took some beatings too, none more so than the three thrashings at the hands of Rangers inside a fortnight in 1982/83. We lost 5-0 at Ibrox in the Premier Division then, having reached the quarter-finals of the League Cup after winning our section, capitulated 6-1 in the first leg at Rugby Park. Davie Cooper was magnificent that night and scored four goals, and it only got worse in the second leg when we let in another half dozen.

Jim and I worked really well together and I thought we were unlucky to be relegated at the end of 1982/83. Jim wasn't really given much in the way of a transfer kitty so we had to rely on our younger players. We also elected to remain part-time on our return to the top flight too. But ultimately what did for us was our away form; we didn't win at all on our travels and picked up just four points from our 18 games played away from Rugby Park.

Kilmarnock never looked like gaining promotion the following season – in March we were mid-table and it would be another ten years before they were back in the top flight – and I started to feel it was time to move on. I still hankered after a managerial job and that opportunity eventually arose when Dumbarton came calling. Billy Lamont had led my old club to the cusp of promotion to the Premier Division for the first time since reconstruction of the Scottish leagues in 1975.

With ten games remaining, they were in the box seats for one of the two automatic promotion places. But in March 1984 Billy was tempted by a move to Falkirk and, all of a sudden, the Sons were on the lookout for a new manager.

Alex Wright took caretaker charge for matches against Clyde and Falkirk and he reported to the media that he had been inundated with applications for the vacancy. Understandably, having built up a head of steam in the race for promotion, Dumbarton's priority was to make an appointment that would not have a detrimental impact on that. That was probably the principal reason they contacted Kilmarnock to speak to me.

I received a phone call from big Jim to tell me about the Dumbarton opportunity and he made it clear he didn't want me to go. He offered me the chance to eventually succeed him as manager of Kilmarnock but the lure of Dumbarton proved too much. Having been in the role before and knowing the club as well as I did, I couldn't resist the chance to go back to Boghead and I was the lucky man entrusted with the job of securing promotion and realising the dream of the club and its supporters.

There were some, however, who viewed the job as something of a poisoned chalice. Myself and my assistant, Billy Whiteford, could carve our own niche in the history of Dumbarton by completing the job and leading them to the top flight. But, on the other hand, if we contrived to pluck defeat from the jaws of victory and failed to secure promotion, we would forever be tagged as the duo who had failed in their mission. To be honest I wasn't even considering the latter as I believed I had the ability to ensure that the team that had done so well up to this point could get themselves over the line and in to the Premier Division.

My first match in charge was, ironically, a visit to Rugby Park to face Kilmarnock. I watched my players fight out a 0-0 draw and the point was enough to take Dumbarton to the top of the league. We were now a point ahead of Partick Thistle and Morton, although both our nearest challengers had a game in hand.

Those outside the confines of Boghead thought our challenge for promotion would eventually peter out, but the following weekend we edged further ahead at the top when two goals from the evergreen John Bourke, who had re-joined the club from Kilmarnock, and a strike from Stuart Robertson gave us a 3-0 win over Meadowbank Thistle. On the same afternoon Morton, managed by another former Rangers winger, Tommy McLean, lost 3-2 against Clyde, while Peter Cormack's Thistle, who had leapfrogged us when they won their game in hand, were defeated 2-1 by second-from-bottom Raith Rovers.

And it was second-placed Thistle that were next up for us on the fixture list when we travelled to Firhill on 24 March. We defended stoically and earned a 0-0 draw, but it was still nip and tuck at the top. Successive home wins over Alloa (2-0) and Clydebank (2-1) allowed us to maintain our narrow advantage, but we were knocked off our perch by Morton on 14 April when we lost 2-0 at Cappielow. It was Dumbarton's first league defeat since Boxing Day.

Although it was a bitter blow to lose, Thistle's home defeat to Kilmarnock still left Dumbarton in second place, four points ahead of the Jags. Yet we contrived to make things hard for ourselves when, the following weekend, we lost 1-0 against bottom side Alloa at Recreation Park. But we steadied the ship and beat Brechin 3-0 and Airdrie 4-1.

Sandwiched in between was a dramatic 2-2 draw against Clyde at Boghead. We were outplayed by the Bully Wee and trailed 2-0 at one point. But Tommy Coyle netted on the rebound after his brother Joe's penalty had been parried and Albert Craig restored parity later in the game. And that was it. Thistle drew 1-1 with Brechin and we had a lead of six points with only two games remaining. Remarkably, little old part-time Dumbarton would be playing Premier Division football in season 1984/85!

Winning the title would have been the cherry on top of the icing on the cake. On the final weekend of the season we faced Ayr United at Boghead – my assistant, Derek Whiteford, had been in a similar role at Somerset Park prior to joining me at Dumbarton – while Morton were up against Kilmarnock.

With our visitors only a point ahead of second-from-bottom Raith Rovers, they needed a win to preserve their First Division status and, on the day, they were far better than us. Robert Connor scored twice and Alan McInally, who was set to sign for Celtic, also scored to give Ayr a 3-0 win. In the end our result was academic as Morton beat Kilmarnock 3-2 to secure the title.

Nonetheless, it was difficult to be disappointed considering what we had achieved. In my ten games in charge Dumbarton had lost just twice and I had done the job I had been signed up for, to ensure promotion to the Premier Division was secured. The challenge now would be to construct a team that had the ability to stay there.

CHAPTER 13

DUMPED BY DUMBARTON

UNSURPRISINGLY, DUMBARTON were immediately installed as the bookmakers' favourites to secure a swift return to the First Division. Although we had surpassed all expectations by going up, most learned individuals reckoned our squad wasn't strong enough to compete with the likes of Rangers, Celtic, Aberdeen, Hearts and Hibernian and significant investment would be required simply for us to survive.

The first-team squad I inherited this time did not have the same young, emerging talent I had had in my first spell. There were no Murdo MacLeods or Graeme Sharps. Instead I had a squad of seasoned pros like Mark Clougherty, Donald McNeil and Pat McGowan. We also had the Coyle clan, brothers Joe and Tommy, and the redoubtable John Bourke, who, along with McNeil, was the only player who remained from my previous stint. John had left Dumbarton, joined Dundee United in 1977 and had also made over 100 appearances in a four-year spell at Kilmarnock. He had, however, come back to Boghead for a fee of £15,000 towards the end of season 1982/83 and in our promotion season was back doing what he did best, leading the line and scoring goals, notching 14 times in 38 appearances.

There were good young players too like Albert Craig and Stephen McCahill. I was particularly pleased to get young McCahill, a promising 17-year-old centre-half from Gleniffer Thistle, as there were about half a dozen other clubs interested in him. But I felt I still needed to strengthen the player pool further. The problem I had was that there wasn't much in the way of money available for buying players.

Simply put, I had to try and sell before I could buy and one of the first to go was my first-choice goalkeeper Tom Carson. I valued Tom, who had been excellent since I arrived, at £100,000, but he was able to move under freedom of contract which meant his transfer fee was determined by a tribunal. There was a bid from Watford but Tom eventually signed for Dundee. However, we received just £50,000 for him thanks to the decision of the tribunal.

That certainly didn't help swell the transfer kitty, but I did manage to pull off a great piece of business when I signed Gordon Arthur from Stirling Albion for £10,000 to replace Tom in goal. It was a bargain. He was a good, solid goalkeeper and would be one of the standout performers over the course of the season. In addition to Gordon I brought in right-back Alan Kay from Partick Thistle and he would play in all 36 Premier Division matches. Jimmy Simpson also joined us from Kilmarnock.

When the players came back after their summer break I was intent on ensuring their fitness levels were at the optimum level when the action got underway in August. I took them on runs up and down Kilpatrick Hill in Dumbarton and, for those readers familiar with the infamous sand dunes at Gullane, the hill there was like a mole hill in comparison to this one! The feedback from the players was that they had undertaken the toughest training sessions they had ever experienced. I had faith my players had the necessary finesse to compete in the Premier Division but I was also keen to ensure they had the proper fitness levels too.

Some of the routes we took were proper cross-country courses and at one stage the lads had to run across a tree that had fallen across one of the rivers that meandered through the hills. For a bit of fun I actually greased up the tree and, sure enough, some of the lads – I think big John Bourke was one of them – slipped and slid as they tried to run across it and ended up in the river and soaked to the skin for the remainder of the training run!

I also wanted our pre-season friendly matches to give us that competitive edge. After playing three matches inside a five-day period against lower-level opposition, we welcomed Watford to Boghead for our final friendly. Owned by Elton John and boasting the talents of John Barnes and Maurice Johnston, the Hornets had reached the FA Cup Final in season 1983/84 so they were the type of high-calibre opposition I felt we needed to face. And we showed that we were ready to hit the ground running by beating Graham Taylor's side 2-1. We drew a crowd of about 4,000 and they watched Albert Craig fire us ahead after 16 minutes. A great goal from Johnston on the half-hour meant we were level at the interval, but big John Bourke netted what proved to be the winner ten minutes into the second half.

I felt that we were moving along nicely but behind the scenes all was not well. Boghead had been put up for sale – the asking price was a mere £100,000 – and the ownership of the club changed when Hugh Fraser came in. And to cap it all off there was a bitter stand-off with the players over money. They had been offered a 100 per cent wage rise but some were steadfast in their refusal to accept the new terms. The result of the pay dispute was that about half of my squad had not yet re-signed for the new season.

Although it's fair to say that that was hardly the ideal preparation for our Premier Division bow, I was adamant that even if I had to send out half a reserve team I would do so as long as I knew they wanted to play for Dumbarton. Thus, we were down to the bare bones when we opened our first-ever Premier Division campaign at Cappielow against Morton. The departure of Carson meant I had to hand a debut to Doug McNab in goal. That would be the only match he would play for Dumbarton but, under the circumstances, we actually played well but lost 2-1. The Greenock side, who had also faced Watford pre-season, losing 3-2, led 2-0 at half-time but we played much better in the second half and deserved more than the solitary goal we got, scored by Stuart Robertson.

We then welcomed my old club Rangers to Boghead. It's fair to say Rangers were in the doldrums at that time – they hadn't won the league since 1977/78 – but the return of Jock Wallace to the helm in October 1983 had galvanised the side. They won the League Cup and embarked on a long unbeaten run in the Premier Division. Such was the impression they made during that spell, they were the favourites for the title in the opinion of some pundits.

In order to illustrate the gulf that existed between Dumbarton and Rangers, the Light Blues had added Iain Ferguson to their ranks in the summer. A tribunal had told them to pay Dundee over £200,000 for Ferguson and that put into perspective the challenge facing me. We could barely find the funds to pay our players, yet here we were up against a side that could afford to break the Scottish transfer record to boost their squad.

But I refused to let the chasm be the reason for us not being able to beat Rangers. In fact, ahead of the game the message from me was loud and clear: our visitors would have to roll their sleeves up and be prepared for a good, old-fashioned scrap for the two points.

And our approach rocked Rangers. We almost went in front after 12 minutes when Joe Coyle shot for goal only for Hugh Burns to clear his effort off the line. But just four minutes later we did edge ahead when Albert Craig rose highest to meet Coyle's cross and head the ball beyond Nicky Walker in the Rangers goal.

Albert almost made it 2-0 midway through the first half – Walker denying him with a superb save – and we were rarely troubled by our visitors, who were booed off the field at half-time by their supporters. My message in the dressing room was simple – just keep doing what you are doing – and for 36 minutes of the second half we did just that.

As the match moved in to its final ten minutes my wee part-timers were still 1-0 up and on course for one of the most famous victories in their history. We had been helped by an inspirational debut display from our goalkeeper, Gordon Arthur, but the game turned on its head inside a minute.

Firstly Ally McCoist, who my central-defensive pairing of McCahill and Clougherty had kept in check until then, expertly volleyed in the equaliser. Although this would be the start of a lean spell for Ally, I knew he would come good for Rangers. In fact, a couple of years later I was playing in an old crocks game in Greenock when I was summoned to sit in the front seat of the Jaguar belonging to the new Rangers player-manager, Graeme Souness. Mr Souness put before me a list of players and asked who I would keep. The only name on the list that I recommended was Ally. I told Souness he would be the one that would score the goals to make Rangers successful again, and after 355 goals in 581 games I think I was proved correct on that one!

Back to the dying embers of the match at Boghead, it was now about holding on for a precious point but my lads had put so much into the match that they just couldn't muster up enough energy to hold out. In the blink of an eye two points had become none when Ian Redford scored to give Rangers a scarcely deserved 2-1 win.

I couldn't have been prouder of the players after that game, and all I asked was they took the positives from the performance into the matches that lay ahead. And they did that, with two Joe Coyle goals giving us a 2-1 win over Queen of the South in the Skol League Cup before a similar scoreline got us our first two points on the board in the Premier Division against Dundee.

On a day of glorious sunshine our victory was orchestrated by Joe Coyle. He scored both our goals in the first half and was at the heart of all that was good about our play that afternoon. Incidentally, our match that day was the only one in the top flight that couldn't be considered a derby. The Old Firm and New Firm faced each other and there was an Edinburgh derby and Renfrewshire derby on the fixture card too.

We were oozing confidence now and were desperately unlucky to lose 1-0 against Hearts at Tynecastle. I sent my team out with a mentality to go and win the game and we could easily have been 3-0 ahead before my old protégé, Willie Johnston, created the winning goal for Donald Park shortly before half-time. Luck deserted us on the day, with Kenny Ashwood particularly unfortunate as he shot against the post and had a goal disallowed when one of the other lads strayed into an offside position.

The Hearts defeat came a few days after we had lost heavily at home to Dundee United in the League Cup. I have to be honest and say we were well beaten by United, for whom Davie Dodds and Ralph Milne both scored twice. However, I felt a bit aggrieved early in the second half when we had a goal chalked off. We were trailing 1-0 when Gerry Crawley crossed the ball high into the box. The United goalkeeper, Billy Thomson, came off his line to collect the ball but big John Bourke rose to reach Gerry's delivery too. In the end neither player made contact with the ball and it travelled over the line. But the referee, Mr Young from Belshill, felt John had fouled Billy so awarded a foul against us. Back in my day it would never have been a foul – burly centre-forwards like Don Kichenbrand used to barge goalkeepers all the time without punishment in those days – but the game was changing and goalkeepers were starting to receive more protection from match officials.

Those two defeats didn't knock us out of our stride too much, though. Next on the fixture list was Celtic, who rocked up at Boghead on the back of an uneven start to the season that had seen Davie Hay's side register just one win from their opening four league matches and exit the League Cup at the hands of our conquerors, Dundee United. And my lads heaped further pressure on the Parkhead side as we managed to eke out a 1-1 draw.

We went into the game with a threadbare squad. Our list of injuries and illnesses necessitated a request to postpone the reserve fixture against Celtic, but the first team I fielded did me proud. Reporting in the *Glasgow Herald*, James Traynor called that match our 'coming of age', although he also wrote that Celtic 'plumbed new depths of ineptitude'. I sent us out with a game plan to stifle the midfield and it worked. Celtic created very little before Frank McGarvey put them ahead after 33 minutes. But try as they might, they couldn't find a second goal. My players took full advantage, albeit thanks to a contentious penalty, awarded by referee Ian Cathcart. Mark Reid was adjudged to have fouled Joe Coyle and Joe picked himself up and made a clinical job of firing the ball beyond Pat Bonner.

The two matches against the Old Firm at Boghead stick out for me as I played my part in swelling the attendance on each occasion. Boghead had a capacity of 10,800 – only 800 of that was seated – so you can imagine when the two Glasgow giants rolled into town demand for a place in the ground was high.

The gates were closed but there were still thousands milling around outside so, after seeking permission from the police, I grabbed three of the lads who worked on the turnstiles and handed them each a black bag. I stuck my head above the wall and encouraged the fans to come and pay cash at the turnstile to get in. By the time the match kicked off each of the lads had bags bursting at the seams with British bank notes. I proudly took the bags up to the boardroom and handed them to the chairman, Mr Robertson, but only after I had given each of my handy helpers a handful of cash for the role they played in gathering the money. Mr Robertson actually questioned what was in the bags – he thought they were full of rubbish and couldn't understand why I was bringing them to him – so you can imagine his delight when I opened them up and showed him the actual contents.

I gave the players a night off from training as a reward for the draw with Celtic and they repaid me with another win the following weekend. We went to Easter Road and beat Hibernian 3-2, with our goals coming from two of the Coyle brothers, Joe, who bagged a brace, and Tommy. We trailed 1-0 after 15 minutes but by the interval we had overturned that deficit to lead 3-1. Joe grabbed our equaliser from the penalty spot and put us ahead four minutes later. He had a hand in our third goal too, crossing for Tommy to knock the ball beyond Alan Rough in the Hibernian goal.

Remarkably, my team now boasted the Premier Division's top goalscorer – Joe Coyle – and had a Scottish international squad member in our midst when Steve McCahill's stellar displays earned him a place in the Scotland U18 squad. I felt the result at Easter Road had been a long time coming. I felt our performances in the opening gambit of the season merited more reward than they had received. We were unlucky on occasion, losing out by a single goal many times, with concession of goals late in games being our Achilles heel.

But I wanted to make sure we didn't get carried away and we got a bit of a reality check after our win over Hibernian when we suffered three successive defeats. That run started with a 2-0 home loss to defending champions Aberdeen but, just like we had done to Rangers and Celtic, we gave them a big fright before succumbing late in the game. Willie Miller was the man who breached our defence with a screamer from 30 yards 13 minutes from time. Willie Falconer sealed the win after 85 minutes but I took great heart again from the fact that we had matched the Dons for large parts of the game.

A narrow 1-0 defeat at home to St Mirren followed – Frank McAvennie got the goal – before I was heading back to Tannadice to lock horns with Jim McLean. As I have said, Jim and I didn't see eye to eye when I was coming to the end of my time at Tannadice, but he had built a fine Dundee United side. They had taken everyone by surprise when they won the title in season 1982/83 and had come ever so close to reaching the European Cup Final the following season, losing out in controversial circumstances to AS Roma in the semi-final. The return to Tayside also afforded me the chance to catch up with Walter Smith, who was now in the assistant manager's role at Tannadice.

You will have gathered by now that my team stood up to the challenges that were thrown their way and when we faced United it was a case of 'same again'. We learned our lesson from the League Cup defeat earlier in the season and held firm against a side containing the likes of Paul Sturrock, Eamonn Bannon and Davie Dodds. We kept them at bay until deep into the second half when their substitute, Tommy Coyne, managed to nick the winner with a goal we felt aggrieved about. I felt that the free kick that led to the goal had been taken from the wrong place and also that Coyne had been offside when he received the ball prior to scoring.

We were back to winning ways the following week when we beat Morton 3-1 at home. Remarkably, we hadn't beaten Morton in 12 previous attempts but in what pundits already had billed as a relegation scrap, we emerged with a precious two points. A bizarre own goal put us ahead after 15 minutes – the Morton defender, Andy Dunlop, lobbing his own goalkeeper from 30 yards – and by the interval we had doubled our lead thanks to another goal from the irrepressible Joe Coyle. A magnificent Alan Kay header gave us a third goal in the second half and we were so good in an attacking sense that I felt, on another day, we could probably have scored another three or four goals.

That match represented the start of the second quarter of the fixture list and the win left us with seven points from ten games. As a manager I reflected on that first quarter and decided, to give us a better opportunity to pick up more points, I would need to change our system. I had a good base to build from – in the first nine games I had five ever-presents and another two who had missed just one league game – but felt we needed a wee change to kick-start our season. And I elected to try out my new system on our first trip of the season to one of my old stomping grounds, Ibrox.

We had shown at Boghead earlier in the season we were capable of matching Rangers and this time we managed to take something from the game. Jock Wallace's side were due to face Inter Milan in the UEFA Cup the following midweek and we showed them how defending stoically could silence the big guns. Admittedly I had Gordon Arthur to thank again for the four or five terrific saves he pulled off in the first half, but we were well worth our point in the end. Remarkably, that was our first clean sheet of the season.

I had managed to secure Gordon for just £10,000 and I commented at the time that I should be in Rio de Janeiro along with one of the infamous Great Train Robbers, Ronnie Biggs, as I felt as if I had got a steal of a deal. Gordon would prove a great acquisition, going on to make over 150 appearances for Dumbarton.

In the wake of the Rangers game there were reports of an infamous media tycoon taking over at Dumbarton. It was no secret that the club were seeking a new owner and an injection of cash. The club had been in a bit of difficulty in the 1970s but had found stability before, in 1980, £350,000 had to be spent on a new stand at Boghead. Money had been tight since then and the rumours going around were that Robert Maxwell, chairman of the Mirror Group and owner of Oxford United, was prepared to purchase Dumbarton and bring to an end any financial worries we may have had. Any possible deal never materialised but, as manager, I was keen to get the situation resolved sooner rather than later as I was hopeful that a new owner would make money available to strengthen the squad to help us in our bid to maintain our hard-earned top-flight status.

But with nothing happening on that front eventually my thin playing squad and the fact we were part-time started to take its toll. While we were enjoying mixing it with the big boys, the lads had other jobs on top of their football commitments. For example, Gordon Arthur was a surveyor with the Coal Board, the Coyle brothers were both joiners, Kenny Ashwood was a refrigeration engineer and John Bourke was a PE teacher. They had to balance the working hours in those roles with playing and training with Dumbarton and that was tough on them.

As much as the draw at Ibrox was a terrific result, it was the start of an eight-game winless run and by the time we faced Rangers again in our last game of 1984, we were starting to struggle. In fairness, this sequence of fixtures included trips to Parkhead and Pittodrie and if my wee team gleaned any points from those games it would be viewed as a bonus.

We went to both venues aiming to play like we did at Ibrox, but we were outclassed, particularly when we lost 2-0 to Celtic. We faced Davie Hay's men a matter of days after they had beaten Rapid Vienna 3-0 in the European Cup Winners' Cup, thus overturning a 3-1 first-leg deficit to progress to the next round. And they continued from where they left off against us and, in the end, we were fortunate only to lose two goals.

When we faced the league leaders, Aberdeen, at the end of November we looked set for a bit of a hiding when Frank McDougall scored for the eighth successive game with less than a minute gone. But my defence held firm as the red tide crashed down on us on several occasions and the game ended 1-0.

As I said, points taken at Ibrox, Pittodrie and Parkhead would have been a bonus, but there were games that we should have taken more points from than we did. For example, the run started with a 1-1 draw against Dundee and afterwards I came in for some criticism for our tactics. After Kenny Ashwood fired us ahead after nine minutes we reverted to the system that had worked so well against Rangers. My priority was to get points for Dumbarton, not to entertain fans the length and breadth of the country, so I encouraged a 'what we have, we hold' strategy after Kenny's goal. And the obdurate defending that was required to execute that strategy would have kept a second successive clean sheet had the referee, Louis Thow, not added on as much injury time at the end of the game, for it was in the third additional minute that Jim Smith equalised for Dundee. Our time-wasting was cited as one of the principal reasons for the extra time, but that left me a little perplexed as at no time during the match did Mr Thow issue any warnings to my players on the occasions when he felt time was being wasted.

A late goal proved our undoing the following week too – Jimmy Bone netting late in the day at a boggy Boghead to give Hearts a 1-0 win – and once again it was such small margins that were costing my team points. We did, however, gather precious points when we drew 2-2 at home against Dundee United and 0-0 against St Mirren at Love Street. But we missed an opportunity to move ahead of one of our closest challengers at the bottom of the table when we drew 2-2 against Hibernian at Boghead in November.

To be honest, that day I struggled to name a fully fit team yet we found ourselves 2-0 up after just 15 minutes through goals from Albert Craig and Patrick McGowan. But we couldn't hold on and twice inside a minute after the interval a young Gordon Durie found the net to earn our visitors a share of the spoils.

My team were back to winning ways ten days before Christmas. We went to Greenock to face our relegation rivals Morton and chalked up only our second away win of the season. Ahead of the match we led our opponents by three points so winning gave us a bit of breathing space at the foot of the table. For once the goalscoring plaudits went to someone other than Joe Coyle; John Bourke was the main man this time, scoring two goals and also striking the bar with a header.

I was really pleased with the Morton result for a number of reasons. Firstly, it arrested our run of matches without winning and I now felt we were starting to add a bit of cutting edge to our play too. That was apparent when we faced Rangers on 29

December, with another two goals added to our tally, but we were undone by a virtuoso display from Ted McMinn.

The enigmatic Ted scored a superb goal direct from a corner kick and there was another stunning goal from Davie Cooper as Rangers ran out 4-2 winners. But I refused to be deflated after the match. As 1984 drew to a close my boys, perceived by many a learned pundit as the whipping boys in the top flight, had fought valiantly to sit five points clear of bottom club Morton, and three ahead of Hibernian, who occupied the second relegation spot in the league.

We had cause to be optimistic when 1985 started with a 1-0 home win over Dundee, but that win was followed by three successive heavy defeats. Back-to-back trips to Edinburgh brought a 5-1 hammering against Hearts and a 3-1 reverse against Hibernian. And then Aberdeen came to Boghead and beat us comfortably 2-0. However, we were still a point clear of safety and had played a game less than Hibernian, who occupied ninth place.

We eked out a good point at home to St Mirren – Tommy Coyle's second-half goal equalising a strike from Frank McAvennie – but we then lost 4-0 at Tannadice and were undone by a rejuvenated Ally McCoist in a 3-1 defeat against Rangers at Ibrox.

I had tried to strengthen the squad ahead of those games by bringing Graeme Sinclair back to the club. 'Sinky' was another from the brood of talented young starlets that had been prominent during my first spell at the club. I worked with him during my time in charge of the reserves and he eventually became a mainstay in the first team. His fine form eventually secured him a move to Celtic for £65,000 in August 1982. But after initially winning praise for a stellar performance against Johan Cruyff and Ajax in a European Cup tie in Amsterdam and picking up a League Cup winners' medal, Graeme flitted in and out of the side during his time at Parkhead and had had a loan spell at Manchester City in November 1984 before we got him on a similar deal.

Graeme made his second Dumbarton debut in the defeat at Tannadice and played well a couple of weeks later when we won for the first time in six games, edging out already relegated Morton 1-0 at Boghead. Little did we know at the time, but the goal scored by Jimmy Simpson that day would be the last Premier Division goal scored by a Dumbarton player.

With Morton doomed the second relegation place was up for grabs. The win over Morton took us on to 19 points, level with Hibernian, and we had a game in hand. However, the Easter Road side, having won at Ibrox earlier in January, plundered Parkhead that same day we beat Morton and picked up two points in a 1-0 win over second-placed Celtic. And Dumbarton were faced with a tough run-in too. In our final eight fixtures we were due to face Celtic twice, Aberdeen away and Dundee United at home.

However, crucially, we had our relegation rivals to play on 6 April at Boghead and that would prove to be the pivotal game. The Easter Road side arrived a point better off than us but I felt our game in hand still gave us a slight advantage. But on the day we were outplayed by John Blackley's side. Willie Irvine opened the scoring and future Hamilton Accies manager Brian Rice added a second to complete a comfortable 2-0 win.

The following Monday the *Glasgow Herald* headline declared 'The Party is Over for Dumbarton', but I was still convinced we had the players to preserve our Premier Division status. But when we lost our game in hand against Dundee all our hopes of survival evaporated. Our return to the First Division was confirmed when we lost 2-0 at home to Dundee United on 27 April.

It had been a fantastic experience managing Dumbarton in the Premier Division and I think we punched above our weight even though we ended up relegated. The margins are fine in the Premier Division, though, and for all our good play and bravery we lacked that cutting edge and that lack of firepower ultimately led to our demotion.

But we were more than capable of bouncing straight back and our target for season 1985/86 was for an immediate return to the top flight. I met with the chairman, Sir Hugh Fraser, and we discussed our strategy for the forthcoming campaign. Sir Hugh had been chairman at the likes of House of Fraser and Harrods and he paid approximately £80,000 to acquire a controlling interest in the club. It was a productive chat as I outlined what I felt was required to achieve our objective. Sir Hugh seemed happy with what I was proposing and he sanctioned moves for the experienced Erich Schaedler, who came from Hibernian, and Gerry McCoy, who joined from Falkirk.

I was absolutely delighted to get Erich on board. A full international and a member of the Scotland World Cup squad in 1974, he was an experienced defender and I felt he could use that to bring on the promising youngsters I had at my disposal. Alongside Gerry he made his debut in a 2-0 opening-day win against Airdrie at Broomfield and we lost just one of our opening 11 matches.

Both Erich and Gerry were top performers in those matches, with Gerry scoring in each of the opening five league fixtures. And when he scored his sixth goal of the season against Kilmarnock at Boghead on 19 October my team were four points clear at the top of the table.

Unfortunately, it was all downhill after that. We didn't win again in the league until we faced Kilmarnock at Rugby Park four days before Christmas, a run of seven games. In that sequence we fell to the heaviest defeat of my second spell in charge, 6-1 against Hamilton at Douglas Park. Willie Watters was making his first-team debut for Accies that day and scored a hat-trick. But although we lost heavily the Hamilton goalkeeper, Rikki Ferguson, played a blinder, pulling off several excellent saves including one from a Gerry McCoy penalty.

Erich Schaedler was at left-back for Dumbarton against Hamilton and I picked him to play there again the following week when we drew 2-2 with Montrose. It would be the last time I would write the name 'Schaedler' on a team sheet. He was in and around the club after that match, turning up to training one day in his Range Rover accompanied by these two Dobermans, but I had no inkling of the news I would receive just before the year ended. I was telephoned with the news that, aged just 36, Erich had been found dead. I had to break the news to the lads and there was a numbness and a silence in the dressing room when I informed them.

Our next league fixture against Alloa Athletic, scheduled for 28 December, was postponed as a mark of respect, and the playing squad, replete in their Dumbarton blazers, and myself attended Erich's funeral. Although he had only been with us a matter of months he was a popular figure and had endeared himself to our supporters with his tigerish tackling.

It was the responsibility of myself and the senior pros to try and turn our attention back to football when the world welcomed 1986. At the end of our wretched run of form before Christmas we were third in the table, four points behind leaders Hamilton with a game in hand. But after starting the year with two defeats in three league games, the last of which was a 4-0 drubbing at Station Park against Forfar, I tendered my resignation.

The heavy defeat to Forfar came just seven days after we had been eliminated from the Scottish Cup by Queen's Park. Although we had fallen to fifth in the table, we were only four points adrift of second place with two games in hand but, for me, it was time to go. I wasn't getting on with Sir Hugh – I didn't think he was much of a football man – and I had to take cognisance of my own health too.

I was part-time at Dumbarton so as Avril's dad wasn't keeping too well, I had taken over the running of his business, which was based in Airdrie, and I was also involved in a pub in Glasgow city centre called The Waterfront. There would therefore be days when I'd be up early to travel through to Airdrie, carry out a full day's work then travel to Dumbarton for training. After that I'd be back in the car and off to oversee things at The Waterfront. As you can imagine, such a hectic schedule puts a significant amount of pressure on you. There were numerous occasions when I would get into bed at 2am only to be back up again at 5am. It's fair to say Avril and the family were getting increasingly concerned and that's why the time was right to call it a day at Dumbarton.

Although disappointed to leave Dumbarton, I felt I left the Sons in a decent position. I was also certain I wasn't finished with football just yet. I was willing to listen to any offers that came my way and, within a few weeks, I was back in the game thanks to an old pal.

CHAPTER 14

DOWN WITH
THE DOONHAMERS

AFTER LEAVING Dumbarton I wasn't sure if I would get another opportunity to get back into football. But my old pigeon-fancying pal John Lambie, manager of Hamilton Accies, called me up and offered me the job as his assistant manager.

I had known John for years. He had been a doughty opponent in his playing days as he played at right-back for St Johnstone and Falkirk and he used to kick lumps out me. He would often joke that the only reason I scored six goals against Falkirk back in March 1962 was because he wasn't playing that day! Away from the pitch our mutual love of pigeons meant we were often in each other's company and that enduring friendship was key in me getting offered the job at Douglas Park.

Moving to Hamilton also saw me involved in the top flight again. Accies had just been promoted to the Premier Division as First Division champions and my Dumbarton side had been on the end of a real drubbing back in December 1985. We were thumped 6-1 at Douglas Park, with Willie Watters grabbing a hat-trick.

Willie left to join Clyde soon after I arrived to assist John – believe it or not the three goals he scored against Dumbarton were the only league goals he scored in 11 appearances for Accies – but there were plenty of characters in the dressing room and also on the terraces. We had Gerry Collins, Ally Brazil and Willie Jamieson, who had both come from Hibernian, and one of the leading marksmen in the history of the First Division, John Brogan.

We also tempted Tom McAdam to the club. I had worked with Tom while at Dumbarton and I was keen to get him added to our squad. He had left Dumbarton back in October 1975 and, after two years at Dundee United, had ended up being converted into a centre-back by Billy McNeill at Celtic. After over 350 games, three league titles and winners' medals in the Scottish Cup and League Cup, Tom had joined Stockport County briefly before John and I brought him back to Scotland. With his experience and the ability to play up front and in defence, I thought Tom would be ideal for Hamilton, but he made only three league appearances before joining our Lanarkshire rivals, Motherwell.

The character I was referring to on the terraces was, of course, Fergie, or Ian Russell to give him his proper name. He became infamous for his expletive-laden rants directed at the players and the management, but despite regularly voicing his displeasure throughout the entire 90 minutes, he rarely missed an Accies game before ill health stopped him going. I used to get quite agitated when he started and would tell him that he'd get himself in trouble with the police. Lambie, who was used to the abuse and would be subjected to it even when we weren't playing, used to tell me just to let him jump around and swear!

In truth, we were relegation candidates pretty much from the start of the season. With only ten of the first-team squad full-time, Accies were always up against it and we only took two points from our first 19 league games. It was 29 November before we chalked up our first win, 3-1 against Hibernian at Easter Road, but that was quickly followed by a 7-0 drubbing against Hearts at Tynecastle and an 8-3 defeat against Celtic. We did give our fans something to cheer on New Year's Day, though, when four goals from Albert Craig gave us a 4-2 win over Motherwell in the Lanarkshire derby.

I had had Albert in my squad at Dumbarton and one of the first things I did when I got the job at Accies was recommend that John send someone to watch Albert in action. As I expected the scouting report was a favourable one and John sanctioned a move to sign him. It proved a shrewd bit of business as Albert's form at Hamilton eventually earned the club a £95,000 windfall when Albert moved to Newcastle United. And the game that stimulated interest from the North East of England was one of the most famous in Scottish football history.

With the run of form Accies were on, you can imagine the last thing we needed was to draw Rangers away in the Scottish Cup at the end of January 1987. They had been reborn under Graeme Souness and were going toe-to-toe with Celtic for the league title. But after a four-day break in Blackpool, we went to Ibrox and shook up the world of Scottish football by winning 1-0. In truth we took a real pummelling but Lady Luck was smiling on us that afternoon and Adrian Sprott's goal took us through.

I vividly recall the celebrations in the dugout after we scored. The dugouts at Ibrox then weren't the cavernous ones that are at the stadium today. They were like wee wooden boxes and when Sprott scored, John Lambie jumped up to celebrate and smacked his head against the roof of the dugout!

That shock victory was the highlight of the season for Accies. We lost to Motherwell in the next round of the Scottish Cup and were relegated to the First Division well before the season concluded with a 7-3 defeat against Dundee at Dens Park.

I was really enjoying working with John and the lads at Hamilton, but I was still on the lookout for a return to management so when I heard Queen of the South were looking for a new manager I duly applied for the post. The Doonhamers were looking for a replacement for the recently departed Mike Jackson. Mike had had a fine spell in charge of Queens in the mid-1970s, leading them to a couple of Scottish Cup quarter-finals. But his second spell in season 1986/87 was not as successful, with the club finishing tenth in the 12-team First Division and only staving off relegation to the Second Division by two points.

The post at Palmerston Park had been advertised such that the club were looking for either a full-time manager or player-manager and the rumour at the time was that Rangers midfielder Bobby Russell was going to be offered the latter role. Bobby had been out of favour at Rangers and was interviewed by the board of directors. Allan Ball, who had played with distinction for the club as a goalkeeper between 1963 and 1982, was also reportedly interested in taking the helm.

However, I met with the chairman, Willie Harkness, and must have impressed him as I was offered the job. Mr Harkness was a significant figure in the Scottish game and had been president of the SFA. I also followed in the footsteps of a couple of Rangers team-mates when I took the job. The redoubtable Bobby Shearer had moved to Dumfries when he left Rangers in 1965 as a player-coach. And, in June 1970, Harry Davis had taken on the role of manager at Palmerston Park, albeit for just one season.

Season 1986/87 was Queens' first back in the First Division following promotion at the end of 1985/86. They had finished as runners-up to Dunfermline in the Second Division but while the Pars kicked on and gained promotion to the Premier Division, Queens teetered on the brink of relegation. The end of the campaign was wretched as the side only picked up one point from their final six matches. But that point, gained in a 0-0 draw against Montrose, was a crucial one as it finally staved off the challenge of Brechin City, who ended up second-from-bottom of the table and, as a result, were demoted to the Second Division.

The squad I inherited in the summer of 1987 had lost a number of the leading lights from the previous season. Winger Jimmy Robertson and club captain Graeme Robertson left for the Premier Division, joining Morton and Dunfermline Athletic respectively. Jim McBride, who had made 37 league appearances in the previous campaign, emigrated to Australia and the club's top goalscorer, Tommy Bryce, asked for a transfer and eventually joined our First Division rivals, Clydebank.

To compensate, ten players were brought in, among them a couple I had worked with at Hamilton. The experienced John Pelosi was one of them and I appointed him captain. And I also recruited Jimmy Sinclair, who joined as player-coach.

One of the first things I did after I took the job was insist that all players trained two nights a week at Strathclyde Park in Hamilton. Previously the lads from in and around Dumfries had trained separately at Palmerston but I felt we all had to be together in order to work on our game plan for the weekend fixtures.

Despite the changes to training, my time in the dugout in Dumfries did not get off to the best of starts. We only picked up two points in our first four league matches before registering our first league win over Kilmarnock at Rugby Park at the end of August. That wasn't our first win of the season, though. Eleven days earlier goals from Jim Doherty and Jim Hughes had earned us a 2-1 win over Premier Division Falkirk in the League Cup. But by the time we beat Kilmarnock we were out of that competition when we fell at the next hurdle, Hibernian beating us 3-1 at Easter Road.

The biggest issue for us was that we were struggling to score goals regularly. Tommy Bryce had scored 20 goals the previous season and I found it difficult to find another number nine who could get anywhere close to that kind of return. We tried to bring in some players on trial, with a view to playing them in some reserves games to cast an eye over them. But that led to frustration as some of them didn't turn up, which left us short of players for the reserve fixtures. That meant I had to pull the boots back on to make up the numbers, but one match against Albion Rovers ended painfully for me. With five minutes remaining I tried to execute an overhead kick but landed awkwardly, breaking my left wrist. That ruled me out for about six weeks, but such was the enjoyment I got out of playing football I was always available to play if required even though I was now 50.

The wrist break also got me into a spot of bother with my wife, Avril. In my infinite wisdom I decided to drive myself to the hospital after I sustained the injury – fortunately the car I was driving at the time was an automatic – and when I informed Avril of this when she met me at the hospital she was less than enamoured. I was also a bit annoyed as we were due to go and see Gerry and the Pacemakers a couple of nights later and my injury stopped me from getting up and jiving!

I did eventually manage to get players on board but over the course of the season five players wore the number-nine jersey, including Alan Bain, who had a goal against Rangers on his CV, who came from Clydebank in October. The vastly experienced Derek Frye was another brought in. But despite having a good track record in front of goal – he had been Second Division top scorer back in 1975/76 and averaged almost a goal every two games during his spell with Clyde – Derek only managed seven league goals in this, his second spell at Palmerston. Indeed, our issues in identifying a regular goalscoring centre-forward can be summed up by the fact it was a midfielder, Jim Hughes, who ended up as our top scorer with 17 goals.

We were also losing goals at an alarming rate, and in successive weekends in November and December we shipped five goals, losing 5-0 away to Meadowbank Thistle and 5-1 at home to Raith Rovers. Those games proved to be a watershed moment, however. They prompted me to change our system and I moved to playing a sweeper system to help give our two centre-backs cover.

The results were immediate. We were unbeaten in our next six league fixtures and kept clean sheets in four of those games, including a 0-0 draw with high-flying Hamilton. We actually did well against my old club that season. John Lambie led them to the First Division title but after losing our first encounter 3-0 at home, we drew 2-2 at Douglas Park in October and won 2-1 on our next visit there in March.

Queens eventually finished in a comfortable seventh position, seven points clear of East Fife and my old club Dumbarton, who were both relegated after gathering only 36 points. We should, in fact, have finished much higher than we did. Only Hamilton, Meadowbank Thistle and Forfar lost more games than us, but our undoing was the number of draws – 15 from 44 league games.

The target for my second season was to build on what we had achieved and push for promotion to the Premier Division. I felt this was achievable as we had a good squad, with the likes of future Hamilton manager Billy Reid excelling in midfield and Dougie Mills and Alan Mackin starting to form a solid partnership at the heart of the defence.

Having lost my first-choice goalkeeper – Alan Davidson took up a job offer in Australia – I went back to Hamilton for Rikki Ferguson and also brought in Gary Johnston, a full-back, who signed from Cumnock Juniors. Although I didn't sign a striker, I hoped Stevie Moore could add goals to his game and I also looked to Jim Hughes to continue from where he left off at the end of the previous season. But it became very clear very quickly that it wasn't going to work out. If we had kept our heads above water in season 1987/88 then we were all but sunk in the early part of season 1988/89.

With the league reverting to 14 teams and 39 matches – for two seasons the First Division had comprised 12 teams and we had played 44 league fixtures – my team weren't considered to be one of the favourites for promotion. But that was the aim for our chairman, Mr Harkness, and he made a commitment to the supporters that he and the board of directors would work hard to deliver top-class football in Dumfries. It didn't happen and, instead of pushing for promotion, we went in to a spectacular freefall. After opening the league campaign with a 2-2 draw against Kilmarnock at Palmerston, my team lost six of the next seven league matches and Dundee hammered us 5-1 in the League Cup. The only game we didn't lose in that run was a 2-1 win over Forfar Athletic at Palmerston and that would be one of only two victories recorded in the league over the course of the campaign.

By the time the second of those victories had been chalked up – another 2-1 win, this time over Meadowbank Thistle on 31 December – I was no longer in charge. A 3-0 defeat at the hands of Falkirk on 1 October saw Queens plummet to the foot of the table and when we lost 4-1 at home to Partick Thistle three weeks later, I tendered my resignation. Thistle had just sacked Billy Lamont and had one of their directors, Bobby Watson, in charge, but they comfortably recorded just their second victory of the season.

My side were now propping up the First Division table and the fans were, understandably, getting restless and were looking for changes in personnel to help arrest the decline. We needed players desperately, something I had made the board aware of at the end of the previous season. I felt we needed at least four new faces to help us push for promotion but, try as I might, I couldn't get the ones I felt we needed to join.

I also got to know that certain members of the board were less than enamoured with the players I had recruited thus far.

There were also murmurings of player unrest and concerns over poor fitness levels. The latter wasn't helped by the fact that the training at Strathclyde Park was dispensed with, leaving us with disparate groups of players training separately.

For whatever reason my resignation wasn't accepted by the board so I was back in the dugout for our next league match against Clydebank. The Bankies were challenging at the top end of the division so it was no real surprise that we lost heavily again, 3-0 this time. Our former striker, Tommy Bryce, was among the goals and during the 90 minutes there were calls from the terraces for the chairman to go.

The following week we lost 3-1 away to Clyde, despite taking the lead through Alan Bain. There was further embarrassment prior to that game when we opened the hamper carrying the kits. The number-ten jersey hadn't been packed so Kevin Hetherington had to don number 12 instead. That kind of thing simply summed up the disarray the club were in at the time.

Remarkably we then contrived to turn in a very good performance to draw 0-0 at home with Dunfermline and followed that up with a 2-2 draw with Forfar. That temporarily stopped the run of defeats, but when we faced Morton at Palmerston on 26 November it would be the last time I would take charge of Queen of the South.

We lost 3-2 to the side that had been relegated from the Premier Division at the end of 1987/88 and a chap called Joe Olabode scored both our goals. This would be the first of just three games Joe played following his arrival on trial from Gateshead. The trouble was I didn't sign him! Indeed, the first time I met Joe was when he arrived at Palmerston ahead of the match.

He had been brought in by the directors as they thought he was the man to solve our problems in front of goal. When the directors start signing players and telling the manager to select them then his position, in my opinion, becomes untenable. I also found out later that the directors had quizzed Joe after the match regarding my decision to substitute him in the second half.

My time was clearly up and I decided enough was enough. The following week I took training for the last time and informed the players of my intention to leave. I informed the chairman in writing of my intentions the following day.

My departure from Queen of the South ended my 32-year active involvement in football. I have so many fantastic memories of that period and I count myself as lucky to have been involved in the game I love for so long and to have enjoyed the success I did. But now it was time to close this chapter of my life and focus on my family and pursue interests outside of football.

I had started working in insurance for a chap called Allan McKay. I had played alongside Allan at Dumbarton and I was able to use the experience I picked up in that role when I became a mortgage broker for Eagle Star. I was still at Queen of the South when I started in the mortgage business, but after leaving football I was now able to focus my attention on that role and I made a real success of it, helped in no small part by the Iron Lady herself, Margaret Thatcher.

Mrs Thatcher had decided that council house residents could buy the property they were renting at a reduced cost. That meant there was going to be a flood of folk looking for mortgages and I seized the opportunity to help them out. I made up business cards and left them with a number of letting agents. When folk that were looking to buy their property came in to pay their rent they would pick up a card and soon the phone was ringing regularly. At one point I was doing in the region of 200 mortgage applications a week! I worked closely with Ian Livingstone, who was chairman at Motherwell, and the Yorkshire Building Society. Ian dealt with the legal matters, the Building Society provided the mortgage and I brokered the deal. It proved to be an excellent partnership.

I kept going in the role for a number of years and thoroughly enjoyed it. After that I moved into security and worked in that field until I decided to retire in my early 70s. Thereafter I was able to focus on spiritualism, something I had become extremely passionate about.

CHAPTER 15

LIFE OUTSIDE FOOTBALL

I HAD two main hobbies outside of football: greyhounds and pigeons. I also enjoyed fishing, photography, shooting and I ran a speedboat for a period of time. I can't recall why I did the latter, though, as I suffer from seasickness and even today I won't go on a boat. I also liked a game of dominoes and I made great friends at the local club. I'd pop in most days for a game and a chat and the pensioners loved it, even the ones who followed Celtic!

I raced pigeons from a young age. However, even before that birds fascinated me and, as a boy, I would always be trying to trap pigeons when I was out playing with my pals. Both my grandfathers had raced pigeons and I remember my grandpa Stevenson, my mum's dad, once bringing home a splendid big trophy. He was part of a pigeon racing club and, having won the trophy on a few occasions, he had now been given it to keep. My granny Stevenson decided to give the trophy to me and I still have it in my house today.

My Uncle George, my dad's brother, looked after the pigeons with me and it was down to him to deal with them when I was playing football. We initially kept our birds in a loft on the railway banking in Newton, but when Avril and I got married the pigeons came with us to our house in Kilbarchan. By then I wasn't just racing pigeons, I was breeding them too.

Typically I would have about 100 birds in the loft, a mixture of old and young birds and stock pigeons we used for breeding. The methods used to train the birds would vary. After spending time outside the nest learning to fend for themselves and getting used to their surroundings, a young bird will start flying around the loft aged about six or seven weeks old. Once they had enough confidence to fly further afield we would put the birds in a trailer and take them on what were called 'training tosses'. This involved taking the birds a distance away from the loft, releasing them and then awaiting their return to the loft. The distances flown would then get progressively longer until we were confident the birds were ready to race.

My pigeons would race every Saturday. A transporter would pick the birds up on the Friday night and take them to the venue where the race would start. The lever would then be released the next day, setting the birds free for the race. Depending on the race distance, there may have been an overnight stopover. However, it mattered little which bird was in front at that stage, it was always a case of first bird home was the winner. Birds would be timed using a specially designed clock that was placed inside rubber rings that were wrapped round the pigeon's leg. A unique identification number would also be on the ring. Timings were then compared and a winner declared.

I soon developed an eye for a good racing bird, and not long after I returned to Ibrox from Baillieston I got a call from Scot Symon to go upstairs to his office at Ibrox. The boys in the dressing room were sure that was me getting the call to play the following Saturday so I was excited as I climbed up the marble staircase. When I went in to the manager's office Mr Symon was there with two chaps who I'd soon learn were Duncan Ogilvie, who built houses and was chairman at Falkirk, and Jock Reid, who was recognised as one of the best fliers of pigeons in Scotland.

Duncan and Jock had brought with them two baskets filled with pigeons. Such was my reputation in the pigeon community, Jock asked me to pick one of the pigeons to enter the prestigious Nantes 600-mile race. You could tell the best racing pigeons by their eyes and the way they blinked so I picked out a grizzled hen. The bird then travelled to France on a transporter where it was released to fly back home. Jock said if it won the race he would give me one of the young birds from that pigeon.

Needless to say the bird I chose for Jock won and I picked out a young bird which was white on its underside and I never looked back after that. In its first race, which was over 420 miles, nobody gave it a chance but it won, and it was an hour ahead of the second-placed bird. In total that bird won 12 races for me.

I was still active in the pigeon community until around 12 years ago. Indeed my passion for pigeons was such that I once travelled over 100 miles to meet a fellow fancier. That was back in the summer of 1969 when I was on tour with Dundee United in the USA. I found out the whereabouts of the gentleman regarded as being the top pigeon expert in the States and took a trip to see him. And we had a great chat about racing our birds before I headed back to join my team-mates ahead of our next tour match.

My father took an interest in pigeons but his passion was greyhounds. One of the dogs he trained came from Ireland and we called it R.O.L., short for Rangers Outside Left. I vividly remember his first race at Coatbridge. My dad, sporting a hat, wellingtons and dungarees, and I were there to watch and clearly the bookmakers thought R.O.L. had little chance of winning as it had odds of 5/1. However, by the first bend it was six lengths in front!

The owner of the dog had placed a bet of £3,000 on it so when it won the race he had earned himself a decent sum of money. Rather than share his winnings he simply gifted the dog to us. And R.O.L.'s winning streak continued. The dog won the next ten races before it broke a hock. This was a common injury due to the force exerted on the feet and legs. Greyhounds run anti-clockwise during a race and the injury usually happens on the first turn, when the greyhound is pushing off with the right hind leg. It was the most common career-ending injury for the racing greyhounds and it was a similar story for R.O.L. After sustaining the break the bone simply didn't knit back together properly and we had to have him put down.

Although I gave up the pigeons and greyhounds a few years ago, I still like to get out and about. And when I do I love to go and watch the Rangers. I have a seat for life at Ibrox and, like all other Rangers supporters, I'm delighted to see my team starting to emerge from what was an horrendous time in the doldrums. Steven Gerrard's appointment has been an inspired one and Dave King must take a huge amount of credit for the role he has played in Rangers' renaissance. Although Steven has had his critics of late following a poor run of form at the start of 2020, I feel Rangers have improved and I hope he and the players can very soon bring the league title back to Ibrox.

CHAPTER 16

FAMILY GUY

AS I mentioned earlier I married my lovely wife Avril in the winter of 1965. Eight years my junior, I love her as much now as I did back then, even though I drive her mad at times!

Our first home was a rented house in Beaufort Avenue as the house in Kilbarchan was still being built. But once the construction was complete we settled in and it was in that house that, after a tragic loss, we starting to grow the Wilson clan.

Avril and I both wanted a family and she fell pregnant pretty soon after we were married. We enjoyed a routine pregnancy until it emerged just before Christmas that our baby daughter was lying in a breech position. Four days before the baby was due, Avril went into the Queen Mother's Maternity Hospital for what was a routine procedure. The doctors were going to turn the baby from the breech position – the procedure is called an External Cephalic Version (ECV) and I believe complications are rare – but the drug the medical staff administered had a catastrophic impact. Rather than relax Avril it almost killed her, with her heart stopping four times. And our baby daughter, who we were going to call Susan, died in the womb. We were numbed by the loss.

Avril eventually gave birth but neither of us were even allowed to hold our baby. All we were left with was a multitude of unanswered questions. At the forefront was how could something that was a routine procedure result in the loss of our child and almost cause the death of my wife? Almost 50 years later we still haven't had definitive answers to the questions we have.

Understandably we were devastated and this was compounded when Avril was told she may never conceive another child. But we resolved to keep trying, and on 29 October 1968, almost a year after we lost Susan, Avril gave birth to our daughter, Sheena.

Sheena was a bundle of joy and, in her younger days, she would come down to Mauchline in Ayrshire with me when I took the pigeons on training tosses. We would buy a choc ice en-route and have a great laugh on the journey down from Glasgow. She loved coming along to the pigeon loft in Newton too and coming with me on walks with the dogs, her two favourites being Ranger and Ally.

Sheena and I would also go shopping together, which she loved. We would get up early and I remember chapping on the windows of the shops to see if they would let us in before they opened as I would have training to go to or we would need to get back to Newton quickly to sort out the pigeons. I always used to buy her an extra pair of shoes but told her not to tell her mum that I had! She tells everyone that I am simply the best dad but I think she's a pretty amazing daughter too.

Sheena was followed eight years later by our son, also David. Avril and I have also been blessed with four grandchildren.

Sheena's daughter, Carly, was born on 23 May 1998 and David has three kids, Harry, Anna and David.

My son, David, didn't play much football in his younger days but became a regular five-a-side player when he was a bit older. But he had to stop when he ruptured his anterior cruciate ligament at the age of 38. He's a runner now and travels the length and breadth of the country to run in marathons and half-marathons.

My grandson Harry is a terrific wee player. He was originally a full-back but now plays in the centre of midfield. I love going to watch him play for his club, Stamperland United – my son is one of the team coaches – and he definitely has a chance of making it as a professional. And I was very proud when, in January 2020, Harry had a successful trial for the Glasgow team, making it into their squad of 22. My youngest grandson, David, has also started playing for Stamperland's 2013 team, and he too is showing real promise.

By the time my son David had arrived we had moved to a cottage in Kilbarchan. It was a lovely wee family home, and I went back there recently with my family to visit the folk that stay there now. The family who own the place are huge Rangers fans and it was great fun chatting about old times with them in our old house.

We eventually left Kilbarchan and plans were drawn up for us to build a split-level house in Whitlawburn, Cambuslang. We were going to be joined by Avril's mum and dad – her dad was in failing health at that time – but the whole project was fraught with issues and we never actually moved into the house. During construction the place was vandalised on numerous occasions and we were taking calls from the police during the night asking us to go and board up windows that had been smashed. Eventually we decided that upon completion we would cut our losses and sell the property.

We moved to a house in Mulberry Road instead and stayed there until Sheena got married. With the family starting to fly the nest, the house was too big for us so we moved for what would be the last time to the house in Newlands that Avril and I currently live in with her mum and our granddaughter, Carly.

I was one of the first to hold Carly after she was born and since then we've stuck together like glue and gone everywhere together. From an early age she would come with me to the nearby supermarket to get a roll and sausage and we'd take long walks with the dogs and pick berries in the park. I'd also take Carly with me to the pigeon loft. She loved holding the baby pigeons and I would let her name them all. Her favourite was a white one she called Snow White and she helped raise it from the moment it hatched to the point at which it was ready to race.

Carly would come with Avril and I on holiday too. I think it was something like four years ago that Avril and I went on holiday minus Carly for the first time for a number of years. The two of us were forever going on one adventure after the other and I have such wonderful memories of these times.

I'm also very close to Carly's boyfriend, Billy. She met him when she was 13 and he was playing for Rangers Boys' Club at the time. I enjoyed going along to watch him and give him some pointers on his game but those that say I gave him advice on how to dive are being economical with the truth!

Carly also helped out when I moved into spiritualism and opened up my own church. I had been raised as a Christian and Avril had a strong faith too. But she had started to attend a spiritual church and was keen for me to attend as well. I was initially a bit frightened, if I'm honest, but I went along one night and had a spiritual reawakening. It changed my life.

This happened not long after we moved to Newlands in 1993 at Langside Halls. The lady who was on the platform was both a medium and a healer. She said she could see things coming through me and I was invited to join her circle. I was initially reluctant but Avril told me it was an honour to be asked so, after giving it a wee bit of thought, I agreed.

I went along to this lady's house one evening and it was some time after her husband, Peter, had sadly passed away. Avril had been before and told me that when the husband had been alive he would always make tea and toast for anyone visiting the house. Well that night as I sat around the table I too was served tea and toast by the husband, with the toast cut neatly in to five strips. The chap had come through me and if ever I needed confirmation that I had a gift then that was it.

I went back every week after that and eventually I felt ready to go up on the platform myself. I don't know who was more nervous on that first night on the platform, me or Avril. There can be times when you are up on the platform and nothing can happen so Avril was praying that that would not happen to me. But Avril told me later she could see my face change straight away and I was able to give out messages to Avril's friends who were attending. I didn't know any of them but I could tell them things about themselves that Avril didn't even know.

After that I started to go along to a number of spiritualist churches until, one day, I decided to set up my own one. That was back in 2004 and we called it the Happy Church. The church, which was located in East Kilbride, was extremely popular and we were there for about 14 years. And the popularity was nothing to do with the fact I was Davie Wilson formerly of Rangers and Scotland as I had now built up a solid reputation as a medium. My wee sidekick, Carly, came with us too and she would be on hand to give out the hymn sheets to the congregation.

However, it all ended for me one night when I had a chastening experience with one of the congregation when they tried to discredit what I was telling folk. When that happens one of two things can occur; it can either sap your confidence or make you stronger. For me it was the former and sadly we had to close the church down, although it has subsequently been reopened by Lynn Duffner in June 2019.

And that, as they say, is that. The life and times of Davie Wilson. As I reflect on what I have achieved in my life I have been extremely lucky. I had a fantastic, successful and enjoyable football career and played for my country. I made friends through the game that I still see today and I have a loving family who make me smile every single day. Aye, not bad for a miner's boy from Newton that some folk thought was too wee to play football!

WHAT THEY THOUGHT
OF DAVIE WILSON

As a player, assistant manager, manager and friend, Davie Wilson had an impact on the careers of a number of people. Here some of those influenced by him share their memories of the man.

GRAEME SHARP

Graeme Sharp was signed by Davie from Eastercraigs and nurtured into an all-action centre-forward. Davie was instrumental in securing Sharp's move to the English First Division with Everton, for whom he scored over 100 goals in one of the most successful eras in their history.

I started with Eastercraigs at U15 level and worked my way through the ranks. Eventually rumours started to surface that clubs were watching me and were going to sign me on the old schoolboy forms. My dad, who came to all my games, would also tell me from time to time that folk had spoken to him to say they were interested in taking me to their club.

But the one scout who was at our games week in, week out was the scout for Dumbarton. He was really keen to get me to Boghead but when he spoke to my dad, Dad told him I was in the middle of doing my Highers at school so it would be after those were complete that I would start looking at what the next step would be.

At the end of that school year Eastercraigs went on a trip to the USA, where we played a couple of games around the New York area. When I got back off the plane on our return my dad picked me up and told me that rather than go straight home, we were going to the Central Hotel in Glasgow. I asked why we were going there and he said we were going to meet representatives from Dumbarton. I was just a raw 18-year-old kid so I left most of the talking up to my dad. But by the end of the meeting I had signed the necessary papers and I was a Dumbarton player.

Although I'd had trials at places like Aston Villa and Aberdeen, this was the first offer that had been made to me and I simply wanted to play football. Alex Wright, who was part of the delegation my dad and I met at the hotel, had been manager of Dumbarton but had now moved upstairs. Davie, who had been assistant to Alex, was now the manager, and by all accounts he was less than enamoured when he found out the club had offered me a wage of £25 per week and a £500 signing-on fee.

I was still at school then at Coatbridge High and I was living in Stepps so I would get the bus home from school every Monday and Thursday, grab my training kit then get a bus back into Queen Street station and from there get the train through to Dumbarton. I would then do that all again in reverse to get home.

I may have only been 18 but I was aware of the stature of Davie Wilson. I had grown up watching Rangers and wingers like Willie Henderson and Willie Johnston. But although Davie had left Rangers by then, as a supporter, you were aware of the history of the club and the players that had played with distinction in the past. And Davie, with his distinctive blond hair, was most certainly in that category.

I joined up with Dumbarton soon after that for pre-season and I was now mixing with older pros like Graham Fyfe, who had played for Rangers, Pat McCluskey, who had been at Celtic, and the experienced goalkeeper Lawrie Williams. And when I joined I also got my first experience of Davie's training. It was brutal! Pre-season training at Eastercraigs had been hard, but I had never experienced anything like this. Stan Anderson, who had been part of the backroom staff at Ibrox, was part of Davie's coaching team. Stan would be the one who would push us physically, while Davie was more about the football and how he wanted us to play.

At Eastercraigs the manager, Bill Livingston, would take us to Glasgow Green and make us run up and down the hills, which was really tough. But at Dumbarton a typical day during pre-season would see us go into Boghead and get changed before embarking on a run from there past where the police station used to be and off into the hills. Davie and Stan would take us on these runs along these country tracks, up hills and across rivers and we were doing this back in the days when Scotland got scorching hot sunshine in the summer.

But I soon learned of a wee dodge to cut out some running. We basically ran round one big loop, but one day I found out from some of the older guys that there was a short cut. We would hide in the bushes until the main group ran past then join back in with them! I don't know if Davie knew about this or not but we were never pulled up for it.

Training didn't finish there though. Davie and Stan would then take us out on to the track at Boghead and we would do sprints. As a boy just out of school this was brutal even though it was only two days per week. But I knew in the long run that Davie and his team were doing this for a reason and it would be beneficial for me.

I knew very quickly too that Davie would be beneficial for my career development and progression. My brother Richard had had a bad experience at Rangers where he hadn't been given many opportunities, but once I spoke to Davie I knew this wouldn't be the case for me at Dumbarton. He basically said if I did well enough I'd be in the team and if I excelled he would be in contact with bigger clubs to try and secure a move for me to a higher level.

And that's exactly what happened. Guys like Ian Wallace, who had ended up at Coventry City before moving to Nottingham Forest, had blazed the trail and shown what could be done and I was no different. I started off in the reserves and endured an early setback when I smashed my cheekbone in a game at Clydebank. But after I got myself back fit again I was included in the first-team squad for a pre-season tour of Inverness. After that I never looked back. With the likes of Donald Hunter, Graeme Sinclair and Alistair Brown also given a chance, Davie was making it clear he was going to give young players an opportunity if they merited it. I was in the team almost every week from the start of season 1979/80, and by Christmas I had scored ten goals.

At that time it was guys like myself, Brian Gallacher, Raymond Blair and Murdo MacLeod's brother Alistair who were grabbing all the headlines. But neither of us had a job so, as we weren't doing anything during the day, Davie would bring us in to do extra work with us. That was a real boost for us all as it showed Davie cared about us. If he didn't he wouldn't have asked us to come back for the extra sessions.

He could quite easily have sat at home outside the times for normal training and matchdays but he didn't. He was engrossed in the team and he wanted to make the team and younger players like myself better. He obviously saw something in that group that he could improve and make better and that's what he did.

It wasn't just teaching and coaching during those sessions either. Davie was still very fit at that time and he would take part with us, crossing balls into the box for us and talking to us about what runs to make.

As a manager Davie could be a hard man and was more than capable of delivering the famous 'hairdryer' treatment. He had our respect because of what he had achieved in the game, but he would get irked with some of the senior pros from time to time as he perhaps expected a bit more from them. But the good thing about him was that he didn't hold grudges. He could also read people pretty well, and if you were a bad apple you wouldn't be there too long.

He had a real attacking philosophy too. He wanted us to get the ball down and push forward. That's the way the game should be played. He wanted to get the fans excited and he would ask us to get the ball into the wide areas and crossed into the box for the centre-forwards and that suited my style of play perfectly. We would play three up front, Raymond Blair on the left, myself through the middle and Brian Gallacher on the right, and we went out every week to score goals.

Davie moulded a decent side, but I think success in terms of promotion eluded him because he wasn't able to keep the team together for any length of time. Once offers came in for guys like myself, the pressure was on from the board to sell to balance the books.

Selfishly that worked for me as I knew the club wouldn't stand in my way if a good offer came in. And that's exactly what happened in the early months of 1980. Firstly I ended up going down to train for a week with Aston Villa – who were my favourite English team at the time – and I thought I did well. The manager, Ron Saunders, agreed with my assessment at the end of the week but no offer was made to Dumbarton.

There was a lot of talk in the papers after that about me moving on – Alex Ferguson at Aberdeen and Billy McNeill at Celtic both wanted me apparently – but nothing concrete so I continued to play for Dumbarton. But after a midweek game against Arbroath on 25 March 1980 – we lost 3-2 but I scored one of our goals – I got a phone call at home asking me to come into the ground. My initial thought was I was in for a rollicking from Davie as I had perhaps done something wrong. I couldn't work out why they would want me to travel all the way through from Stepps otherwise.

But I went to the ground and ended up in the boardroom. The chairman, Alex Wright and Davie were there and Alex was on the phone. It turned out he was talking to Gordon Lee, the manager of Everton. The phone was passed to me and Gordon invited me down to see the facilities at Everton, both at Goodison Park and the training ground at Bellfield.

A couple of days later my dad drove me down and after a tour of Bellfield we ended up back in one of the lounges at Goodison Park for lunch. I had no idea what was about to happen next. Unbeknown to me, it transpired that Davie had travelled down with Alex Wright to broker a deal to sell me to Everton. After lunch my dad and I went to the office of the club secretary, Jim Greenwood, and a contract was presented to me. I had had no involvement in the negotiations and these were the days before agents too. Davie and Alex must have been involved in the negotiations and they got a great deal for Dumbarton and I ended up being offered £125 per week and a £5,000 signing-on fee. But that wasn't the pull for me. Everton were a fantastic club and were on the verge of becoming a top side in the English First Division so I signed on that basis.

There was a bit of a stramash afterwards between Davie and Ron Saunders as Ron thought he had been hard done by as he had put in an offer. But the contract offer from Everton was the first one I had received, and within three weeks of signing that contract I was on the training ground as an Everton player.

But there is no doubt that Davie was instrumental in getting me that move. He believed in me, gave me my chance in the first team, encouraged me, took time out to do extra training with me and, ultimately, helped secure my move to the English First Division.

GORDON SMITH

Part of a famous footballing family, Gordon Smith joined Rangers from Kilmarnock in 1977. He won the domestic treble in his first season there and also played for Brighton and Hove Albion, Manchester City and at the top level in both Austria and Switzerland after his days at Ibrox were over.

I actually grew up supporting Kilmarnock and the first game I went to was a game against Rangers. Davie Wilson was in the

Rangers team that day but my eyes were fixed on the player that I wanted to be, and that was Jim Baxter. I was a huge Baxter fan but I also became a fan of that Rangers team. I could name them all and I actually went to watch them again in the Scottish Cup Final against Dundee in 1964. My dad had taken me to watch Dundee play Kilmarnock in the semi-final and I kidded him on that I wanted to go back and watch Dundee when they made it through to the final. In actual fact, I just wanted to go back and watch that Rangers team.

Jimmy Millar was the big, strong centre-forward and Ralphie Brand used to feed off him. In midfield you had Baxter, who was the playmaker, and John Greig, who was the tackler, and on the wings you had Willie Henderson and Davie. Willie was your typical winger, skilful and loved to run at his man and beat him before getting his cross in. But Davie was different. He played in a great era, was highly regarded and part of a great Rangers team but, although he played on the wing mostly, he could also play as a second centre-forward and he was a real goalscoring threat. His talent was to steal in at the back post when the ball was on the opposite side of the park so he could get on the end of things if a cross came in. That meant if the centre-forward missed the ball, he would be there to have a chance at goal instead.

When I was just a young kid I played for Kilmarnock against Dumbarton in the early 1970s, and after the game I got some excellent advice from Davie. He played in the game and afterwards told me that I was a good player, but I was spending too much time on the wing. As I wanted to copy Baxter, as a young boy I started using my left foot all the time. As a result my manager at Kilmarnock, Willie Fernie, used to deploy me on the left wing. However, I also had a good right foot so, like

Davie, I was two-footed. Davie recognised this and advised that I needed to come inside more often as that would catch teams off guard as most of the time the full-back and central defenders wouldn't see you coming.

Not long after that I took Davie's advice and scored a goal against Alloa by coming in off the wing, but I ended up getting into bother with Willie Fernie. He told me I was a winger and shouldn't be doing what I did even though it had ended up getting us what proved to be the winning goal!

I have been fortunate to meet Davie on a number of occasions at various functions, and what strikes you is how humble he is. He was one of my heroes when I was a youngster but he's not one to talk about his career and his achievements unless you ask him about it. He's a proper gentleman.

ALISTAIR BROWN

Part of a clutch of youngsters brought to Dumbarton in the mid-1970s, Alistair made his Dumbarton debut at the age of 17 and went on to make almost 300 appearances for the club. He made 115 of those appearances when Davie was manager of Dumbarton.

I lived in a small village called Roseneath and was playing with Vale of Leven Juniors. The scoutmaster in the village went to school with Ian Hosie, who was the club secretary at Dumbarton. He recommended that the club come and take a look at me and, after attending a couple of training sessions, I was offered a contract.

At that point Dumbarton had a really good youth system and I was part of the intake that included Murdo MacLeod, Ian Wallace and Graeme Sharp. Davie played an integral part in that youth system and a lot of those players that he brought through went on to achieve great things in the game. The youngsters also got their chance in the first team fairly quickly and I was just 17 when I made my debut.

When I signed, Davie was assistant manager to Alex Wright and he ran the reserve team. As a kid I was a Rangers fan, so Davie was like an idol to me and I was in awe of him. And I wasn't just training with my hero either. Davie was extremely fit and there would be a few times when he would play for the reserves too.

We also had some big names in the squad at that time – guys like Graham Fyfe who had been at Rangers and Willie Wallace who was a Lisbon Lion – and Davie was instrumental in bringing them to the club. The senior players were quite influential, but we had an interesting mix of experienced players and youngsters.

Davie was a mentor when I joined the club and if there was anything he did for me it was give me confidence. In my early days, in particular, I thought I would get found out eventually, but Davie was such a good motivator of people and you never saw him down; he was always upbeat and giving encouragement.

Davie and Alex Wright worked well together, but their managerial style was different. Davie was more of a 'tracksuit manager' and he was all energy and emotion. He would make you believe that the stand was full of scouts at every game and they were there to see you. Davie, who had a great sense of humour and loved a wind-up, was very good at getting your head in the right place ahead of a game. He was also very patient with the players and had a lot of humility.

In summary, Davie Wilson was inspirational. He was very humble and patient and his motivational skills meant he built good teams. People in the game had a huge amount of respect for him and I don't recall anyone ever falling out with him.

MURDO MacLEOD

An integral part of the Celtic team that won numerous domestic honours in the 1980s, Murdo was in the embryonic stages of his career when he worked under Davie at Dumbarton in the early 1970s. He also played with distinction for Borussia Dortmund and Hibernian and won 20 caps for Scotland.

I signed for Dumbarton on my 16th birthday. Alex Wright was the manager at that time and Davie was his assistant. I had a chance to sign for another couple of clubs, but Alex pretty much told me I would be going straight into the reserve team and that sealed the deal for me.

Although he was assistant manager for the first team, Davie also looked after the reserves and we all looked up to him given what he had achieved in his own playing career. He was always positive and it was great to have him about the football club. He looked after us and we always talked about football. During those chats Davie would give us great advice and, as a young boy, that was terrific for me.

I made my debut for the reserves against Dundee at Dens Park the night after I signed, and after a few games I got a phone call from Davie to say I would be on the bench for the first team for a First Division match against Queen of the South at Boghead. And that Saturday afternoon in October 1975 was where it all started for me as I made my debut when I came on.

In that era Dumbarton had a really good team. My younger brother, Alastair, signed just over a year after I made my debut, and we had guys like Tom McAdam, Colin McAdam and Ian

Wallace who, like me, went on to play at a higher level. But we all got an excellent grounding at Boghead and Davie was a huge part of that. You always knew Alex Wright was the boss and he would do the team talk and organise the set plays ahead of every game. But Davie would have a voice too. He would either do this addressing the team as a whole or, on other occasions, having one-to-one chats with individuals. And if you had a bad game Davie would still be full of positivity, coming up and putting his arm around you and giving you good advice on how you could improve next time around.

Davie was instrumental in training too. As a 16-year-old up against hard-as-nails guys like John Cushley it was a tough baptism, but Davie made sure there was always a football, it wasn't just about fitness. Apart from pre-season, when we did a lot of running, training during the season was about keeping us sharp so the runs would be a lot shorter and we would be developing our skills with various dribbling and shooting drills. Everything was football-related as that's what Davie had liked when he was a player, so he simply adopted a similar approach when he became assistant manager.

Over the next couple of seasons I became a first-team regular at Boghead and my performances were such that the Celtic manager, Billy McNeill, saw fit to bid £100,000 for me. I found out about the bid from Alex Wright, but both he and Davie were big Rangers men so wanted me to go there. There had always been rumours during my time at Dumbarton that Rangers were watching me, but nothing came of it, although I had trained at Ibrox prior to signing for Dumbarton.

Nonetheless, Davie and Alex accompanied me when I went to Celtic Park to meet big Billy. I was nervous going into the meeting, but having Davie there was great for me. He and

Billy knew each other, having played against each other in their playing days and with Scotland too. That helped to break the ice and calm my nerves considerably and, by the end of the meeting, I was a Celtic player. And Davie was fully supportive of my decision. He made no secret of the fact that he would have rather I had gone to Rangers – any time I see him nowadays he always winds me up about not going there – but he was delighted for me that I got the chance to go to one of the biggest clubs in the country.

I'll always be grateful for what Davie Wilson did to help develop me as a player. He's a top man and I'm delighted to have had the opportunity to pay tribute to him in this book about his life and times.

WILLIE JOHNSTON

One of the finest forwards ever to don a Rangers jersey, Willie, or 'Bud' as he's better known, famously scored two goals on the night Rangers won the European Cup Winners' Cup in 1972. However, back in the fledgling days of Bud's career, Davie played a significant role in supporting and developing the talented youngster.

When I was breaking into the first team at 17, I wasn't an outside-left, I was a silky inside-forward! That's where I wanted to play, but Willie Henderson got injured and Davie was moved to outside-right. Moving across to the other wing just showed how good a player Davie was. But I got a chance since I was mostly left-footed at that time so I came in at outside-left.

Davie was like a father to me. Even when wee Willie was fit again and I got kept in the team while Davie lost his place, he always helped me. If I was up against a certain opponent he would sit with me after training on the Friday before the game and give me some advice about how to play against them. There was no bitterness; Davie was a great professional.

This wasn't my first experience of playing with Davie. If he had been out injured he would usually have a couple of games in the reserves before getting back in to the first team, and I was part of the second team at that time. He was a great outside-left; in fact, he was great in all the forward positions. He knew where the goals were and could score for fun. While I was more a creator of goals, Davie was a goalscorer. He would hit shots from anywhere and was really good with both feet.

Davie was a real character in the dressing room, a man about town. He had greyhounds, pigeons and an E-type Jaguar and was very funny in the dressing room. I stripped next to him for training every day and he helped me throughout my career. When I left Rangers to go to England I would always go out my way to meet him when I came back up to Scotland.

We didn't really socialise after games. I was a Fifer and he was from Glasgow, but we would sometimes go back to the St Enoch Hotel after games for dinner and a few drinks. They would be non-alcoholic drinks for wee Davie, of course, as he wasn't a drinker. We would then go our separate ways and meet back up again for training on the Monday morning.

Alongside Jimmy Baxter, Davie was instrumental in helping me in the early stages of my career, they both made it easy for me. He was a fantastic footballer, a brilliant professional and he's a great man.

WILLIE HENDERSON

The youngest member of the famous attacking quintet that wreaked havoc in the early 1960s, Willie is a Rangers great. After winning several domestic honours he left Ibrox in 1972 and played for, among others, Sheffield Wednesday and Hong Kong Rangers.

Davie Wilson is a real nice guy. He was an excellent player for Glasgow Rangers and Scotland and is without question the best goalscoring winger I played with.

TOM MILLER

Instantly recognisable as the voice of Rangers TV, Tom grew up with the magnificent side moulded by Scot Symon in the early 60s. Davie was among his favourite players in that celebrated team.

Davie Wilson is an absolute gentleman and very worthy of a terrific career being captured in this book.

My early memories are of his performance for Scotland at Wembley in 1963, filling in at left-back after Eric Caldow had his leg broken by Bobby Smith. He excelled getting up and down the left flank with incredible energy. I also recall him celebrating at Hampden in the blue-and-white vertical stripes and sporting a bowler hat after the 1964 Scottish Cup Final.

Davie was a rarity, being right-footed, but, while most comfortable on the left, could play anywhere across the front line. For a wee guy, he scored his fair share of headers and I recall him scoring six goals in one game against Falkirk. His relationship with Brand and Millar was almost telepathic while he thrived on deliveries from Jim Baxter tucked in behind or just inside him.

He was only 28 when he left for Dundee United. Rangers were struggling to arrest the rapidly developing Celtic winning mentality and a wind of change was blowing through Ibrox, particularly in the wake of the Scottish Cup loss at Berwick.

Davie was still part of the squad that travelled to Nuremberg for the European Cup Winners' Cup Final in 1967, but despite Rangers being without a recognised centre-forward – a position Davie had played in on a number of occasions – Scot Symon instead asked Roger Hynd and Alex Smith to provide the goals. For me Davie would have been a better option. He loved the European stage under the Ibrox floodlights, but, despite scoring in the semi-final against Slavia Sofia in the 1967 Cup Winners' Cup campaign, he was overlooked.

The emergence of Willie Johnston probably accelerated Davie's departure too, but the fact he continued to deliver for Dundee United and also won a place in their Hall of Fame suggests Rangers were too quick to move him on. He has also been recognised in the Scottish Football Hall of Fame, a fitting accolade for a true Rangers and Scotland great.

I still see Davie at Ibrox when he attends home games and love to have a chat with him. He's an icon. When he goes on holiday to Tenerife, invariably I get the call to arrange a lift from his hotel and a seat for him near the TV at the Ibrox Bar to watch his beloved Rangers. When he phones he always says 'Hi, it's wee Davie,' and that, for me, says it all. He's a real old school gent with no airs or graces and he deserves to be classed as a Scottish football legend.

ARCHIE MacPHERSON

Regarded as one of the finest football commentators ever produced by Scotland, Archie has over 50 years of experience covering football across the world.

My principal recollection of Davie is that he was one of the most determined wingers I ever watched. He was direct and accelerated brilliantly over a few yards, which made him difficult to defend against. He won a lot of penalties, as I recall, for that very reason.

Of course he blossomed in one of the greatest periods for Rangers and benefitted by having great players around him. In my time covering the game the forward line of Henderson, McMillan, Millar, Brand and Wilson is the one I recall more than any.

BOBBY TAIT

A former grade-one referee, Bobby has known Davie for a number of years. They still meet up regularly and travel together to watch Rangers.

I grew up watching Rangers in the 1960s and wee Davie was one of my heroes. I firmly believe Scot Symon let him go too early. He brought in Orjan Persson in his place and, no offence to the big man, he wasn't in the same class as Davie and was never likely to score the same amount of goals that Davie would have scored for us. Symon did the same with Jim Forrest – another player I really admired – and decisions like those set the club back at that time.

I've known Davie and his family for years as he comes from Newton and I come from Cambuslang. We are also members of the same Masonic Lodge. After he finished his career I would drive him to dinners and take him to Ibrox and we've been to loads of places together to attend supporters' functions like Dubai and Bahrain. For me, it's great just to sit and listen to him talking about football and the players he played alongside. For a guy like me it's manna from heaven and the stories are laced with humour too. In fact he used to randomly point out houses during some on the journeys and tell me that he had bought pigeons from the owner of the property!

What has always struck me about Davie is that he's a gentleman. I've never met a player or referee that had a bad word to say about him. When we went to dinners he couldn't spend enough time with the supporters. He would ask for a cup of tea and then sit and chat away, and the punters loved him for that. He also loved to sign autographs on photos, programmes or pieces of paper, saying that that was a wee personal touch for those who had attended the dinner.

There are numerous stories that I could tell about Davie, but there are two in particular that stick out. When Davie went back to manage Dumbarton in the 1980s I was a grade-two referee. While I wasn't covering games at first-team level, I would often referee reserve fixtures. Ahead of one of those fixtures at Boghead there had been torrential rain which meant a pitch inspection was required to establish if it was playable. I arrived, and when I went on to the park I saw two individuals with pitchforks trying manfully to drain away any excess water. One of them was the Dumbarton groundsman, a lovely man called Dick, and I went over to chat with him. The rainwater was dripping off him and I asked who the other chap was that was helping him out. He told me it was wee Davie. Here in the bucketing rain was the first-team manager, soaked to the skin with a pitchfork helping his groundsman out to ensure a RESERVE game went ahead. I went over to speak to Davie and I asked him why the hell he was doing what he was doing. He told me a couple of the first-team players were coming back from injury so he needed the game to go ahead so these boys could get back to fitness and be available for selection for the first team. Dumbarton were in the Premier Division and had a really small first-team squad so Davie needed players to stay fit if he was to have any chance of keeping the club in the top flight. And lending a helping hand like that summed Davie up, no airs or graces, never afraid to muck in and help out.

Around that time he also made a playing comeback. He was in his late 40s then but still took part in training, and I'm told he ran around the same way he did when he was in his 20s. Well, I arrived at Boghead this night to referee a reserve game and it turned out Davie was short of players so listed himself as a sub. I was handed the team lines before kick-off and have to confess I didn't even recognise Davie's name on the piece of paper. But there he was, stripped for action, and with about ten minutes to go he decided to put himself on. As I said, Davie and I belong to the same lodge so prior to coming on he called me over and said, 'I trust I can rely on you to give me a penalty kick, brother?' to which I retorted, 'If you can get yourself in to the penalty box at your age then you deserve a penalty.' As I turned to walk back on to the park I heard wee Davie say 'ya cheeky bugger'! I wind him up and tell folk he didn't get a kick of the ball when he came on, but I can't recall if he got the penalty he was after or not. But Davie is adamant he did and he tells anyone who will listen that not only did he get the penalty, he got up, took it himself and scored!

I still pick him up every week now and he still has that wee zip about him. I'll pull outside his house and he'll come out and do a wee sprint across the street to get to the car as if he was still 20 years of age. And the first thing he'll do is talk about football. He'll talk about going to watch his grandsons play and, of course, he'll talk about the Rangers. He loves the club and when we go to games he always makes a point of speaking to any of the current playing squad we meet. And when we walk down to the stadium from the car he never walks past anyone, he'll always stop and sign autographs and pose for pictures. But he doesn't just get that at Ibrox; wee Davie could go to any ground in Scotland and the same thing would happen. As far as wee Davie is concerned, he is still representing Glasgow Rangers and he is proud to do so. He's just a great guy.

SAMMY McGIVERN

A member of the Scotland U18 squad that won the European Championships in 1982, Sammy worked with Davie during the early years of his playing career at Kilmarnock. He subsequently played for Falkirk, Ayr United and Dumbarton.

I have to confess I didn't really know too much about Davie Wilson when he came to Kilmarnock as assistant manager. I was only 17 at the time but my dad, who was a Rangers fan, couldn't contain his excitement when I told him I was going to be coached by wee Davie.

I owe the wee man so much as he showed a great deal of faith in me. I eventually established myself as a centre-forward, but back in the early 80s I was too lightweight to play there. Instead I was played at outside-left and, as I soon found out, there were few better to coach and advise about playing there than Davie. He must have seen something in me and he pushed the manager, Jim Clunie, hard to give me a chance in the first team.

At that time we played two up front – big John Bourke and Brian Gallacher – and I thought it would be difficult to get into the team and help us push for promotion. I didn't think we would play three up front but we did and, when we did get promotion, Davie then pushed even harder for me to stay in the team once we went into the Premier Division.

But prior to that Davie also convinced big Jim to keep me in the team when we drew Aberdeen in the quarter-final of the Scottish Cup. I thought I had no chance of playing, but Davie pulled me aside in the days leading up to the game. He told me he was trying to convince the manager to play me and that whatever big Jim asked me to do then I had to agree to do it. At that time Stuart Kennedy played right-back for Aberdeen and he was famous for making attacking runs down the flank. When big Jim told me I was playing he said my job was to mark Kennedy. I thought that meant I would be playing at left-back but Jim said no, I was still to play at outside-left.

Despite my marking duties I managed to put Kilmarnock ahead after a minute, but thereafter I simply chased Kennedy up and down the park as per the manager and wee Davie's instructions. We ended up losing 4-2, although it took two penalties from Gordon Strachan to take Aberdeen through to the semis.

Davie was a cracking fella, but you knew he wasn't to be messed with. In the 'good cop, bad cop' scenario, Clunie would be the hardy one, while Davie was usually the good guy. But you knew there was a steely edge about him too.

When he came to Kilmarnock he still took part in training and he could ping a ball better than anyone in our team, even though he was in his 40s. In fact, he even turned out in a reserve game for us one night! He still had that youthful look about him and we used to joke about how his hair stayed the same colour of blond that it had always been!

Although he had been a legend at Rangers, Davie was never one to boast about what he had achieved in the game. There were discussions in the dressing room about his career but they were always started by someone else. Even when I've listened to him on the after-dinner circuit what strikes you is how humble he is. He's a gem of a guy, a gentleman.

SIR ALEX FERGUSON

Alongside Jock Stein, Sir Matt Busby and Bill Shankly, Sir Alex Ferguson is regarded as one of the greatest managers Scotland has ever produced. He used to watch Davie play for Rangers from the terraces at Ibrox and eventually played against him when he was with St Johnstone, Dunfermline and Rangers, the latter games coming after Davie had joined Dundee United. They also pitted their wits against each other during their managerial careers and have been friends for over 50 years.

My first recollection of Davie Wilson is when I watched him play for Baillieston Juniors against my local side, Benburb. What struck me was that he had a fantastic enthusiasm for the game. It was around 1959/60 before he really broke into the Rangers team and became an important player for them. He had a real bubbly enthusiasm and he had great stamina that meant he could run up and down the line throughout the match. He was also a great passer of the ball. As an outside-left who was right-footed, coming off the line he had to have a good pass as he wasn't lightning quick to get beyond players like other wingers could. He was sharp, though, and his knowledge of the game in the last third, coming in off that left-hand side allowed him to score so many goals. He had a real knack for scoring goals and, for a winger, to score the amount of goals he did for Rangers was amazing. For about five years he was scoring over 20 goals in a season, and, although I grew up watching the famous Rangers team with the 'Iron Curtain' defence, to my mind the team Davie was part of in the early 1960s was the best Rangers ever had. He didn't just contribute in an attacking sense either. Unlike some other wingers, Davie also understood what he needed to do when he lost the ball, he knew he had to get back and help out the defence.

When you go to a club like Rangers what can make you is the way you perform against Celtic. Jimmy Millar used to terrorise them – big Billy McNeill was fantastic in the air but he couldn't handle Jimmy – and Davie had a great record against them too, scoring a few crucial goals.

One of my outstanding memories of Davie was from my second visit to Wembley. I had been at the 9-3 game in 1961 but, on this occasion, Scotland beat England 2-1. Eric Caldow got his leg broken and Davie played left-back. He was phenomenal that day and that should be one of his proudest moments. I also recall being at the game when he scored the first goal against England at Hampden a year earlier.

Davie was still at Rangers when I joined in 1967, although he left for Dundee United less than a week later. However, during that brief spell I sat beside him in the dressing room and, although he knew he was leaving, he wished me all the best and told me I was joining a great club. Jimmy Millar left around that time too. He was my favourite player. He was honorary president of the Partick Rangers Supporters' Club and he passed that on to me, which I thought was really nice of him.

I did, however, think Scot Symon let Davie leave the club too soon. He brought myself in, and Dave Smith and Alec Smith had been added the year previously. Eric Sorenson and Andy Penman came in too but our squad lacked that Rangers knowledge that someone like Davie had. Without question, retaining Davie and Jimmy Millar would have made a huge difference at that time. They may only have played a handful of games but they had that experience that the likes of myself didn't have. In my first season we only lost one league game, the last one against Aberdeen at Ibrox. Scot Symon had been sacked after a 0-0 draw with Dunfermline earlier in the season, but we looked good for the title when we were 2-1 up against Aberdeen with 15 minutes to go. But we lost two goals and Celtic won the league. Had we had someone like Davie at outside-left, holding the ball up and using his experience to help see the game out it might well have turned out differently.

The fact that Davie had five years at Dundee United after he left Rangers when he could quite easily have walked away from the game said a lot about his character and enthusiasm.

I came close to working with Davie when I was at Aberdeen. Just after we won the league in 1980 my assistant manager, Pat Stanton, told me he was going back to Edinburgh. For Pat's replacement I was looking for someone with tactical nous, a presence, experience and a strong CV as a player. Davie, who I felt had also done a decent job at Dumbarton, therefore came into consideration, but in the end, on the recommendation of Jim McLean, I went and spoke to Archie Knox, who was manager at Forfar Athletic. I was impressed and Archie got the job but that was no slight on Davie as he would have undoubtedly done a fine job too.

Davie obviously ended up back at Dumbarton after that and I remember playing against them when they were in the Premier Division. As a manager Davie had exactly the same enthusiasm and personality as he did when he was a player. And that's an outstanding thing to say about someone, that they had a great character.

Davie Wilson is one of the friendliest people you could meet. He had a fantastic career and his enthusiasm to play the game was extraordinary. Every game meant something to him and I think that's important when you play for a club like Rangers.

DENIS LAW

Winner of the European Footballer of the Year award in 1964, Denis Law was a world-class inside-forward who found fame with Huddersfield Town, Torino, Manchester United and Manchester City. He won 55 caps for Scotland and scored 30 goals. Fifteen of his international caps were won as part of the same team as Davie.

I played alongside Davie for Scotland and he was a fantastic player. He was one of the best left-wingers I played with, but he wasn't just a winger, he was a goalscorer too.

One of the best things ever to happen to a football player is to be selected to play for your country and Scotland had a really good team when we played. We had the likes of Jim Baxter, Billy McNeill and Willie Henderson, fantastic players. But back in our day there weren't that many international matches so you have to get used to playing with each other fairly quickly. However, such was the quality of the Scotland team at that time – and Davie was among the best of the bunch – we made it look as if we played together every week.

That Scotland team should have achieved a lot more than it did. Although we got battered by England [9-3 at Wembley in 1961] we were unfortunate a couple of times to pick up a few injuries. On our day we could match anyone but for guys like myself and Davie, who had dreamed of playing for Scotland when we played football on the streets, it was just special to get picked.

Although the game is much different today than it was when Davie and I played, there is no doubt that Davie would still have been a star. I think the players from yesteryear are still a little bit above the players of today so Davie would have been a standout. He was special and is a good guy too.

I haven't seen Davie for a wee while. I mostly go to Aberdeen when I come back to Scotland from Manchester so with Davie being based in Glasgow we haven't had a chance to catch up. But when we do we'll probably end up talking about football and I'll also get the chance to remind him that he still owes me money. Back in the early 60s when I was at Torino I sent him across several pairs of football boots and he still hasn't paid for them. And they say Aberdonians are tight!

AVRIL WILSON

Avril Finlay married Davie on 30 November 1965. She is the love of Davie's life and it is fitting that the last word of his autobiography is given to her.

I couldn't wish for a better husband, father and grandfather to our family. David, you're not only my husband, you're my best friend. This book will be a lasting legacy for our family and I am so glad Alistair contacted us to ask to write about your life.

CAREER STATS

Honours

Scottish League Championship Division One	1958/59, 1960/61, 1962/63, 1963/64
Scottish League Championship Division Two	1971/72
Scottish Cup	1959/60, 1961/62, 1962/63, 1963/64, 1965/66
Scottish League Cup	1960/61, 1961/62, 1963/64, 1964/65
Glasgow Merchants' Charity Cup	1956/57, 1959/60, 1963/64*

* First two successes were with Rangers, the third was as part of a Glasgow Select XI

Hall of Fame Inductions

Rangers	2014
Dundee United	2017
Scottish Football	2014

APPEARANCES AND GOALS

Rangers (1956–1967)

League	227 appearances (includes 2 as substitute), 98 goals
Scottish Cup	38 appearances (includes 1 as substitute), 21 goals
League Cup	71 appearances (includes 2 as substitute), 28 goals
Europe	37 appearances, 10 goals
Other Matches	36 appearances, 6 goals

Dundee United (1967–1972)

League	121 appearances (includes 7 as substitute), 20 goals
Scottish Cup	11 appearances, 3 goals
League Cup	24 appearances (including 4 as substitute), 4 goals
Europe	5 appearances, 0 goals
Other Matches	33 appearances (includes 4 as substitute), 8 goals

Dumbarton (1972–1973)

League	48 appearances (including 3 as substitute), 2 goals
Scottish Cup	4 appearances, 0 goals
League Cup	8 appearances, 1 goal
Europe	N/A
Other Matches	1 appearance, 0 goals

First and Last Games

First game for Rangers	v The British Army at Ibrox 18/12/56
Last game for Rangers	v Motherwell at Fir Park 24/05/67

First game for Dundee United | v Sheffield United at Tannadice 05/08/67

Last game for Dundee United | v Hibernian at Easter Road 08/01/72

First game for Dumbarton | v Stenhousemuir at Ochilview 12/02/72

Last game for Dumbarton | v Dundee United at Boghead 28/04/73

Goals

First goal for Rangers | v The British Army at Ibrox 18/12/56

Last goal for Rangers | v Clyde at Ibrox 22/04/67

First goal for Dundee United | v Aberdeen at Tannadice 16/08/67

Last goal for Dundee United | v Motherwell at Fir Park 27/03/71

First goal for Dumbarton | v Dundee at Boghead 20/09/72

Last goal for Dumbarton | v Dundee at Dens Park 10/02/73

MANAGERIAL CAREER

Dumbarton (1977 to 1980)

Played	128
Won	51
Drawn	38
Lost	39
Win Percentage	39.8%

Dumbarton (1983 to 1986)

Played	72
Won	22
Drawn	17
Lost	33
Win Percentage	30.6%

Queen of the South (1987 to 1989)

Played	64
Won	16
Drawn	19
Lost	29
Win Percentage	25%

DAVIE WILSON SEASON-BY-SEASON

		League			Scottish Cup			League Cup			Europe			Other		
		A	S	G	A	S	G	A	S	G	A	S	G	A	S	G
1956/57	Rangers	6	0	1	0	0	0	0	0	0	0	0	0	3	0	0
1957/58	Rangers	12	0	2	4	0	0	3	0	0	2	0	1	2	0	0
1958/59	Rangers	15	0	2	1	0	0	6	0	2	0	0	0	2	0	2
1959/60	Rangers	27	0	8	7	0	7	5	0	4	8	0	3	5	0	0
1960/61	Rangers	34	0	19	3	0	1	10	0	1	8	0	1	5	0	1
1961/62	RANGERS	29	0	15	7	0	4	11	0	9	6	0	1	5	0	1
1962/63	Rangers	32	0	23	7	0	5	7	0	3	4	0	1	5	0	1
1963/64	Rangers	16	0	6	4	0	3	9	0	6	1	0	0	0	0	0
1964/65	Rangers	25	0	10	0	0	0	9	0	2	5	0	2	1	0	0
1965/66	Rangers	12	0	6	4	0	1	5	0	0	0	0	0	2	0	1
1966/67	Rangers	17	2	6	0	1	0	4	2	1	3	0	1	6	0	0
1967/68	Dundee United	30	0	8	2	0	1	5	0	1	0	0	0	7	0	3
1968/69	Dundee United	21	4	4	3	0	1	3	0	0	0	0	0	12	3	3
1969/70	Dundee United	30	2	6	2	0	0	4	1	0	1	0	0	8	0	2
1970/71	Dundee United	33	1	2	4	0	1	6	0	3	4	0	0	N/A	N/A	N/A
1971/72	Dundee United	5	3	0	0	0	0	2	3	0	0	0	0	2	1	0
1971/72	Dumbarton	14	0	0	1	0	0	0	0	0	0	0	0	0	0	0
1972/73	Dumbarton	31	3	2	3	0	0	8	0	1	0	0	0	1	0	0

INTERNATIONAL CAREER

Davie Wilson won a total of 22 caps for Scotland, scoring ten goals. The following is a breakdown of the international matches he played in:

Date	Opponents	Venue	Competition	Result	Goals
22/10/1960	Wales	Ninian Park, Cardiff	British International Championship	Lost 0-2	
09/11/1960	Northern Ireland	Hampden Park, Glasgow	British International Championship	Won 5-2	
15/04/1961	England	Wembley Stadium, London	British International Championship	Lost 3-9	2
03/05/1961	Republic of Ireland	Hampden Park, Glasgow	World Cup Qualifier	Won 4-1	
07/05/1961	Republic of Ireland	Dalymount Park, Dublin	World Cup Qualifier	Won 3-0	
14/05/1961	Czechoslovakia	Tehelné Pole Stadion, Bratislava	World Cup Qualifier	Lost 0-4	
26/09/1961	Czechoslovakia	Hampden Park, Glasgow	World Cup Qualifier	Won 3-2	
07/10/1961	Northern Ireland	Windsor Park, Belfast	British International Championship	Won 6-1	1
08/11/1961	Wales	Hampden Park, Glasgow	British International Championship	Won 2-0	
14/04/1962	England	Hampden Park, Glasgow	British International Championship	Won 2-0	1
02/05/1962	Uruguay	Hampden Park, Glasgow	Friendly	Lost 2-3	
20/10/1962	Wales	Ninian Park, Cardiff	British International Championship	Won 3-2	
06/04/1963	England	Wembley Stadium, London	British International Championship	Won 2-1	
08/05/1963	Austria	Hampden Park, Glasgow	Friendly	Won 4-1	2
04/06/1963	Norway	Brann Stadion, Bergen	Friendly	Lost 4-3	
09/06/1963	Republic of Ireland	Dalymount Park, Dublin	Friendly	Lost 1-0	
13/06/1963	Spain	Santiago Bernabeu, Madrid	Friendly	Won 6-2	1
11/04/1964	England	Hampden Park, Glasgow	British International Championship	Won 1-0	
12/05/1964	West Germany	Niedersachsenstadion, Hannover	Friendly	Drew 2-2	
25/11/1964	Northern Ireland	Hampden Park, Glasgow	British International Championship	Won 3-2	2
10/04/1965	England	Wembley Stadium, London	British International Championship	Drew 2-2	
27/05/1965	Finland	Olympiastadion, Helsinki	Friendly	Won 2-1	1